KT-500-620

MY ROOTS
A DECADE IN THE GARDEN

'I have been on holiday for the past fortnight. I told everyone that I was going to Norway, which was a surprisingly effective means of closing the conversation down. In fact I sayed at home and gardened, blissfully, all day and every day, not leaving the curtilage for days on end. The weather, of course, was better than Norway, or Barbados for that matter. Perfect.'

Monty Don's weekly dispatches from his Herefordshire garden have been a fixture on the *Observer* for more than a decade now, and this book is a collection of some of his favourite pieces.

By turns intimate, poetic, down-to-earth, funny and charming, they express the very particular outlook of a writer for whom gardening and life are one and the same thing.

MY ROOTS

A Decade in the Garden

Monty Don

BBC

LARGE
PRINT

First published 2005
by
Hodder and Stoughton
This Large Print edition published 2006
by
BBC Audiobooks Ltd
by arrangement with
Hodder and Stoughton
a division of Hodder Headline

UK Hardcover ISBN 1 4056 4806 6
UK Softcover   ISBN 1 4056 4810 4

Copyright © 2005 by Monty Don

The right of Monty Don to be identified as the
Author of the Work has been asserted by him in
accordance with the Copyright, Designs and
Patents Act 1988

All rights reserved.

British Library Cataloguing in Publication Data available

Printed and bound in Great Britain by
Antony Rowe Ltd., Chippenham, Wiltshire

For Sarah

Publisher's note:

Due to the constraints of the large print format, the author's footnotes have been inserted into the main body of the text in square brackets ([]).

Contents

Introduction

I first heard that the *Observer* was looking for a new 'Gardening Editor' from a friend who worked in newspapers. I had written a couple of pieces for the paper over the previous few years, and she said that I should apply—so, emboldened, I did. I was asked to supply a couple of columns as a kind of literary audition. None that I have written since has been so agonised over, but a few months later I received a call from the editor to say that the job was mine. I was to supply 52 columns a year, each of around 1200 words. A figure was mentioned, with the apologetic 'It will hardly change your life, I am afraid'. He could not have been more wrong. The money, although meagre by journalistic standards, was a lifeline. I was skint at the time and deep in debt. Other than a succession of manual jobs and working for myself, it was the first proper job I had ever had. But it meant more than just money. The job itself was—and remains—completely life-changing.

The really important aspect of it to me was that the *Observer* has always had an honourable tradition of valuing and nurturing good writing—regardless of the subject-matter. I grew up wanting to be a writer, not a gardener. From childhood I wrote obsessively: poetry, plays, short stories, long stories and a journal that ran to thousands of words daily. A lot of this was dreadful, but I was learning the trade. Anyway, whether it was good or bad, writing was the *real* me and through it I made sense of the world. This is as true today as it has ever been. I gardened because I loved it and it kept me sane and well, but I never once thought about writing about it until I was well into my thirties. In some papers gardening is seen as the very outer reaches of purgatory—indeed the phrase 'gardening leave' is a metaphor for banishment from the centre of all worldly business—whereas the *Observer* has fostered a long line of garden writers dealing with the centre of their own universe.

I suppose that is at the heart of these pages. It all really matters to me. Occasionally I churn out an article that is a quasi-essay (none of which appears in the following pages, I assure you), and I hate doing it and hate myself for succumbing to hackery. Because I am a rank amateur, without any formal training and, crucially, with no links to the world of commercial horticulture in any guise, there is no point in being anything other than subjective. As a consequence, I nearly always write about my own garden and the effect it has on me and my family. Everything here is personal.

It is pure coincidence that the *Observer* job exactly coincides with the making of our garden. It was an open field until April 1993 and now, twelve years on, has twenty separate areas or gardens that probably appear ageless to most visitors. Making all this has been grist to the *Observer* mill—about a million words of grist—but absolutely nothing has been done *for* the column. I have merely used it as an excuse to justify some of the expense of what I was going to do anyway.

I was recently quoted as saying that I prefer my own garden to any other that I have seen, and I certainly do. But I mean this in exactly the way that

I prefer my wife to anyone else's wife that I have ever met, or my children to any others. The bond is inextricable and soil-deep. Everything in my garden has meaning and memories attached to it, from individual plants to the broad sweep of design. Therefore my family, animals, meals and events are all an important part of my gardening life and crop up within these pages along with all the unhorticultural bits and pieces of life that do not suddenly vanish when I set foot into the garden.

This is the second volume of my *Observer* pieces. The first, *Gardening Mad*, was published in 1997, so the bulk of this selection is chosen from the last eight years, although I have tried to get some kind of representative spread to span the entire period since I wrote the first article. The format of the book is based upon the calendar, with the 52 pieces starting on New Year's Day and running sequentially through the year, although quite happily leaping years or even a decade in the process. Between September 1998 and July 2004 I wrote a 500-word extra bit each week, called 'My Roots', which was a kind of blog of what I had been up to in the previous seven days. Unlike a blog, it actually referred, because of magazine lead times, to events of two weeks or more before publication, but I loved doing it and the feedback I received was tremendous. However, this did not stop it becoming a casualty of one of the inevitable 're-designs' that newspapers feel the need to impose on their readers. I have included one of these shorter pieces alongside each of the 'main' articles. However, the two run parallel and if they both come from the same date it is entirely coincidental.

During this twelve-year period I have appeared a

great deal on British television, mostly on programmes about gardens and gardening, culminating with *Gardeners' World* on the BBC. Whilst I enjoy this enormously and it is clearly perceived to be my main job, the limitations of television are potentially frustrating. Words are always secondary to pictures, and everything is inevitably the result of a team working together. At best it pools the disparate skills of a harmonious team to create a sum greater than its parts; at worst it is art by committee, with all the compromises and frustrations that inevitably ensue.

But the beauty of a column is that it is a solo effort. So this book is my voice alone and I take full responsibility for all opinions and views expressed. Any mistakes are a result of my own ignorance or carelessness. However, I should like to thank the two editors of the *Observer* Magazine of the past ten years, Justine Picardie and Allan Jenkins, who have both encouraged and helped me in every way possible. Also my editor at Hodder, Richard Atkinson, who, as ever, has been a profound and entirely benign influence. But by far the most important person in this book is my wife Sarah. She reads everything I write before it goes to press and invariably makes astute suggestions, not least in tempering my own instincts to burn bridges and leap over cliffs. The most significant thing is that we garden together as an indivisible team and have done so now for 26 years. I may sit in this room overlooking the garden writing on my own, but I have absolutely no concept of gardening alone. The garden—and all my work—is of her and to her and from her.

January

01.01.95

The passing of December to January changes little. Things look sullenly the same. But it is a chance to take stock and make resolutions. Here are mine:

1. Make people take gardening less seriously. If you garden with gaiety then you are immediately at the heart of a great mystery that will unfold new revelations for the rest of your days. If you garden with solemnity you will rapidly become—if you are not already—a boring old fart. Remember—'All things fall and are built again/And those that build them again are gay'. [W. B. Yeats: 'Lapis Lazuli'—should be required reading for all gardeners—and politicians.] Good gardeners are people who build again.

2. Make people take gardening more seriously. This is a matter of integration. All those who get real fulfilment from gardening have it suffused into their lives. But gardening is generally perceived as a 'hobby' (such a dismissive word!) or something to do when you have time—as though there is only time available when everything else is spoken for. I realise that most people (myself included) have too little time to spare, but you can design your garden around and into your life so that they are in harmony rather than at odds with one another.
   Books, television programmes and articles

have a tendency to treat gardening as a series of tasks to get done and out of the way in order that one might get on with the pleasurable business of living. This is a pity and a mistake.

3. Keep a diary. This must be a record of everything that happens in the garden, as it happens. I was advised to do this in my business career by a successful money-maker who told me to 'diarise' everything. The word put me off for a year, but since then I have, and it works. You write down everything after it happens, as a future reference. You should note the weather, everything sown and planted, what is flowering, all failures and disasters, what is ordered and tools bought. One year I did this in a beautifully bound book, with hand-cut pages and 'Garden Journal' inscribed on the frontispiece in my best handwriting, but it did not work. It was too fancy to be a workaday tool. Get a page-a-day desk diary and treat it without deference, getting mud on the pages, using whatever writing tool is to hand, but above all using it. [This is pure pontification, as I didn't take my own advice. I regret this very much as I would have liked a more complete and intimate record of the creation of my garden.]

4. Propagate. Seeds are cheap and cuttings cheaper, layering is easy and budding good fun. By propagating busily you dramatically increase your stock of plants and, perhaps more important, control their breed and upbringing. You are also making something from scratch,

8

working much more closely with the garden. A direct analogy is in the kitchen, where if you make a soup from home-made stock, paring the vegetables and chopping the herbs fresh from the garden, it is immeasurably more satisfying than if you buy a can containing the same ingredients that you merely heat and serve.

5. Spend! Spend! Spend! Compared to other parts of my life that only give me a fraction of the pleasure, I am mean and scrimping about garden expenditure. I know that I am not alone in this. People begrudge a hundred pounds on a dozen plants that will last as many years whereas they will blow as much on a bad meal with friends they don't really like. With credit cards and excellent catalogues, buying plants has never been easier. I resolve to be generous to my garden.

6. Make better paths. Unless you have exceptionally well-drained soil or look after the grass well so that it is thick and well-rooted, I think that much used paths must be hard-surfaced. This costs money and is a palaver to do, but not difficult. You do not have to use one consistent material and you can play with patterns and combinations. Don't be superior about concrete slabs. They are seldom as beautiful as natural stone but are often not a bad second choice.

7. Get gaudy. I am fed up with cool good taste and pastels. I shall plant more rich, sumptuous colours along with bright oranges, yellows

and crimsons.

8. Take a photograph from the same few positions each weekend. It is easy to forget how much things change over the year, and all planting and planning depends upon an awareness of these changes. A pictorial record of the garden taken from the same aspects at the same time of day is a great help, good fun and a good record. [Digital cameras changed my horticultural life. I treat them like the day-to-day diary and these thousands of snaps provide source material for all my written work.]

06.01.02 **My Roots**

Real New Year resolutions are edged with failure because they imply a need for radical change. They reek of make-over mentality. Of course I don't let a little thing like that get between myself and a whole batch of fresh resolutions still warm and unbroken from New Year's Day. The main trouble is that they are old resolutions repeated. Yes, I want to plant new bulbs, but only because I didn't plant the bulbs that I promised I was going to this last autumn. Yes, I must renew all the hurdle fencing, but if there was a good source of hazel I would have done it before, because it is easy and I enjoy it. Of course I want to spend more time in the garden, but that is only possible if I am either more efficient with my time or get paid more for doing less. The former is a lost cause and the latter is a desire hardly limited to

New Year.

There is actually one good thought that I do intend to stick with this year and next: keep the edges crisp. I know that it will work, because I have been doing it for the past month and it is easy and makes all the difference in the world. I think that this is a spin-off from having the garden constantly photographed. (I have two separate photographers coming every few weeks for a book I am doing, and this will continue for the next eight or nine months.) It makes you look with the unforgiving eye of a lens. If you analyse photographs of all the really good gardens, they share a certain sharpness of focus at all exits and entrances and along all straight lines. This then allows a high degree of softness and fuzziness in other places. It is a tightening of structure that allows liberation within it. I have been going round the garden trimming hedges and edges for just that reason and it has made a huge difference. Our hedges are the most dominant aspect of the garden from November through to April, so it makes sense to have them looking really good at that time, whereas I have always seen hedge-cutting as a summer activity. A winter trim also stays trim until March.

Lest this all sounds a bit anal, I have also been wasting time in a carefree sort of way, tooling around doing little things in between the gaps in the weather. I shifted strawberry plants about to make better use of the space. I can't pretend that this had anything to do with keeping the edges crisp. It was more like rearranging the plates in the cupboard, which, if I am honest, was one of the reasons I liked doing it.

11

02.01.05

You get older, you slow down. Failure feels like less of a humiliation and more of a balanced return. My dog is getting old and she is lying at my feet as I write this—as she has done for almost every article I have written for these pages over the past nine years—snoring and groaning and farting. I took her to the vet because the groans seemed to be increasing, and she had a cancerous tumour removed a year or so back with a seventy per cent chance of remission. I dreaded the stoicism at my feet. It turns out that she's fine. She has arthritis. She's getting old. But the advice to us groaning old dogs is to keep moving. Stay still too long and it gets harder to start again every time.

Well, this is a start of sorts. The garden does not acknowledge the calendar in any kind of handy way, and if there is a 'new year' in the garden then it probably happens around the end of October—but increasingly I feel that we are confused about all that sort of stuff. There are no gardens without us. The garden does not really exist, or at least not independently of us. So it is perfectly reasonable to take stock and to impose a fresh start on the garden and ourselves. It is all part of keeping moving or, at least, of not grinding to a groaning halt.

One of the things that I want to do in 2005 is rely less on labour-saving kit. I am starting to feel profoundly irresponsible using endless noisy machines to do jobs that could be done as well by hand. It might take a little longer and be slightly harder work, but there are few bits of mechanical baggage that improve the quality of the garden and equally few that improve the quality of life for the gardeners and their neighbours. I am thinking of hedge cutters, mowers, strimmers, rotavators, vacuum blowers, chainsaws, ride-on mowers—all the toys that boys fall on so intently. There are millions and millions of gardeners burning fuel, making noise and, equally important, distancing themselves from the place behind a barrier of mechanical sound and fury. It is not good.

Now, I must put in a qualifier. I use all this stuff. It is like cars. I hate and detest what cars have done to this country and the world at large, but I use them all the same. But I think that simply to accuse myself (before you do) of being hypocritical is a cop-out and intellectually lazy. In order to do anything practical about what seems to me to be a transparently bad situation, there has to be a series of workable compromises.

This year I am going to try and cut out as much mechanical kit as possible. It will mean more physical work, but the old groaning bones need that. For years I measured the quality of my soil preparation by the silkiness of the tilth that I prepared by repeated rotavating, but there is no logic to this. A fork and rake will do the job well enough. Seedlings and plants in general cope pretty well with a fairly coarse soil finish, and the soil structure seems to get active benefit, becoming less compacted and being much slower to form a crust or 'cap'.

If someone developed a genuinely well-made push-mower I would certainly use it, for some of my grass at any rate. When we lived in London I had an old one which I bought for a few quid in a junk shop, and it was great for our bit of grass. I am sure that must be true for most urban gardens. It goes without saying that there would be a huge exercise benefit. [This is a running sore in the Don household. I have trained regularly in some way or other for the past thirty years, and every single time I put on tracksuit, running shoes or whatever, Sarah will say, 'Why can't you do something *useful* with all that energy?' And every time I know that she has the high moral ground. And every time I take no notice of her.]

Hedge-cutting is another modifiable activity. Shears are now hardly used by anyone, but they do a good job, and are quick, safe and quiet. Obviously electric hedge clippers are better than petrol ones, but you can buy an awful lot of shears for the same money and you will not be restricted by the length of electric cable or dry weather.

Thinking along the same lines, it always amazes me that people have so readily bought into the notion of garden centres. They are simply another type of supermarket, with all the limitations that this implies. People are beginning to wise up to the nefarious stranglehold that supermarkets have on our food, but is it any better with garden centres? Are their plants and products produced ethically and with all the considerations of fair trade? Perhaps they are. But I think we should always ask, and get an answer. I don't want garden centres to go away, but this country has an under-used resource of thousands of small nurseries, all run by experts and all producing superb material at bargain prices. Why do we not use them more than we do? Is it really so hard to shop by mail order or

14

the internet or by making a short local journey in the dreaded car?

Talking of supermarkets, I shall be focusing more than ever on growing good food from my garden this year. I always try but always feel that there is room for improvement, and especially so in the past few years. The secret is a continuous low-level attention to detail. This means sourcing good varieties and seeds, sowing and pricking out when it is best for the plants rather than when it fits round all my other various activities, weeding and watering when it will do most good, and harvesting when things are at their tastiest. Put all those little things together and it makes a huge difference. I started this past year to alter my soil preparation regime, digging much less and adding less manure. I am inclined to think that as long as all compaction is broken up and an inch of garden compost is worked into the surface just before planting out or sowing, then there is no need for any other cultivation. Deep digging has its place, but only where there is very poor soil structure and the need to add lots of organic material. I am also mindful that digging adds carbon to the atmosphere, and if it is sensible to cut down on the use of fossil fuels in the garden then it is equally sensible to cut down on digging.

Finally, I want to set in motion some hawthorn topiary. We all tend to think of topiary as an exclusively evergreen thing. But it doesn't need to be at all, and I think that the bare winter branches could be really good. There we are: I have ended as I mean to continue—on a positive note.

16.01.00 **My Roots**

Seeing as it is a new century and all that, let me deconstruct a journalistic pretence. I write these words at least two weeks before you read them, and at certain times of the year, especially Christmas, one stockpiles columns to meet holiday deadlines. So the last time I wrote about my garden was in fact four weeks ago, and this is the first 'My Roots' of this year. The contents of the last two columns were based partly upon what I had already done before Christmas and partly on good intentions. I am glad to say that almost all these good intentions were drowned in alcohol and sloth.

The truth is that I did precious little over the holiday period and feel not the tiniest shred of guilt about it. The weather had something to do with it as we went from minus 12 to snow, tempest and then flooding in Christmas week. Although it meant we could not have a bath or use the dishwasher or washing machine over the Christmas period (the septic tank is absurdly close to the flood line and to move it would mean major reconstructive surgery to the garden—I would rather go unwashed), the garden seemed to cope. The most visible loss was all the top growth from the artichokes and cardoons, which had been very lush, but that was always chancing it a little, global warming or not. As ever the flooding brought a mass of debris into the spring garden, but it was an excuse to tidy it up and I spent a happy day doing that. The snowdrops and hellebores are racing each other for the best show. The snowdrops will win the first lap but the hellebores will take the race unless there is a catastrophe.

I made my first batch of soil blocks with the new soil blocker and sowed onion seed. All have germinated and the blocks seem OK. It is hard to know how good or bad they are, as I have not handled them and do not intend to until there are sufficient roots to hold them together. They are on the mist propagation bench, which seems to be keeping them at the right state of moisture to stop them drying up and cracking apart. For the record, I used three parts coir, three parts sieved garden compost, two parts sharp sand, two parts sieved loam. These soil blockers were always intended to have peat as the main binding agent, and the coir is a substitute for that, but I want to cut it out if possible and shall be experimenting accordingly.

I also cut all the hornbeam hedges to a uniform height, just using my secateurs. It involved taking off up to four feet in some places and just a few snippets in others, treading carefully through flower borders, veg and shrubby growth. Whilst this might seem excessively pernickety, the job was spread over about ten meditative and enjoyable days.

04.01.04

It is no coincidence that New Year resolutions are made when the garden is at its bleakest. You are, after all, giving yourself an easy ride. Things can only get better.

In fact I am deeply cynical about resolutions of any kind. They are founded upon a core of guilt and tend to be a list of what you ought to have done last year rather than what you really plan to do this coming twelve months. If you are serious about doing something, then put your energies into doing what you can today. I speak as someone whose desk is piled high with unanswered letters (if one of them is from you I am truly sorry—and ashamed) and whose list of unwritten books grows longer every year—which may be a blessed relief to the book-buying public but is a real source of dissatisfaction to me. But at least I don't believe my own excuses any more. I do not do things that I profess to want to do because, at some level, I choose not to do them. Simple as that.

Better to set targets for today and stick to them. I am a great believer in the one-day-at-a-time approach to getting things done. It certainly works in the garden. Dig just a little every day and a big area soon gets dug. Doing something—anything—for just fifteen minutes every day invariably gets more done over the months than great bursts of activity leavened by guilty inaction. And to get the full benefit this should not be too structured or measured. Simply potter.

All the best gardeners are potterers. The secret

of pottering is to see it as an enjoyable activity in itself rather than as a good way of ticking things off a list. I have a standard question that I ask myself if I get struck by teleological doubts: would I continue doing this if I knew that in thirty minutes' time I was about to have a heart attack? But if I am to go early then I am as happy to go whilst pottering in the garden as at almost any other moment. This is something I have always loved and I will continue to potter for as much of 2004 as I can.

I have now been in this garden for twelve years, which is longer than any other in my life, and the structure is largely there now. If I was passing on any single resolve for the coming year I would say take whatever steps you can to get the structure of the garden in as soon as you can. It is never too late to make a big difference. There is a paralysis that takes hold when, after a few years of making a garden, you think that you have missed the boat with the structure. Hedges are not there, and it feels too late to do anything about it. In fact it never is.

Even from scratch—especially from scratch— you can always quietly come up on an outside lane and transform the outlines with a batch of cuttings. Even if you have the money to buy any quantity and quality of plant you fancy, be modest. Buy small. They always grow better and faster than enormously expensive mature plants. Forget the dramatic transformations and actions. Resolve to potter.

23.01.00 My Roots

Every garden has its own weeds. They are part of the genius of the place. In my parents' garden in chalky Hampshire it was ground elder. In our last garden the horsetail was king. Here it is bindweed. We have nettles—horrible ones with roots the colour of a baby bird's gaping beak and a sting like a second-degree burn—but that does not daunt us. Nettles can be bashed and cut and composted and swamped. We have thistles and docks and creeping buttercup, not to mention the couch grass in the vegetable garden and the horseradish in the holly hedge. We have more of all of these than bindweed, but bindweed is what wakes me sweating in the eye of the night. (Well, OK, that is a slight exaggeration, but you get the drift.)

There is a patch of the stuff in the garden that we have tried to limit to one area. The problem has been that this area contains the cross junction of two hedges, and the bindweed has coiled in amongst the hornbeam roots with sneering permanency. But we have now removed one of these hedges to extend the jewel garden and have unearthed barrowloads of pale bindweed roots, looking like a cross between spaghetti and stretched maggots. Every tiny brittle section is a future infestation, and hours have been spent trying to pick bits out of the mud with frozen fingers.

I had planted a dozen different types of species roses along here some years ago—*Rosa sericea, pteracantha, moyesii, willmottiae, et al.*—and they have grown well. Hugely well. I like species roses; they have an uncomplicated vigour allied to subtlety and delicacy. To disturb them in any way would undo the years of health and lose the really impressive structures that they had, for the most part, become. But the bindweed had snaked under and into them and, having started the eradication process, there was nothing for it but to cut them all back brutally, dig them up—no little job as their vigour worked below as well as above ground—and pot them up whilst we went through the ground with our version of a fine-tooth comb—a fork and fingers. I know that this is precisely the right course of action and that the roses will survive this kind of upheaval remarkably well, and that I would always have regretted missing the opportunity of radical action against the bindweed, but at the same time it is a shame.

Some years ago I was given a *Clematis cirrhosa* 'Freckles'. This is the delicately lobed, evergreen, winter-flowering variety. I had previously grown *cirrhosa* var. *balearica* without any problems and loved its hanging bells of lemon flowers at this time of year. 'Freckles' got hit by frost each of its first three years. Every time I thought it had been killed, and every time it regrew. It is now, after six years, sprawled all over a hawthorn but without a hint of flower. Yesterday I was peering up into it and saw the first few buds and half-opened flowers. It is a heart-lurch of pleasure. The prodigal returns.

17.01.99

A new year and little green shoots are pricking up out of the ground and the buds are swelling on the bare branches. It would seem that the ground is creaking to life after the kind of death of midwinter. That is good and exciting—but not true, of course. Like the pathetically hopeful message on Victorian gravestones, the garden was not dead but sleeping. This is a kind of virtual dying, like the cancer scare that is enough to make you realise just how lucky you are to be alive. This ontological gratitude lasts only for a moment or two before life kicks back in and makes you realise just how difficult it can be to exist. That's fine. Gardens are complex and messy and, as in life, there are few easy fixes. A better motto for gardening than Victorian headstone whimsy is the reply of the Buddha when asked what dying was like: 'It changes.'

It is one of the curious contradictions of modern life that whilst we are presented with a stream of instant experiences and as wide a range of choice as possible, steady revolving change is often judged to be threatening. I know that a lot of inexperienced gardeners would like things held at a perfect static moment and treat the variations of growth and season as an encroaching tide that ruins the sandcastle. This is not the way that it is. Gardens have seasons, not lives, and a better analogy than a tide is to think of the garden as a running stream with occasional pools and waterfalls.

But some changes in the garden involve real, irreversible death. I have been writing for months now about my yews in the front of the house which are sick and, I now concede, dying. The reality of this is that I face not just the loss of slow-growing, expensive plants that were just hitting their aesthetic stride, but also a radical change in the landscape, as hedges have to be grubbed out and burnt. It is the death of a scheme and a view that had become part of the household, as well as the death of the individual plants.

Some years ago—January 1990 to be precise—we had a great storm in western Britain every bit as bad as the more famous one of October '87. Eleven mature trees were blown down in our garden in a fifteen-minute blast. It was brilliant. Two years' worth of firewood (although none of it was burnable for two years) and spaces where there had previously been immovable fixtures. Mind you, there was a hell of a mess to clear up, with torn roots leaving gaping craters in the ground and branches all over the place, but nothing that a chainsaw and tractor couldn't fix. By April, long-dormant daffodils were growing where roots had been, and those clumps that had been shaded by the canopies were flowering twice as well as before. The new grass grew. It changed.

This happens all the time in woods, of course. A tree crashes down, a space is made and plants like primroses, violets and bluebells respond immediately to the new levels of light and increase accordingly. The puny seedlings of the tree that fell, which have struggled to survive in its shade, become vigorous saplings. And so it goes.

But each season there are losses in the garden

that seem to carry no good with them. Nothing seems to fill the space so well. It is odd how the same plant put in the same place is somehow never the same. Only change will do. I think that this is because the thing is the accumulation of its past and final form, as well as its future potential. If you are able to find another plant, identical in size and form, you might just replicate the most recent manifestation of the plant that is lost, but still forgo all the past, without which it is sham.

Plants need a personal history if they are to have meaning in your garden. This is why 'instant' gardens never convince. Without meaning, plants merely become a theme park or show garden. But if you go back to beginnings and put in an immature plant that in time should by rights become very similar, then you are investing enormous faith in the future, with the real risk that by the time it becomes the thing you want it to be, other things will have moved on and it will be irrelevant. I know that this is a constant debate within National Trust gardens—playing off the opposing demands of running living, evolving places against the public's desire to see a garden embalmed at the point at which it was handed over. Visitors want a museum and a memorial, but the truth is that only living, vital gardens awash with constant change are at all interesting.

Even more problematic is the extent to which death in its less dramatic manifestations should be displayed. Should one leave withered fronds to overwinter, or should you cut back hard and tidy death away?

Northern light becomes the subtle browns and bleached umbers of dead foliage and stems very well. However, while lingering, dry death has a faded beauty, sodden death is merely depressing. Any foliage that starts to rot should be removed as a lost cause. You can plant to maximise the decorative qualities of the slow death each winter. Grasses such as most miscanthus, molinia and pennisetum hold well into winter, even one as dank and miserable as this. Dried beech and hornbeam leaves look fine on a hedge but must be swept up once fallen—that is a death too far. The dead stems of evening primrose are now rattle-bone dry and the opened seed pods—looking as though cast in bronze—make more attractive dry 'flowers' than the conventional blooms of summer. In my opinion. Fennel stems, feverfew and old man's beard (*Clematis vitalba*) are all positive attractions in the winter garden, their dried dead husks defying the wettest weather.

I like dead trees too. William Kent carefully 'planted' a dead tree at Stowe so that it created exactly the right effect for his carefully contrived picturesque landscape—much to the subsequent derision of plantsmen, but it seems a reasonable thing to do. That kind of starkness can only come with death. Perhaps a better reason for not cutting down a dead tree is to provide a slowly rotting environment for insects and therefore birds within the garden. As ever, too much tidiness is an ecological disaster, inside the garden and out. If a tree or shrub, or even a perennial, does die on you, and you are determined to clear it away and replace it, do not consider it truly dead until it has appeared to be dead for a year. It is astonishing how many things will revive from a seemingly hopeless position.

27.01.02 **My Roots**

The natural order of things has returned. The hens are laying again. This is a slight exaggeration as they have produced the grand total of three eggs in the last eight days, but this is a 300 per cent increase on the previous three months, so celebrations are unconfined. I am only half joking. The first eggs of spring don't just seem a culinary treat as they are incomparably nicer to eat than any eggs you can buy, but it also has real significance for the garden. It sets the natural order of things straight. I have been pouring food into the birds for week after week, locking them up at night and letting them out first thing, spent hours moving their fencing so that they can have fresh grass, and been forced to make that fencing good, because I fence the chickens not so much to keep the foxes out as to keep the birds firmly in. I know that in the ideal organic scheme of things they would be earning their winter keep by charmingly working their way round the orchard, eating all the leatherjackets and bugs, but they run as fast as their stumpy legs will take them straight to the newly planted hedges that have been painstakingly mulched, and systematically work along the hedge-line, scattering the mulch into the long grass so that it cannot be properly regathered—assuming that one had the time for such things.

Before Christmas, I bought a bag of tulips from the local farm shop. They are two hundred 'Queen of Sheba' and one hundred 'White

Triumphator'. They were happy to clear their stock and I got them for a song. The plan was to rush home and plant them immediately and not to worry if they came up a little late. I did the rushing home bit and did not think about them again until I discovered them in their bags in the potting-shed, quietly sprouting. However, we have planted them all the same, just putting them in about an inch deep. Whether they will develop enough root structure is debatable, but something might be salvaged. The truth is that this kind of careless neglect and general all-over-the-shopness is not atypical. But let him who is without sloth and chaos cast the first rotten bulb.

20.01.02

An A–Z of Gardening in 2002:
Annuals are the nearest that you need to come to quick fixes or instant gardening (see below under M for enlargement on this theme) as everything, from seed to seedhead, happens in a season, which is invariably a lot less than a year. You don't need a greenhouse or even a seed bed to grow them. Sow direct where they are to flower and for the price of a dud perennial from a garden centre you can have dozens of different flowers and hundreds of plants.

It is taken as given by half the population that gardening is **Boring**. Whilst accepting that people have the right to be bored by whatsoever they choose, although football, opera and local politics might seem more natural candidates, there is a certain lack of logic in this. No one ever accuses farming or cooking of being boring. It is true, however, that lots of gardens are as dull as dishwater. This is because they strive after the 'finished' thing, thereby missing the whole point. Gardening is about doing and being, not what has been done and has been. So here's to the endlessly diverting process of quietly gardening, about which not enough celebration is made.

It is a problem for people with a small garden to get enough material to make a decent **Compost heap**. All the devices for getting round this are pretty useless. Yet to have a healthy organic garden (or even, wash my mouth out with soap and water, a non-organic one) you must have a supply of your own compost. Why doesn't every council take compostable rubbish away and make it available as the finished article?

Decking is, and always has been, a very bad idea. It only ever looks good as the flooring for a veranda that overhangs a slope, and even then it must be roofed, or else in our wet climate it is too slippery to walk on. It was promoted entirely as a result of being a cheap, easy option in television make-over programmes. And I know about these things.

E is for **Evergreens**. This is a bit of a cheat, as I really mean year-round green, but G is already spoken for. The more I garden and the less that I know that I know, the more I realise the importance of green in the garden. You cannot have too much of it. I don't just mean having it— which, on the whole, is not too difficult to organise in this country—but making the most of the hundreds of different greens available.

F is for **Flower shows**, which I love as long as

they are put on as a jolly celebration of all that is vital about the gardening world. The best ones tend to be locally based, like Southport. In the past the grand shows have been hijacked by the horticulturists (see under B for boring) and at present are in danger of being taken over by corporate PRs (see under W for waste of space).

I got ticked off by my elder sister over Christmas for not paying enough attention to **Garden centres**, where 'most of us get our plants'. I can see that it is easy to be snotty about them and treat them as an organic foodie might look down at a supermarket, but most of them *are* horrible. Expensive horrible at that. But I promise to try and visit them more often and to learn to love them better. Perhaps.

Hazel (*Corylus avellana*) is a magical plant, as important to me and any garden of mine as sweet pea, rose or lily. Its leaves, lit by May sunshine, are stained glass, its stems more useful than any piece of machinery, its nuts the only ones I really like and, best of all, it makes its own ecosystem of plants, birds and insects that delights more with every passing year.

I would like to be buried in a hazel coppice.

I am a great fan of Hugh **Johnson**. I know that he is famous for wine and I know that he is no lyrical poet, but for grown-up clarity there are few to match him in any age. Try *The Principles of Gardening* or his *Encyclopaedia of Trees*. Trees are not gardening, huh? See T below.

Kit is bad, tools are good. The trouble is, like all boys and most gardeners, I love kit. But the garden kit market is flooded with useless rubbish. All gardeners should have hand tools that they love and cherish, but go through your gadgets and

29

gizmos and whittle them down to what is really essential. Be especially tough on anything that claims to be 'labour-saving': this is usually a lie.

It will never win any prizes as the most beautiful, fragrant, dramatic or romantic of plants, but summer would not be complete without **Lychnis coronaria**. [Blimey—the barrel was being scraped a bit blatantly there.]

Make-over is an ugly word. I particularly hate make-overs on television. They make gardens look like a horticultural version of a shopping mall. They also devalue the process of transformation that happens naturally and surprisingly quickly through time and hard work. What makes it even more annoying is that some of the programmes— and *Ground Force* is a case in point—are extremely well made.

I have taken pot shots at the **National Trust** on these pages over the years, and it is an easy target, sitting in the water like a staid old duck. But if it did not exist we would have to invent it in a form remarkably similar to that which it has today, although perhaps a *little* less solemn and reverential. National Trust gardens are an amazing resource and remarkably accessible and good value. More power (and money) to them.

Time to wave the **Organic** flag again. There is no easy, quick solution, save a gradual realisation that we have sorely abused this planet and must start to respect it and ourselves a little more. This has to begin at home if it is to be anything beyond pious hot air. It is up to us. There is no need to join or renounce anything. Just garden organically, quietly and modestly at home. This way we will change the world.

Primroses still make my heart sing, and I saw my first one in our little coppice last week. This is what I garden *for*.

Quantity not quality is often much nicer and better in a garden. We still suffer from the Victorian hangover of reverence for specimens, which makes for interesting but ugly gardens. Gardeners fall into two camps: those who use their plot to house a growing collection of plants and those who want to make a beautiful space. Whilst the two are by no means mutually exclusive, I belong firmly in the latter school and I am growing increasingly fond of ordinary plants used confidently with a sense of scale.

The **Royal Horticultural Society** behaves as though the horticultural world is all one large country estate, with shows and gardens that we, the visiting public, are kindly allowed in to share as long as we keep our noses clean, don't ask awkward questions and don't frighten the horses. At the same time it does genuinely good work and, like the National Trust, would probably need to be invented if it did not exist. But why so pompous and stuffy? Why so out of touch with life as it is generally lived? And why, oh why Wisley? [When I wrote this I was not making television programmes for anyone and managed to offend the BBC, garden centres, the National Trust and the RHS all in one go. This slightly embarrasses me now, but at the time I was warming my January bones by burning some bridges.]

Snobbery is still too prevalent in the gardening world. It is rooted in the fact that to climb through the social classes in Britain you must acquire a large country house somewhere along the way with a large well-stocked garden attached to it. It is not necessary to garner any love or knowledge of gardening, although a smattering of Latin plant names goes a long way to ensuring social success. It is a middle-England thing, this snobbery, genteel and vicious and without any redeeming features. These people's respect for those in authority has an edge of desperation that feeds their contempt for those beneath. Surely it is time to chuck all that on to the compost heap of aspiration?

Trees are garden plants too. The make-over mentality does not suit their cultivation unless they come ready-grown and delivered by crane, but there is a huge pleasure to be had from growing trees from small saplings, even in a very small garden.

Underneath our feet is the great undiscovered frontier. Science has barely scratched the surface of knowledge about the billions of small creatures that live in the soil, working to digest organic material and create a rich and balanced humus. It is an underworld of infinite complexity and wonder, and we treat it with contempt simply because we cannot see it. Farming has done its ignorant best to destroy the soil, egged on by foolish governments and bribed by greedy 'food' manufacturers. Gardeners at least can learn to love the earth they tread upon.

It is important not to trust any politician, scientist, manufacturer, even journalist, until you have established exactly what their **Vested interests** are. Science, in particular, is held to ransom by chemical and food companies as increasingly these are financing research. For the record my own motives, if not vested interests, are money, vanity and anger.

Westbury Court in Gloucestershire is a wonderful garden. I went there about seven years ago with my family and for three hours we were the only visitors. I must make an effort to go back this spring, when the tulips are out.

Xerophytic plants (look it up) are not the only ones that cope without water. We seem to have got obsessed by watering. Other than when you plant anything, there is hardly any need for it except for plants in containers, greenhouses or annuals. We get more than enough rain to do the job.

Youth culture still obsesses television and advertisers. This is partly because an astonishingly unrepresentative number of people who work in television are under thirty and regard life after forty as an unimaginable, beslippered old age. The upshot is the absence of grown-up representations of gardening on television—part of the general juvenility of modern life—even though the demographic make-up of the nation is steadily getting older. There is a notion that things have to be whappy! and zappy! and fun! to be interesting and entertaining. They don't.

Zzzzzzzzz. That's quite enough.

February

04.02.01

It is snowing. The flakes stream into the torchlight like a crowd flowing across a bridge, each one unknowably different, all exactly the same. But look up and the snow piles out of the dark like a weightless waterfall, tumbling from a black nowhere to your face. Snow at night is like the roof falling in, quietly. I suppose that the quiet is as much the essence of my garden at night as the lack of light, and that is one of the privileges of living here out in the sticks. Another man's nocturnal weather is accompanied by a soundtrack of traffic roar and people noisily doing what night people do. Our silence is complete for moments at a time and I have always felt compelled at night to move silently, carefully, aware that the space I fill is a clumsy intrusion. Our dark is measured by the moon and stars and their relative obscurity, not by streetlamps, shop lights or headlights. The effect of this, with its stillness and gaze into the vast mass of the universe, is slightly perversely to make the garden at night a fine and private place.

I have always loved my nightly walk round the garden, even in weather a lot less romantic than snow or frost. Which is just as well, given that it is normally not snow cutting through the torchlight but rain and more rain. The lack of light puts a fresh face on the place. The garden is simplified but not reduced. The good bits are coloured by memory and the bad bits smudged out. In fact, although we do sometimes have complete silence (but not often, of which more anon) we never have complete dark. The moon figures a lot and I am always aware of its stages, from the shiniest fingernail rim in the late afternoon, to a full, fat, orange harvest moon in September. Talking of which, we had the most marvellous exhibition of the full lunar eclipse the other day in a completely clear sky. It had the effect of not just making the moon a russet colour but of giving it more dimension, so that for an hour or so it was this amber ball in the sky rather than its usual disc-like self. I have tried to become knowledgeable about lunar planting and have read various books prescribing to the day when and what to put in the ground according to the phases, but it seems that there is something a little mechanical and unsubtle about this. [Whilst I still do not practise lunar planting for the simple reason that I grab what time I can as and when it presents itself, I would not be so dismissive of it now. I see it as self-evident that anything that tunes you into the rhythms and flow of nature will make you a better gardener and person.] It reminds me of feng shui, which, although based on common sense and intuition, is undoubtedly a load of old rubbish as soon as it becomes a marketable creed. You need the irrational, harassed, all-too-human element to make gardens come alive, and that invariably means putting the beans in when the moon is on the wane (or vice versa), just when the book says on no account plant legumes until the moon is waxing (or vice versa). The lunar flow to go with is inside your veins, not a book, and if you spend ten minutes or so outside in your garden every night you will soon tune in. It must be outside of course—looking through the window is cheating.

You need the wind. You need the rain.

I take the stars for granted because, when there are no clouds, they are always there. Masses of them, billowing and shifting like a blizzard. I am no astronomer but I can edge my way round the sky, finding the Plough and from there the Pole Star, locating the square of Pegasus and working up to the only galaxy visible to the naked eye (and that only if you look away and catch it shimmering right at the edge of vision). When I was thinking about this article I realised that the night sky belongs almost entirely to my garden. I hardly ever come across it anywhere else. I take it on trust that other people have access to it too, but for all its billions of miles and galaxies and planets and moons, it is as local and personal as this year's crop of beans or the knobbly outline on the pruned limes.

I mentioned that we have total silence from time to time, but it is perhaps only for a minute or two a week. In modern life that is quite a lot, but for most of the night the garden is busy with noise. The loudest and most shocking of the lot is heard at this time of year: the scream of the vixen looking for her mate. Nothing is more bloodcurdling or inhuman than that. Part of me loves to hear it, because it is a privilege to have foxes prowling around at night, but another part immediately does a mental check to see if I have locked up the hens. No doubt it will become a thing of the past if the absurd anti-hunting bill goes through and all the country foxes are wiped out by gun and gas, as surely they will be, in the countryside at least. [The bill did go through. All parties involved got very cross. We shall see how the fox fares—and what legislation pursues anglers, falconers, ferreters and people walking their dogs. The whole process has been an unedifying aspect of being British.] We have tawny owls and little owls, although the latter make most noise at dusk and dawn. In our last house and garden there was a large orchard rising on a slope immediately behind the house. One year an owl nested and had two young that stayed within the orchard after they had left the nest. As they grew they tested their voices more and more, answering each other hoot for hoot. By the end of August they were getting good at it and would scream and blare for hours at a time with astonishing volume just a few yards from our bedroom window. The memory is a treasure, but the experience was notably devoid of sleep.

In a week or two the first curlews will come back and start their fluting, warbling call before it gets light. As we go into March and April this carries on almost through the night and the day and is perhaps the best, most haunting birdsound that there is. When I was a student my father made me a tape of the dawn chorus in early March, standing in his garden at 6 am with a primitive tape recorder, and sent it to me. I could only bear to listen to it once. It was a heartbreaking, deeply disturbing sound, like glimpsing someone you love passing on a train. The robin, blackbird and thrush slowly breaking the dark and going insane with song as the dawn rose. Now I would rather lose sleep than miss any of it at all.

I have to admit one thing that I hate about night. Bats. The only tolerable bat is a dead one and I would willingly cause all bats in the UK to die today of a mysterious disease. I know that this sort of thing provokes flurries of outraged letters, but save your ink, [Fat chance. The letters of outrage duly poured in.] because this is a deep-seated irrational loathing based on fear and not open to any reason. I know that bats eat thousands of noxious insects in every garden, and I know that they do no known harm, but that kind of knowledge is not enough. They literally make my flesh creep, and a bat in the house is my yardstick of hell. From April to October they bombard me as I work or walk in the garden at dusk and only willpower makes me do it night after summer night. I think I hate them most for making me feel so frightened, along with the knowledge that the fear is unreasonable and therefore cannot be reasoned away. I suppose that I am frightened of something else and they are the unbreakable link to that thing—and I shall never know what it is. A bad dream. Having said this, I do like to watch the noctules flying above the river about half an hour before dusk on a summer's night. They look just like swifts or swallows until they suddenly fall vertically to take a flying beetle, pulling up into another rising soar without breaking speed at any stage. Noctules are among the few bats that never live in buildings, and that, coupled with their very high flight pattern, almost makes them acceptable.

I was going to write about the way that the grass is carbuncled with tens of thousands of snails after a shower at night, crunching and bursting underfoot, but I am so bored with slugs and snails. We all know about them and they will force their way into these pages before the year is out.

Now it is the end and I have not mentioned the night flowers like nicotiana and stocks and their opulent scents. Well, they will have their day.

01.02.04 **My Roots**

A pinch and a punch and here's a kick for being so quick. February is here again and there is a spring in my step if not the air. I know that there are people who find February one of the toughest months to get through, but for me it is one of the good ones. Everything gets better in every way every day. This is where being a gardener really helps. Apart from the purpose that comes with the growing sense of there being things to do that must be done soon (and without the stress that will come in a month's time when exactly the same list of jobs remains undone), there is almost daily evidence that things are growing. Spring is unstoppable, and the odd passage of hard weather will do little to slow it down.

Having said this, it snowed the day before yesterday, and this morning we woke to find the meadows and part of the garden flooded. Both were lovely and welcome as part of the full winter package. We have far too much of the anodyne winterish weather to complain if meteorological muscles get flexed. The effect on the garden seems to be minimal. It gets cold, it gets wet. The sprays of *Stipa gigantea* were flattened, but bounced back as it melted. The real danger of snow is when it freezes, and I have known just an inch completely buckle an aluminium fruit cage. There was a sharp wind that set the snow hard on the netting, even though the air temperature was only just zero, and the weight of all those thin reticulated interstices of ice did hundreds of pounds' worth of damage.

But nothing can stop the measurable daily growth of the tulips that are now pushing their snouts by the thousand through the soil of the jewel garden. It would be nice to affect a kind of languid detachment from this, but in truth we are excited and pleased with ourselves. Thousands and thousands of bulbs, mostly tulips, have been planted in this garden, and if it doesn't look overwhelmingly spectacular we will feel cheated. [They were fabulous. We had thirty people to a 'tulip lunch' on 25th April and the sun blazed all weekend, the garden fulfilling all fantasies and expectations.] Planting in November or December is an act of faith, but by February the evidence is accumulating that it is actually going to happen and you are like a child counting the days to Christmas. Well, I am.

14.02.99

There was a couple who used to help me in our last garden. Their story is impossibly romantic but long, so suffice to say that after lives very much lived they met when George was going on sixty and Rose past forty, fell in love and married. I have never seen two people so content with each other's company. George was one of those men who can fix anything. Nothing was beyond him. If he had not done it before, he would work it out. To call him an odd-job man or handyman was to belittle

43

his dazzling array of skills. But he knew his limitations. He wouldn't go up ladders and always claimed not to know a weed from a wisteria. Nevertheless he could dig and cut grass and did so superbly. Rose had always liked gardening and was good at it. Her dad always used to win the big prize at the village flower show. So, if they were working in the garden, George would be cutting grass or mending fences or machinery and Rose elsewhere, weeding, pricking out or tying stuff up. They had cups of tea together and then went to their separate jobs. Then George got very ill [George was a genuinely heroic figure and a key part of our domestic family for over ten years. He was very ill for the last five years or so of his life but never complained or even mentioned it. At one point he went into Hereford hospital to have a kidney removed. I rang the hospital from a filming trip in Thailand. The ward sister told me that he had 'gone'. Fearing the worst, I asked, 'Where?' 'We don't know,' she said. 'He's vanished.' My father-in-law tracked him down in the pub where he had gone because the hospital was 'too hot'. When asked about the stitches, George replied that there was a bloke down the pub that said he would remove them for him.] and it seemed wrong to make them work apart. They became a team. When they were fixing things Rose became George's mate, and when they were gardening George followed her lead.

Shyly, over many months, they let out that they were starting to tackle their own garden. They would even come home from working in ours all day, have some tea and then go out to work. They really got into it and loved it. The result is a

44

fabulous garden, loaded with character and the humanity which is so often missing from conventionally acclaimed gardens. It was an extension of them and their relationship.

But there is one feature which I would never have guessed at in a million years. The vegetable patch was divided in two by a path. And one side was George's and the other Rose's. Neither was allowed to cross that line.

There was nothing coy or precious about this. They grew vegetables to provide fresh, cheap food. But it was cultivated in direct competition with each other. They only grew on their own side what they individually liked to eat, and where these tastes overlapped they watched over their relative growth with possessive pride. As soon as the process left the garden and entered the kitchen, everything became mutual again. They ate the same food and happily shared the fruits of each other's separate labours.

At first I thought this very eccentric, but on reflection I think it is an indication of how sorted they were, because gardens can split you asunder.

For a start there is the stereotypical role-playing that goes on. The longest-standing and most atavistic is that women do the house and men do the outdoors. That stance is made complicated and fractious by the evidence that more women garden than men and, if one can make such judgments, are better at it. The other role that is still sometimes played out is that women are in charge of the kitchen and men control the kitchen garden, as though the two were not umbilically connected. This could work very well as a division of labour if there was complete agreement on the end that was aimed at—making good food. All too often men grow vegetables as an end in themselves, dumping them in the kitchen as though the cooking was an afterthought. All vegetable classes in flower shows are a testament to that attitude, with the veg judged on size, shape and conformity, with never a reference to taste. Mad.

Usually the differences follow less clearly defined lines. The garden often starts out as an extension of the same home-making process that both partners have shared from the moment the house was purchased. One might be better at dealing with the builders and the other at getting the details right, but it is rare (and disastrous) for one partner to abdicate all involvement in the setting up of a home. The garden is more often than not tackled in the spirit of sorting it out and making it nice rather than as a means of horticultural or human expression. With the experience of the house behind them, a couple will stroll, metaphorically, through the early stages, hand in hand. But then something happens. One of them gets into it. One of them finds it a chore. One of them finds their horticultural ignorance a challenge, and the other is completely overwhelmed by how little they know. The roles shift. One starts to make more decisions than the other. It becomes 'his' garden or 'her' garden. The couple's loss is the individual's gain, because gardens are often the best means of self-expression and creativity that a person has access to, so they subtly reinforce their role as the gardener of the household and are reluctant to surrender it, however much they publicly lament the lack of help. There is a geological shift of the heart, and a chasm, much wider than the garden path, opens up.

Where both partners are keen you have a different set of problems. We have had to negotiate this at home. Both of you can love your garden equally. Both of you can have strong and creative plans for it. But if the garden is to be a successful reflection of your joined personalities those plans will not agree, because if they did it would merely reflect the boring harmony between you. You need a clash to create some kind of dynamic entity that is more than the sum of its parts.

But it is a dangerous game. A clash too far and one partner will feel dominated and put upon and the garden will become a cypher for the unequal relationship.

I think that gardens only work if everyone involved puts something significant into them. You cannot have one person making all the decisions and the rest of the household simply walking around admiring it or liking it best as a place to sit and read the papers sipping a gin and tonic. That is a charade. As soon as you grow something yourself, put it into the ground with your own hands and tend it, then it has meaning. Good gardens should be ballasted with private meaning and memory or else they will not stay afloat. And if this means splitting parts of them down the middle to create private spaces, then so be it. But George and Rose's divided vegetable patch has one important factor: its shape is a perfect circle and their two halves together make a whole.

07.02.99 My Roots

The other day Mr Good arrived with an old Luton van filled with oak stakes. They all had been cut from his woods on Wenlock Edge, that wonderful spine of wooded hill that starts about twenty miles north of here. The trees that provided the timber had been planted the year he was born, 59 years ago. I had ordered a hundred three-foot stakes, forty eight-foot and thirty six-foot. Each one was riven with wedges, so that they are all roughly triangular with a portion of bark on the outside and the grain running straight and true down its length. No two are alike but each piece of wood is a joy, strong as iron, grown out of the land of one of the most beautiful parts of Britain. He opened the back of the van and that delicious smell of green oak poured out into our cluttered farmyard. These cost no more than machined softwood posts from a sawmill or garden centre, all identical, all grown anonymously somewhere, anywhere in the world. But that is the horticultural equivalent of junk food. Fences, gates and posts all matter as much as plants in defining how the garden feels and looks.

The tall stakes are for supporting the hazel hurdles I ordered from Hampshire in December. The smaller ones are the uprights around which I shall weave fences with locally cut hazel around the individual borders in the vegetable garden. These are to replace the ones I did six years ago when we first moved in and which have now rotted. The posts are set about two feet apart and banged two feet into the ground, leaving one foot above. It is a lot of banging. No one told me how to do it, but I copied it from pictures in medieval manuscripts. I expect that there is a much easier method, but I don't care because I am in my element. Working in this garden with wood that has real meaning and provenance, to make the framework for the plants that will dominate midsummer, makes me completely and utterly happy.

15.02.04

I used to be a jeweller, and for a few years we had a shop selling upmarket costume jewellery in Beauchamp Place. St Valentine's Day signalled the end of the post-sales slump. Every year we did a little Valentine's Day collection—all hearts and cupids and bows. Sold like hot cakes for a week between the 7th and the 14th and not much after it. Most sales were to men buying Valentine's Day presents. They nearly always fitted one of two modes. The first was brash and breezy with lots of bonhomie that very thinly masked deep anxiety at buying this sort of stuff, and they nearly always bought the first thing you showed them and got out as quickly as possible. The second type was much more sheepish, and the whole process took ages, with much head scratching and trying things on the shop assistants. There was always a terrible choice to be made, and the skill was in trying to sell at least two items to help them out in their dilemma. Then in the following week at least half these pieces of jewellery would be returned by the recipients and exchanged for something that they actually wanted.

I have always glossed over Valentine's Day for anything other than professional reasons. Going to an all-boys boarding school rather limited the exchange of cards, and I have never given nor received one. But 15th February is Sarah's birthday, so for the last 25 years the two days have been collated into one love celebration. This year—today—Sarah is fifty. She is not coy about this. Hiding your age seems to lie in the same territory as plastic surgery. You only fool some of the people some of the time. Nevertheless, it is a landmark by anyone's standards.

So what has this got to do with gardening? For me, almost everything. When we got together, 25 years ago this summer, I was a keen and well-practised gardener but clumsy, impatient and wonderfully ignorant of most plants. She had never really gardened at all but had a real feel for flowers. But it was not a case of horticultural gender stereotyping, where the man does the broad design and the woman fills in the pretty details. Her background was, and still is, in design, and she thinks in terms of structures and volumes as much as plant details.

When I was wooing her she had a house in Cambridge with a tiny back garden. Her lawn needed cutting and she had no mower, so I cut it with a pair of kitchen scissors. It was slow and wearisome, but love drove me on. Since then we have always gardened together. When we looked for a house in London, the size and shape of the garden was as much a determining factor in what we bought as the building itself. Throughout the 1980s, when we spent our days working in the fashion business and our contemporaries were spending their nights and weekends in clubs and other such larks, we were gardening at home. Making our garden was as important as making our jewellery. Perhaps that is why the business went down the tubes, but that is another story.

The point was that it was *our* garden. We shared it absolutely. There was no division of labour beyond personal preference. I am stronger than her, so do most of the digging and heavy work, but she gets stuck in with gusto. Sarah hates machines of any kind and I have never seen her touch a mower, rotavator, hedge cutter or anything of that kidney. But then she has never mastered a computer either. I love flower arranging, seed sowing and pricking out. She loves bonfires, clearing and cutting back. Both of us spend a great deal of our gardening energy working on plant associations and colour combinations. Set your gender lines where you will.

Nothing is planted or removed in this garden without discussion and a level of agreement. Together we always do things better. Despite doing it pretty much continuously for the past fifteen years, it still remains a slightly uncomfortable oddity that I go away and garden for television without Sarah.

I tend to leap into jobs and get cracking on the basis that things can always be changed and fine-tuned later, whereas she will think for as long as it takes before acting. This can be an infuriatingly long time . . . Often I get things almost right and she will come along, look at it, consider carefully

51

and spot exactly what is needed.

But because we have gardened together just about all our adult lives, I recognise that, like buying jewellery, there are certain things that are essentially male and some things that are female.

I, in a male way, like to impose myself on the landscape. I like the lines and structures of seventeenth-century Dutch gardens and like all landscape art. The spaces between plants seem to me as interesting and beautiful as the plants themselves. I prefer to contextualise everything, so that the sum of a good garden is a coherent whole.

Sarah is more reflective and reactive. She will work out from a certain point, adapting and adding to what she has done rather than infilling broader outlines. She is better at detail. I love it when the hedges are all cut, the topiary trimmed and the sharpness of the outlines revealed. She loves a degree of shagginess and misrule to be always present. She has often said that her horticultural ideal is a perfect piece of countryside—a bluebell wood or a hedgerow over a bank frothing with cow parsley. I think mine is probably a hybrid of a zen garden and vegetable allotment. This is a game, of course—we all like all sorts of conflicting things, but there is no doubt that Sarah and I arrive at agreement from different positions. Are we typically male and female in this? I don't know.

The real point is that we garden well together because we are not the same. It is not our similarities that make us good partners but our differences. We disagree about all kinds of things. But in the process of disagreeing we come to an agreement that is different and better than either of our original thoughts or positions. Together we make each other—and our gardens—whole. For 25 years we have had gardening as an essential component and expression of our love. The prospect of 25 more is genuinely thrilling.

13.02.00 **My Roots**

I keep a garden diary, not for your or anyone else's consumption, but it is incredibly useful to me. The records are brief and often insufficient, but never inaccurate. So I can go back to 13th February 1998 and see: 'Exquisite morning—big full moon in blue sky—thrush singing—snowdrops, hellebores and crocus perfect. Planted 2 "Doyenné du Comice" pears and onion sets 75 x "Turbo", 75 centurion F1, 75 "Stuttgart Giant" and 50 "Sturon". Sarah potted 9 regale lilies and did bonfire. Best Feb weather ever. HOT! 17°C.' Funnily enough I have no recollection of this day. Without the diary it would have been lost. And why only fifty of 'Sturon' when there were 75 of the others? Then last year the 13th Feb entry went like this: 'Grey damp day. Very raw. 22 hazel bundles delivered. 8 more to come. Visited Bryansground and Usk castle. Both v. good. Venison for dinner with chard, red cabbage and apple, roast potatoes, hot damson sauce. V. good.' I am beginning to sound like Parson Woodforde. The truth is I remember a year ago clearly. We had American visitors checking our garden out for a photo shoot, and it looked as bleak and unappealing as it possibly could do. Dead. The venison and hot damson sauce were much more interesting. From 13th Feb 1989, writing about our previous garden, I read that 'the wind has streamed the branches off the trees all day, rattling the glass in the windows like false teeth. I have done nothing all day . . . I realised in the middle of last night that the paths in the kitchen garden are far too deeply dug out. The earth from the beds will be constantly spilling on to the finished paths. I can't think why I didn't work this out before. Too pleased with myself. Shit. Too damned pleased to think straight.' I was harder on myself in those days. I am more forgiving now. I also typed everything then, clacking away in the dark, hoping not to wake the children. I miss the punchy solidity of my typewriter but am irretrievably tied to a computer, although the garden diary is now always written with a fountain pen in a big desk diary. If I write at the end of a day's gardening I can scarcely hold the pen with my lumpen fingers, let alone shape words clearly. But that does encourage brevity.

The point is that this is all gardening. The garden runs through our lives like a river through a field, like air in our lungs. The garden does not end in space any more than it does in time. The flowers grow as much in our minds as in the soil. There are very few nights when I do not lie in the dark, everyone else sleeping inside this creaking, bony house, and go through the garden, seeing it with the clarity of a dreamer, taking it to pieces and putting it together again, mending everything in my head.

29.02.04 [This is a radically curtailed version of the piece I wrote for 29th February 2004, and I include it because it gave me a very rare opportunity for long-term rumination and because I think it unlikely that a similar opportunity will crop up again during my tenure at the *Observer* . . .]

I am sure someone else will have pointed out that not only is this a leap year but also this four-yearly 29th February only falls on a Sunday once every 28 years. I remember the last one well. I was twenty and working on a farm in a village called Ellisfield in Hampshire. February was cold and dry, and a burning hot spring and summer followed. The soil was dry and we got all our seeds in by mid March. If, back in February 1976, I had had the opportunity and prescience, what would I have planted in a garden expressly to enjoy now, 28 years later?

This is a long time in the life of a garden. I remember asking the head gardener at Levens Hall in Cumbria, Britain's oldest surviving garden (and by that I mean the oldest garden with its original planting), how long it would take to recreate the extraordinary and huge topiary and hedges. His answer astonished me. 'About thirty years,' he said. 'Everything after that is about control and restriction.' So on one level you could sit down this afternoon, plan an entire garden, as one does, and know that in 2032 it would be at its peak. This is not at all surprising for borders or the average deciduous hedge, but it also means that a maze or ambitious topiary on the scale of land art could be created and seen in its maturity between one Sunday, 29th February and the next.

Of course large trees would still be young and

growing, but it is astonishing how they grow in 28 years. Given a good start and a bit of luck, most trees from oaks to cypresses will establish a good presence in a generation, but some would really get established.

But I think that the one thing that I would really like to have done in February 1976 is to have got hold of a field—which back then would have cost no more than £1,000 an acre for the very best land, or six months of my wages—and planted a hazel coppice. By now it would be in full rotation, having borne at least one good crop, and ready to repeat that every ten years or so for the next three or four hundred years, as well as provide the most exquisite eco environment for flowers, birds and butterflies. I planted a mini version in this garden six years ago and it is already the real thing, although not ready for coppicing yet.

I would also like to have planted an orchard of standards. The modern mini-orchards are mature after five years and past it after ten, but full standards would hit their sumptuous maturity at around a quarter of a century.

On a more common-or-garden scale, snowdrops, crocuses and wild narcissi planted now would spread by seed really well in 28 years, creating that massed effect that just cannot be faked by anybody other than the show gardener. Finally a holly hedge is worth planting for the next generation. I put one in ten years ago at the same time as a yew hedge, using plants of the same size for both. The yew, traditionally so slow to get going, is now solid and ten foot tall, whereas the holly is much thinner and shorter. But give it another ten years and it will be a corker.

March

03.03.02

All over the country the air is thick with the song of a thousand thousand lawn mowers. The grass is lapping ankles and the first wands of spring sunshine trigger the internal lawn mower in every manly chest. This is not gardening, this is manhood and conquest and the solemn, atavistic rites of spring. Mock if you wish, but tread softly because grass cutting in general, and the first cut of the year in particular, are things that should be celebrated. That first tang of mown grass, the intense distillation of new green, is pure intoxication. You cannot cheat this. It does not work in November or January. You have to have some heat from the sun, spring growth and a certain quality of light to make that fragrance. And a lawn mower. Scissors would not do the trick. The grass has to be crushed as well as cut. The combination of blades whizzing round, either cylindrically or horizontally, and a roller following in their wake, squeezing the last trace of fragrance and imposing lines across the landscape of uniquely satisfying order. Stripes work. However much you throw the accusation of a bourgeois, philistine aesthetic, there is an unarguable universal truth: a lawn articulated by alternating stripes of flattened grass makes the world a better place.

The key thing about a lawn is to keep the grass at a uniform length. In this a lawn is really a form of topiary. Beyond a certain length (two inches? Three? Is there an exact point where an extra millimetre slips the lawn into meadow?) it ceases to be a lawn at all in the same way that a topiary peacock becomes just another bush if left with leafy feathers uncut. But, up to that critical point, the secret of a lawn is not how long but how *even* it is. Uniformity is all in a lawn. The odd rogue tuft can ruin an acre of otherwise immaculate stripes. Obviously an even cut is the most important factor in this, and I shall come to the best means of getting this in a moment, but it is not just down to the mower. First there is the matter of the grass itself.

A lawn is, after all, no more than ground cover, an interwoven mesh of plants that happen to thrive when regularly cut. There are dozens of other plants that try and grow amongst them, but very few like being topped and gradually grass will swamp them. When I first started to make this garden from the field that it was, I did not sow any grass at all but merely mowed the very coarse meadow until, remarkably quickly, it began to assume a lawn-like sheen. Even more dramatically, the vegetable garden paths were left as trodden earth which gradually were occupied by self-sown weeds and grass. I mowed these dirt-tracks once a week, and after three months the weeds largely gave up the struggle and the grass got established.

But if you are going to deliberately sow seed or lay turf, which grass do you choose? If you are growing grass from seed you must decide between a perfect lawn or something which can withstand hard wear and tear. The two are incompatible. The latter will have rye-grass (and timothy and meadow grass) and the former will be mainly bents and fescues, with Browntop (*Agrostis tenuis*) and Chewings Fescue (*Festuca rubra commutata*)

60

predominant. Chewings Fescue will not compete well with a more vigorous grass like timothy or perennial rye-grass, and the tougher rye-grasses and meadow grasses will not thrive when cut as short as a bowling green or other fancy lawn.

Rye-grass mixes are much cheaper than grass for fine lawns, and price is likely to be as accurate an indicator of what you are buying as anything else. In practice it is pointless making a so-called 'luxury' lawn if you are going to do much more than walk gently across it. If you intend to wheel barrows, ride bikes and hold world cups and test matches, choose a coarser grass and live with the social shame. The only temptation to avoid is cutting it too short—which most people do.

But cut it you must. Which mower does one use? Cylinder mowers used to be best for lawns, and rotary for rougher or longer grass. But rotary mowers are pretty good now and many have rollers attached to give that stripy finish. If you are to restrict yourself to one mower—and these are the sort of belt-tightening sacrifices that are being forced on a once-great nation—it makes sense to get a rotary. I prefer petrol models to electric, as they are more powerful and don't have a lead that you have to be careful not to cut through, but electric are quieter and cheaper. Meanwhile an old-fashioned push mower is by far the cheapest and most energy-efficient way to cut a small area of lawn.

It is a mistake to leave grass clippings uncollected unless we have a full-on drought, and the compost heap can recycle them much better than the lawn can. Actually, most compost heaps are wrecked by lawn mowings. This is because they have a very high nitrogen and moisture content and decompose far too fast. The result is a vile-smelling, greeny-black sludge. But if you mix the grass with an equal measure of straw, shredded paper, bracken or any other very dry, high-carbon vegetative material, this will turn the mix into fragrant, crumbly compost. But when I say 'mix', I do mean it—don't put it in layers but thoroughly mix it all up as you go.

03.03.02 **My Roots**

'Here again (she said) is March the third/And twelve hours singing for the bird/'Twixt dawn and dusk, from half past six/To half past six, never unheard.' Edward Thomas was born on this day 124 years ago, and 24 years ago I spent the day walking around Froxfield and Steep, in Hampshire, looking for centenary clues and nurturing an obsession for the poet, but finding only primroses and violets, which, of course, were all the keys I needed. Still are. Our little hazel coppice, a tiny homage to Hampshire, is scattered with primroses at their best and violets with scent Shakespearean in intensity. It was Sarah's birthday the other day and I got up at first light to pick her a bunch whilst she was still asleep, but when I got there every flower was frozen solid, prostrate with frost. It is that curious half season, wanting to be spring but not quite allowed to be free of winter yet. And the jobs crowd in on the days as they lengthen. What was reasonably resting over winter is now either languishing and needing assistance or raising itself from sleep. What was seasonable drabness is now untidiness. Things can no longer be left undone. Although I have written about mowing this week, in fact my own grass is still uncut because I do not have a mower at the moment. This is about to be rectified, but when I wrote about the smell of new-mown grass I was digging deep into memory whilst looking out of the window at shagginess.

We have finished pruning the lime walk and I hacked back the hornbeam hedges that grow beneath it as they were creeping above the first row of pleached lime branches. Hornbeam is amazingly hard: a stem as thick as two of my fingers will almost defeat the biggest loppers whilst the same growth of lime is a sensuous pleasure to cut with just secateurs. Cutting the hedges back—as opposed to trimming them—feels like a slight betrayal of the initial impulse to plant them, which was mainly to provide shelter from the scouring wind. But everything has grown enough to be able to push aesthetics ahead of practicalities. Nevertheless I planted two new hawthorn hedges up the top, to close off the new area of raised beds, which are otherwise horribly exposed. I also sheltered the sheltering hedge with hazel hurdles, to give it a chance to get going and do its protective job all the faster. The wind never ceases to amaze me in its ability to nip growth in the bud more effectively than any lopper or saw.

04.03.01

I am always terribly aware of the date at the top of this page. Not least because it is not today's. I try to throw myself forward the fortnight that divides delivery and publication of these words although at this time of year we oscillate wildly between winter and spring through a thousand shades of grey. Maybe I am not enough of a gardener to do 52 timeless horticultural essays, but whatever the reason, it pleases me to try and be as pertinent and reflective of that date as possible. Meaning is inextricably bound up into the season, the weather and the context of *events.* No garden is an island, however hard we try to make it so.

One of the ways that I make sure I am tuning into the right kind of future is by checking back over my garden diaries. I have been keeping these for the past thirteen years [This is a complete lie. I made very random diary notes that *started* thirteen years before this date but did not become remotely regular until 1998.]—always a desk diary, a day to a page—and I try to write the weather, what looks at its best (or worst), what was sown or planted, what was eaten from the garden and what jobs were entrained. Lots of days run to no more than 'Wet and grey. Indoors all day.' But the picture does slowly emerge over the weeks and months. The jobs that you know you did assume form and pattern when given a date. For instance, exactly a year ago I moved thalictrums, took melianthus and dahlia cuttings, thinned rocket and planted 150 'Turbo' onion sets. So much for the industry. The important bit is 'Primroses in great mounds in coppice and violets *extraordinary*—never seen anything like it. I hope they last as well over the next few years. Cowslips out—perhaps a dozen or more—weirdly early. Hyacinths in kitchen fabulous. *Lonicera fragrantissima* good. Lovely dawn—bright, clear, cold. Wonderful sunset.' You can tell that this was written that evening, still glowing from one of the first proper spring days in the garden.

The violets are not so good this year. Too much competition from grass, I think. Perhaps they will make a late burst for glory in the space between my fingers writing this and your eyes reading it. And so the same things happen year after year, but happen differently. To dismiss this seasonal rhythm as boring would be like disdaining to listen to the St Matthew Passion at Easter because you had heard it last year. But every violet or daffodil is the first one ever, and every successive year enriches its freshness with experience.

These sparse diaries—more white space than black ink [Up to four years' white space' . . .]—are slyly eloquent of one's life. So, ten years ago there are just three notes, two of them seemingly unconnected to gardening but as clear a picture of my garden as a government enquiry. They are: 'Prepare statement of affairs for liquidation meeting'; 'Fax strand material to Rosie on trees', and 'Hedging pm'.

The liquidation meeting was that of our own company and was part of the process of losing every material thing that we had. A fortnight earlier we had sold our house and garden to put into the liquidators' pot and we had moved in, all five of us plus two dogs, with my parents-in-law. I was gardenless, sort of. This qualification is because we had retained a field from the sale with the half-baked plan to build a house on it one day. In the event the house never got past the dreaming stage, but I did dig a patch of it for an allotment that summer, driving the four miles to it after the children had gone to bed. It was lovely. The Rosie in question was Rosie Millard, now in front of camera and microphone as arts correspondent for the BBC, [Rosie has since retired from this job.] but then a fledgling director for Granada's *This Morning*. My only source of income at that stage was sporadic appearances on that show, either filmed or live, and I was desperately trying to drum up enthusiasm for more work from me. In fact this was to dry up altogether after a few more months, and the entry for 3rd March 1992, exactly a year later, reads: 'Sign on at New St, Leominster'. Which, for the uninitiated of you, means signing on the dole.

But the third entry for 3rd March 1991, 'Hedging pm', is the good bit. To preserve my sanity, which is a glib phrase but in those circumstances entirely accurate, I was laying a long hedge between the field that we had retained and the garden that we had sold. With hindsight this was a kind of masochism, but it felt completely right and healing at the time. The hedge bounded a small wood and was completely invisible from anywhere other than our field. There was no one to observe me make a fool of myself. It was mainly hawthorn, with some field maple, elder and ash mixed in. I had never attempted to lay a hedge before and had had no instruction. I now know that it was extremely difficult because it was very overgrown, more a line of small trees than a hedge, but with a chainsaw, billhook and ropes I slowly got it done. It was tricky and dangerous and fun, and because I had to concentrate completely in order to do it at all, it eased my mind better than anything. Across the field from this garden a man has laid a similar hedge in half the time I took and with twice the degree of competence. It is a beautiful object.

I have not laid a hedge since, but have earmarked one in this garden for my next foray into that area, and hopefully it will be just hedgecraft rather than hedging-as-therapy. The hedge in question is hawthorn and divides the coppice from the orchard. It was planted in the crudest possible manner, by lifting a line of turf and heeling the young plants in slits. The whole operation took two men about an hour. On one side it is six foot tall and thriving, but on the other, where it skirts around some trees I planted eight years ago, it is stunted and thin. This is because the trees are taking all the moisture and goodness. The moral of the story is that if you want a hedge to grow away strongly you must remove any competition from weeds. And, in this instance, two cherries, a field maple and an ash count as weeds. Anyway, I reckon that the hedge will be ready for laying in about five years' time. To introduce that kind of combination of agricultural skill and aesthetic beauty into the garden from the hedgerow (as opposed to hedge) to the garden risks being pretentious, but if it works it is lovely.

I have been preoccupied with hedges because we have been planting a whole load down the end of the garden. This area is very loosely orchard but except for a few months in summer that looseness becomes a rag bag of compost heaps, orchard, chickens, tunnel, borders and play lawn. None of these things is objectionable in itself, but they do not interrelate in any kind of harmonious way. It is as though the garden breaks up at this point and is less than the sum of its parts. A garden should be as spatially connected and balanced as a beautiful house, and at best this bit of my garden has vitality, but on a grey, muddy afternoon it is plain ugly. The plan is to integrate them in such a way that the spaces flow together and work independently without losing any of their usefulness. A garden hedge has to do one of two things in a garden: either it acts as a frame to set off the elements it contains, or it is a screen. In both cases it defines space, and the space between plants is always the single most important element in any garden.

I plan to extend the coppice where the orchard formerly spilled over the main path and box it in with more hawthorn hedge. I particularly like this notion of boxing in areas of garden so that the contents spill out of them like a jack-in-the-box. The hedges need to be kept lower than the contents—not difficult in the case of a wooded area—and act like a corset, accentuating the voluptuousness of the planting through restriction.

I think that most gardens underdo hedges. Maintaining them is not much work—certainly much less than a lawn or border—and even a very small garden can usually be improved by subdivision. Hedges do not have to be four-square. A cloud hedge looks great (there was a good one in the winning garden at Chelsea last year sponsored by, amongst others, the *Observer*), and hedges can just as easily snake and bend as march in a straight line. The important thing is to get the height right in relation to the space that the hedge bounds. As a rule most hedges are too low. Just as a high ceiling tends to improve the proportions of a room, so high hedges make a garden seem bigger and more beautiful. And there is the added bonus that the higher and longer your hedges, the more bird life you will have in the garden.

14.03.99 **My Roots**

It has been a busy week, involving a film crew, mulching, planting and clearing ground, but one thing has completely overshadowed all this: I have just buried my dog Beaufort in the garden. He was a big dog and needed a big hole to plant him deep, out of the reach of foxes, plough and the most ardent horticulture. In a week of wind and rain I dug beneath a blue sky in the shiny light of early spring, going down below topsoil, subsoil, pebble layer and into the soft red sandstone. I tried to dig a good grave, clean-sided and generous. He was very old and I had known that this was coming for a few months. [The truth was that I delayed having him put down for at least a month until I had finished writing *Fork to Fork* for the purely selfish reason that I did not think that I could cope with the combined distress of his death and the strain of completing the book to the required deadline, even though I was acutely conscious that he was suffering.] His back legs and kidneys were packing up and his dignity was lost in the mechanics of dying. If you own a dog you know that its death will almost inevitably precede your own. It is not a tragedy. Their death is part of looking after them. Digging a grave is a literal, physical link between life and death.

He was as much part of the garden as me. I cannot remember being outside here without him. His mother came from Tuktoyaktuk, high in the Arctic, and the wildness of ice and snow never left her pale eyes, but Beaufort was a gentle, if nervous, dog, and completely bonded to me. He would quietly ignore anyone else and spent all my waking hours by my side. He sat beneath this desk every time I wrote, and every time I went out into the garden he came too, lying a yard or two from where I was working and rising to shadow me when I moved away.

I got him thirteen and a half years ago with his brother when we still lived in London and before our children were born. Both dogs were pitch black and grew huge and shaggy and slept in a heap, often literally one on top of the other. But as they matured their play fights became serious and they inflicted terrible damage on each other. With small children this became dangerous, and I gave Baffin to a couple off the west coast of Scotland, where he roamed a thousand-acre island and swam in the sea with the seals. In his absence Beaufort blossomed and relaxed. He learned to trust and enjoy the children.

Then we moved to Herefordshire and he had free rein over the small farm we bought. He came to this garden and was present almost literally in every moment, every detail of its shaping. I have an abiding image of him from one of the first few visits to what was then a wildly overgrown paddock. I was lost in plans, pacing out the territory, when I noticed him half a mile away across the fields and called for him. He looked up and raced back, never breaking stride as he dived into the river, which was in full and frightening winter flood, swimming it effortlessly, ran across the meadow and finally leaped the five-foot sheep fence before arriving at my side and soaking me with a shake. All that bursting energy became a hobbling, very tired old dog, but the memory is a source of vitality itself.

It is all over now. Everything changes. The garden seems unbearably empty.

24.03.96 [This was one of the first pieces that espoused a unity of gardening, cooking and eating, which later became a TV series and book called *Fork to Fork* and which is absolutely central to our domestic life.]

Being wholly self-sufficient in fruit and vegetables is an exercise in vanity, on a par with drinking only home-made wines. It is Luddite and ludicrous and went through its death throes in the 1970s as a last kick against the pricks of refrigeration and jet transportation. [I wholly disagree with this now and probably, if I'm honest, did then.] However, for most people it is not an option, even if they would like it to be, because they simply do not have enough space in the garden. But there are very few gardens so small that they cannot provide the raw materials for a delicious dish or two. This seems to me to be the right way to go about growing fruit and vegetables. It means that you plan your menu before you start planting and thereafter every stage of the growing process is part of the savouring of the meal. It makes gardening into exquisite foreplay. It means wooing the plants, gently enticing them into the perfect pitch of ripeness and then plucking them, taking them into the kitchen and subtly preparing them before consummation. The links between the ultimate site of fulfilment, a table—preferably outdoors—and the stages of horticultural seduction, through choosing varieties, planting, feeding, thinning, protecting against birds, picking and cooking, are all unbreakably forged.

My lust for summer pudding starts to get roused now that spring is unequivocally here. I can smell it, see its firm consistency on the plate, dribbling a rich red, the white bread bruised with the same juices. [Sorry. This is all terribly OTT.] I am sure that there is a supermarket near here that would sell me an item masquerading as summer pudding every day of the year, but it is to the real thing what sex on the internet is to a long night of passion with a true love. Once you have eaten a home-made summer pudding with ingredients fresh from the garden, every imitation is pointless. This seems to me to be the criterion that one should set when deciding what to grow in the garden. Strawberries, asparagus, pears, new potatoes, tomatoes—all are shadows of their real selves when harvested from a supermarket shelf. But let's stick to summer pudding.

Elizabeth David says one should use only 1lb of

raspberries and 1/4lb of redcurrants. Jane Grigson suggests a mixture of 'blackcurrants and raspberries or a mixture of raspberries, redcurrants and blackberries'. The wonderful *Concise Encyclopedia of Gastronomy* quotes Sir Daniel Hall: 'Prepare enough fruit to fill half a soufflé dish, i.e. Black, White or Red Currants, Raspberries, also Strawberries, mixed in any way you fancy (small, wild strawberries are best).' The Reader's Digest *Food From Your Garden* (not to be sniffed at) advocates only the use of red- and blackcurrants. Henrietta Green says anything currant or berry except strawberry. It seems that there is room for interpretation, but I personally like to have currants and raspberries in my summer pudding. If blackberries are ready, they do no harm to the mix. Incidentally, in the sixteenth century blackberries were valued much higher than raspberries.

Begin with currants. You cannot have a currantless summer pudding. Blackcurrants (*Ribes nigrum*) are different from red-currants (*Ribes rubrum*), which are similar to white currants (*Ribes sativum*). So focus first on blackcurrants. They grow on bushes and do not respond well to training into more controlled shapes and sizes. Nevertheless, there is no reason why a bush should not flourish in a good-sized pot. They need really rich soil, so put as much manure or compost as you can into the hole before planting. It is best to plant in autumn, but it could be done before Easter. They will grow in shade, but prefer sun, and need plenty of air (but not cold draughts). The bushes will live long and get pretty big, so allow five feet between them. Firm them in well and keep them well watered at all times. After the first year, prune back old wood and the straggliest growth to the ground. This should amount to a third of the bush each year. Commercial growers sometimes coppice the entire bush every other year, taking only one (very heavy) biennial crop. Remember, it fruits on young wood, so pruning, which instigates vigorous new growth, also ensures a better crop.

If left to their own devices (which they usually are) redcurrants will make a sprawling bush, inconspicuously living for years except for the annual orgy of red fruit which the birds will gobble up in days. Unlike blackcurrants, however, they can be trained into cordons, goblets, fans or whatever takes your manicurist fancy, which makes them very suitable for a small garden. They will grow in shade and can be trained against a north wall. They do not insist on such rich soil as blackcurrants either, but should be given a mulch of compost each year. Whilst they need to be planted five feet apart as bushes, cordons can be put in the ground just eighteen inches apart.

They fruit on spurs growing off mature wood (like apples), so the principle of pruning them is to shorten laterals by about half after fruiting, and again in winter. These laterals are kept on a permanent framework of whatever shape you have a mind to establish. Like gooseberries, redcurrants respond well to a feed of potash in spring. Firewood ash is fine, or sulphate of potash.

White currants are redcurrants that are white, so treat them identically.

You have to protect all currants from birds, or else you will be summer puddingless. A temporary frame made out of canes tied together with a fine nylon net will do, or you can establish a fruit cage with a permanent construction. But something is essential.

Raspberries are the queen of fruits, far better than strawberries and in many ways far easier to grow, as well as taking less space. They like cool, damp conditions and prefer the soil to be slightly acidic, so add a dressing of sulphur if you live in an area of limey soil. Add plenty of compost as you plant, and it is best to prepare a trench with manure dug into it, because they need as rich a soil as possible. Put the canes fifteen inches apart, not too deep as they are surface feeders, but make sure they are firmly in the ground. Cut them back to about a foot and mulch them, both to feed them and keep the weeds down. Raspberries are difficult to weed because their roots are so shallow, so keep the mulch really thick. They need supporting, and wires strung between strong posts are best, but they can also be grown up a tripod or winding round a pillar.

There are two types of raspberry: summer- and autumn-fruiting. Given the culinary imperative, we shall be growing summer raspberries. You must prune these by cutting all fruiting canes back to the ground after harvesting, tying in the remaining canes for next year's crop. At the end of the winter the tips of these are reduced by about two feet.

Don't be put off growing any of these fruits by the apparent complexities—that is only a result of compacting a wodge of information into a small space. None of it is more complicated than making a summer pudding. Think of the whole process, from soil to table, as the preparation of a delicious meal.

17.03.02 My Roots

Have I said that the curlews are here? Just as it takes until June to get blasé about the cuckoo, I haven't got used to them yet. Each time I hear them I stop in my gardening tracks to marvel. The curlew's call is a sound whose sadness makes you glad to be alive. Mind you, the garden is fairly jigging with spring, bubbling under with bud. It is hard not to feel the pulse of it, even under a remorselessly leaden March sky. Sarah and I spent an entire Sunday gardening together in the jewel garden, broken only to chauffeur teenage children around the countryside. We pruned back all the roses, moved two clematis *viticella* '*Purpurea Plena Elegans*' and '*Niobe*', the former with an enormous rootball which I had to chop back dramatically just to lift), moved grasses and about fifty tulips that were all too close to the box hedge. Hedges around or behind borders are a wonderful thing, but you do need to allow a no-plant zone of at least a foot if it is a little box hedge and a metre if it is a proper hedge of beech, hornbeam, yew or whatever. So these tulips and alliums have been airlifted out and used to fill gaps. Hope to God they flower. This—the effect of moving things on the immediate future—has an added tinge of anxiety tacked on to it because of the constant process of photographing the garden that is happening this year. I know that the tulips can look wonderful. I know that Sarah and I will be completely satisfied and amazed by them—but will they be good *enough*? When I used to do the late lamented *Real Gardens* for Channel 4 I was always blithely telling our real gardeners not to tart the place up, to relax and let it be itself, warts and all, but I didn't convince myself, let alone them. You always want the shaft of light 'just so' when the camera is turning, and the once-in-a-year combinations of colour and light and form that you happen upon whilst idly pottering with a mug of tea to all be gathered together within the lens as the photographer clicks.

I have never been anything but profoundly disappointed by pictures of this garden, although this may be to do with a wholly unrealistic, inflated opinion of its beauty. But it is more, I suspect, to do with the way that our gardens are so much more than the sum of their plants. Curlew cry, the tightening of dried mud on your hands and the knowledge that there is only another half an hour before a child has to be collected and a meal cooked are all necessary ingredients of the magic.

26.03.95

Happy New Year. Today the clocks go back and today we start the year anew. The calendar has as much to do with it as a set of scales does to the way you look. In the 1980s I was involved in the fashion business and lived and worked in London. Gardening and fashion are both dominated by seasons, but one has an unhealthy, silly addiction to change and the other cannot help but flow with the changes of the year. One of the ironies of fashion is that all the work for 'next' season's collections take place at times of year when the seasons proper are making dramatic, if stealthy, changes themselves. So we would retire to our studio in the high summer of August, and emerge blinking at the end of October after the buyers had gone home to find that the world had changed utterly. Whilst we had been working on our summer collection, constructing artificial changes for an artificial season nine months ahead, summer had turned to autumn and we hardly even noticed. At Christmas it would start again, and we would hunker down over drawings and samples, never seeing or smelling fresh air, leaving and returning home in the dark, working seven days a week until the end of March. [This all sounds exactly like writing a book.] Then, beside ourselves with frustration, exhaustion and contact with the most absurd group of people on the planet, we would step out into our neglected garden.

For a day or two we would get home at six and not know what to do with ourselves. Months of slumping in a heap needed to be worked out of the system and translated into action. But all that lassitude was shrugged off at the weekend when the clocks went back. That weekend was always devoted to the spring tidy-up of the borders, going on into the Sunday night until it was eventually too dark to see the trowel in one's hand.

To plunge the hands that had fawned on buyers from chain stores across the world into the moist earth was exhilarating. They were soft and weakened by hibernation, but soon regained clumsy familiarity. Even the brittle sting of tiny nettles was a reminder of sensation more real than the glitter and frocks of fashion. After months of floral fabrics, hothouse flowers in hotel rooms, perfumes and flowery, vapid speech, I can't tell you how clean and intoxicating the air of our Hackney back garden seemed.

If the weather was fine that weekend—and, like childhood summers, I always remember it as fine—the garden got its first attention of any horticultural kind for six months. It was a fashion victim. The surprising thing was that it did not mind very much. One weekend spent with the two of us pottering would tidy it up, weed it, mulch it and prepare for more serious stuff ahead.

But there is a key lesson for small gardens amongst this whimsy: you do not need to do anything very much for most of the year if you grasp the moments that do matter with both hands. If you are at all organised and enthusiastic you can gear the garden specifically to suit your timetable. So if you invariably take to Tuscany or Butlin's [Tuscany or Butlin's? Now it would be Puglia or Centerparcs.] every August it makes little sense for the garden to peak at that time (it would be an interesting garden that did, but that is beside the point). If, as we did, you find yourself too busy to garden between September and March, that need not stop you from having a good garden. It rules out much digging and means that, by conventional standards, all tree, hedge and shrub planting has to be done very late in the season, but in a small garden this hardly matters because everything can have such close attention. In fact we used to plant and move anything at any time of the year. Nothing died as a result.

For those of you (not us any longer, thank God) living in towns, this is your chance to get back to an absolute reality. Very few people need the land to live, either to provide employment or food. But most of us need contact with the land to live fully as human beings. I have always thought of urban gardens—most gardens—as islands, where we create our own kingdoms, acting out our need for land, nurture and nature. On this weekend all these tiny islands wake again, each one crammed with insects, birdsong (often far better in town than country) and slow-moving people emerging into this gift of extra light.

Whether you have never gardened before in your life, or you are a gardener of fifty years' standing, makes no difference: stop reading this and get outside. Happy new garden.

21.03.04 **My Roots**

This is it. We are being here now. The vernal equinox is when my year tips gently into delight. Everything speeds up, gathering rosebuds as it may. We may not be virgins, but Herrick's urging to 'make much of time' never seems more appropriate than at this time of year. Next week the clocks go forward, and for the gardener everything seems possible. It is as I imagine the first few days of a three-week holiday must feel; all the possibilities and limitless time expanding out ahead to make them real. My overriding sensation is one of excitement and expectation.

Perhaps this is one of the bonuses of being a

bloody depressive. A bit of controlled mania is the consolation prize for coming through winter. Not that it is glamorous or novel in any way. The work is rhythmic and particular and deals with earth and weather and patient preparation.

Talking of earth, the soil we used for the dry borders was all taken from our turfstacks. These are objects of joy and beauty. Well, an inner beauty perhaps. Whenever we lift any turf, which (given that every square inch of our two acres was originally turf and is now almost entirely cultivated) has been a great deal over the years, we do so as carefully as possible and stack it all, laying the turves grass to grass. This means that they get no light and the grass dies after a week or so. Gradually all the roots and organic material bound in to the top inch or so of soil beneath the grass decomposes too, and what remains is a block of exceptionally crumbly, fibrous soil about the size of a small van. When we come to use it a year or so later we slice down through it with a spade, like cutting the side of a trench. There is more to this than unchanging practicality handed on from century to century—although you would think that that was intoxicating enough. There is also the lovely ritual of doing things just so, of enacting a pattern worn as smooth as the handle of a much loved spade. It has the same attraction as folded linen, as a table well laid or the nap of an autumnal lawn as the leaves are swept into piles. Simple, but powerful magic.

26.03.00

Fritillaries sound like nothing else on earth and now, damn her, I can never see one or hear it named without thinking of the bag lady of Finchley. 'He's frit,' crowed Lady Thatcher in one of her more lucid moments, aiming her remark at the much maligned Neil Kinnock, and I am still not sure if it was a result of her increasingly gormenghastian dentistry that made her mispronounce 'He's fit' ('Whoar,' you can see her thinking, 'I could fancy some of that.' A bit far-fetched, I admit, but a delicious thought) or whether she was just thinking floral and the word fritillary burst unbidden to her lips, only to be nipped in the bud. We shall probably never know, but that's the wonderful world of gardening for you, rich with imponderables.

And, if you are lucky, rich with fritillaries. Rich is the right word. The common snake's-head fritillary, *Fritillaria meleagris*, is as opulent as a harem, chequered stained-glass petals hunkered over spangled light. No snake's head was ever so beautiful, although they do have a kind of sinister, reptilian quality, especially before they open out, the pointed flower head hooked over from the straight stem with its evenly and sparsely spaced leaves—hardly more than thin green grooves. Look at the chequered petals closely and you will see how they are a perfect combination of blocked precision and smudged expressionism—perfect because it is not predictable or measurable. I like their folk name of sulky ladies—it exactly catches their pouty appeal. It is a bulbous wild flower found in wet meadows (although perhaps a garden escapee—the first record of them as a wild flower postdates their record as a garden plant by fifty years). Until the 1930s they grew freely in 27 English counties, but now this is reduced to about two dozen individual fields across only nine southern counties. This reduction is mainly because, although a wildflower, it is dependent on a rhythm of agriculture that has largely vanished. It thrives in wet meadows that are allowed to grow for hay under the Lammas land regime. This is cut and harvested between 1st July and 12th August and then grazed until 12th February. This exactly dovetails with the fritillary's growth pattern. The bulb goes dormant after June until August, when it grows new shoots that stop just below the surface and also go dormant in response to cooler night temperatures. As soon as the weather warms up in spring they start to grow fast from this poised position, so that they can flower and set seed before the grass gets growing. Man and flowers rubbing along fine. Cowslips spread in the wild under an identical regime in dry, limestone meadows. Call me an old hippy, but given the nature of our agriculture, a harvest of sulky ladies or cowslips for people to walk to and enjoy before the hay harvest seems to me a better use of land than chemically forced junk-grass respected only as part of the process of making a hamburger. But the lesson can and should be heeded for the garden. Snake's-heads are best planted in wet ground with gentle summer shade, although I saw a very happy little colony beneath a Kilmarnock willow in a garden whose soil seemed to be pure sand. Winter wet is the key, and it is wonderful what a hosepipe can do to mimic rain. They should seed themselves and spread to establish a colony if, like the meadow grass, they do not have to compete as they establish. They can be planted as bulbs in August or in flower at this time of year. I bought and planted three dozen, including about ten white-flowering ones, on 10th April last year, which was right at the end of their flowering period. They all seem to be coming up fine this year.

There is a new book by Rod Leeds, *The Plantfinder's Guide to Early Bulbs*, which is geared towards the keen bulb grower rather than the general gardener and is rather heavy on botany and horticulture and light on inspirational anecdote, but has the following wonderful image: 'On a sunny day, the bulb frames [note the plural] containing fritillaries will draw queen wasps'... which fertilise the plants'... These insects seem to be the main pollinators of the early fritillaries...' What an amazing fact! What an added texture of opulence that adds to the plant!

Although they are the best known, snake's-head fritillaries are by no means the only ones. There are over a hundred different species of this member of the lily family. The only other one that we grow is the crown imperial, *F. imperialis*, which is quite another beast altogether, and is just coming into flower now. With a tuft of shiny green punk leaf seemingly growing out of the middle of the circlet of hanging orange-yellow bell-flowers growing on a thick stem one metre high, it is as stridently in-your-face as the snake's-head is shyly beautiful. It stinks of tomcat too. In fact the bulbs—great squashed things that they are—smell almost poisonous in an acrid, chemical way. You plant the bulbs on their side, the pointed end horizontal to the ground. We have *F. imperialis* 'Lutea' in pots, which has clear yellow flowers, and orange ones in the jewel garden. I like the look of 'Rubra' with its almost helleborean flowers. At the moment there are three in the spring garden, where they look rather louche against all the rest of the seasonal subtlety. I think that this year I shall dig them up (always a good idea every three years or so anyway, to replant them with more organic material under them so that they flower with noticeably extra vigour) and put them into pots. They are really a specimen plant to be enjoyed as a freak show and then tucked away to bake over the summer and be repotted in the autumn. Thinking about it, all fritillaries look good in pots, just as, increasingly, I like all 'wild' or naturalised flowers in pots. Even if you only have a tiny space, this is a really good way of getting touches of the water meadows, woods and hills into your back garden.

If you do want to grow a muscular, bunched kind of fritillary instead of enjoying the delicacy of so many of the species, then I think that *F. camschatcensis* is a much handsomer plant than the crown imperial. It comes from the other side of the world (the crown imperial is from Turkey, whereas *camschatcensis* is from the Pacific rim). It will grow best in damp shade (but not too shady) and in June has a deep purple, almost brown, cluster of flowers borne on a strong eighteen-inch stem. The bulbs are made up of rather dry scales so are fragile to handle, but probably worth the trouble. I shall try it.

I like the look of *Fritillaria pyrenaica*, which has yellow flowers washed over heavily with burgundy/

purple. The edges of the petals are turned up, revealing a golden interior as the light streams through the thin flower walls, and that tiny detail is enough to replace all the languid menace of the snakeshead with charm. It comes from the Pyrenees and therefore needs more sunlight than *meleagris*, but is obligingly easy to grow and will form clumps. The only drawback seems to be that it does not come true from seed, the seedlings being rather paler than the parent. Does that matter? Perhaps.

F. orientalis are a good tone darker, without the bonnet-like flicked-up rims. I really like the look of them although I am slightly perturbed by Bill Chudziak's caution in the excellent *Bloom*: 'Fanatics might enjoy the challenge of . . . *F. orientalis*'; whereas Rod Leeds merely comments, 'This is a good garden plant that will thrive in semi-shaded positions in the open ground.' Perhaps he is a frit fanatic anyway.

That brings me back to Lady Thatcher—and Michael Palin. And how does he fit in with the frits? Unfortunately for him he is inextricably yoked to Mrs T in my mind. I was at one of those terrible showbiz award lunches where Michael Palin was given some kind of lifetime, awfully good chap award. Lady Milk Snatcher was wheeled on to read the nominations and weirdly announced the winner to be 'Michael Par-lin', thereby spurring the saintly mispronounced comic into a wonderfully funny acceptance speech entirely at Mrs T's expense. Tears of joy ran down the audience's cheeks and, best of all, the old girl stood by his side throughout, oblivious to any part of the joke. Another golden gardening moment.

28.03.04 **My Roots**

Some years ago I helped a friend with her garden 1400 feet up on Exmoor. We planted hundreds of roses, choosing the toughest, most vigorous varieties and species that would cope with the climate, exposure and pretty horrible soil. Ever since then I have always thought of her whenever I have planted, pruned or even looked at any of the hardy roses. This was at a time when I was unwell and had little work, and the commission was an act of generosity as well as faith in whatever abilities I had. It was—is—a magical spot, and they planted thousands of trees, made large ponds, farmed the land and bred the dogs that I have had for the past eighteen years. This friend died suddenly last month, and yesterday was her memorial service on Exmoor. I have known too many untimely deaths, but this seemed a particularly shocking and sad one, not least because I had been unreliable about keeping in touch.

It is hard to feel positive about these things, but obviously the death of a contemporary focuses the mind on the present and the need to make the most of every second. For me this inevitably takes me into the garden. It doesn't really matter what I do there as long as I do it fully, being properly aware of everything around me. Now that the clocks have shifted forward, the garden is suddenly offering more than just another hour to play in. The quality of that hour seems immeasurably richer than the gloom it has replaced. I never feel so grateful to be alive as in the final hour before dusk in early spring—perhaps the first week of April—a little body weary and always emotionally and mentally exhausted, but happy to be that way. The sunset in this garden is often spectacular, even after a day of cloud, and every week it is moving further along the horizon. Now it is setting over the chicken house, and in a month's time it will be down along the end of the orchard. It is this garden's private sunset. The dawn chorus at this time of year is ecstatic, but the dusk chorus is in many ways better in its defiance. Those last ten minutes or so of extra daylight, riven with song, is time measured by depth, not length. And tomorrow I shall order some more roses that will grow and flower against any odds.

April

07.04.96

In 1992 I rented a farmhouse in Herefordshire attached to a dairy farm. One day the dairyman went past our living-room window with a dead cow in the front-loader of his tractor, its four feet sticking grotesquely in the air. We watched him go across the fields, dig a hole and bury it. For all except that cow, life went on. A month or so later I had a load of manure from that farm delivered for my new garden. I dug it into the ground, grew vegetables, ate them, thought no more. Life went on. The vegetable plot was fertilised by fish, blood and bone which I sprinkled on by (ungloved) hand. The shrubs and trees I planted were all fed with a handful of bonemeal. Since then hedges have had a feed of dried blood each spring.

All these things can now be seen to have been potential time bombs, ticking away beneath the surface of my garden. All bonemeal and dried blood comes from beef, almost all of which is imported. Bovine tissue was only banned from horticultural products in 1993, although bonemeal has always been the ground residue of bones, after removal of the gelatine or fats by steaming. It is used in the garden as a supply of slow-release phosphates, being about 20 per cent calcium phosphate and 3 per cent nitrogen. Because it only breaks down slowly, the plant can use the phosphate—which it needs to develop strong root growth—as it grows. There has long been a potential risk of anthrax and salmonella from bonemeal, and one has always been recommended to use it wearing gloves. There is no serious question of the prion protein or a BSE virus being passed in the bones. The only safety question might be whether the steaming process was adequate or whether minute residues of tissue might remain, which could contain BSE. Heat alone—the sterilising process—would not necessarily destroy the virus or the prion protein. (There is doubt which of these is the infective agent. There is doubt about every aspect of this disease.) So the blanket assurances of sterility from manufacturers are less than convincing. However, the consensus is that this is a very, very remote chance and simply not worth worrying about, either in the general scheme of things or in the paranoid world of Creutzfeldt-Jakob anxiety.

The irony of this new area of anxiety in the hitherto tranquil zone of the garden is that for years garden writers like myself have been urging people to use organic products such as dried blood, bonemeal, and blood, fish and bone as alternatives to chemical fertilisers. Not only were they as practical but also regarded as worthy symbols of purity and wholesomeness, uncontaminated by the influx of chemicals that was pervading all areas of horticulture and agriculture.

Dried blood is used less commonly by the average gardener, although it is a good source of nitrogen and particularly useful for giving evergreen hedges a boost in spring. As a layman I wonder where the blood comes from. Could this handful have been swilling around the veins of the brain of a BSE-infected animal?

If you try to get to the bottom of the question of the potential link between BSE and bovine garden products you meet the same fog of uncertainty, conflicting information and ignorance as elsewhere on the subject. I spoke to an importer of bonemeal and dried blood who brings all his product in from Argentinian beef, and he assured me that there was no possible risk of infection as all his bonemeal was sterilised at 150 degrees Celsius. It was completely, unquestionably safe. I then rang HRI, Horticultural Research International, at Brogdale in Kent, who said that there had been no proof that BSE could be killed by heat, and that heat alone was not a guarantee of sterilisation. It all depended on how long the material was exposed to the heat . . . I questioned them about the risk of infection through manure from infected cattle and was assured that there was no chance whatsoever. The insides of cattle were almost completely sterile and it would have to be a 'very, very sick animal to produce bacteria'. Surely a cow with BSE would be 'very, very sick'? Um, yes. Also salmonella manages to pass successfully through the guts of animals, especially chickens.

Dr Stephen Dealler, consultant microbiologist at Burnley General Hospital, told me that faecal material is likely to be infectious. But above all, we do not know. No one, especially not the scientists like him who have been researching in this field, is sure of what is going on. This makes it doubly sickening to hear the knee-jerk denials of any risk from Ministry officials and the government.

For certain, Dr Dealler said, the infective agent of BSE is not destroyed in the soil. Land treated with cattle-based fertiliser that has been made from infected cows could hold the disease.

And so the uncertainty goes round and round.

The chances of getting BSE from a load of dung delivered to your garden or allotment are tiny, but we also know that there are cows with BSE right through the system. Do you want the manure from a cow dying of BSE nurturing your potatoes this summer?

I spoke to Professor Tim Lang of Thames Valley University, who made the point that behind the obvious alarm at contracting Creutzfeldt-Jakob disease, the real issue is a moral one. Although there is no evidence that BSE is contained in bonemeal or dried blood or manure and the risk is probably not worth worrying about, it raises a central issue: do gardeners want to be a repository for the waste products of the meat industry? In a sense the organic movement has been hijacked as a way of unloading this animal refuse. [Nine years on one comes across more and more instances of cynical manipulation of the organic ideal by the 'food' industry complying with the letter of the organic law and driving a coach and horses through the spirit. It is an industry that has become more perverted than any other.]

I have seen a farmer in Herefordshire spraying abattoir refuse on his land, filling the landscape with an indescribably disgusting stench for days. I guess that this is as much a form of waste disposal as fertiliser, the abattoir being glad to unload their rubbish and the farmer pleased to have free fertiliser so that he can grow more. Not better, you note, just more.

The BSE issue is more complex and more far-reaching than most people want to make it. According to Tim Lang, we have become obsessed with meat products, are far too restricted in our

94

production of food, both agriculturally and horticulturally, and we eat far too much meat and dairy products. These should be reserved for feasts. [The vast majority of meat is junked for animal food, as modern western consumers will only eat a tiny selection of the carcass. Yet the majority of cereals such as soya, maize, barley and wheat is grown to feed these animals. So you have a vicious, malicious, wasteful cycle of food production whilst half the world starves.] The consumption of fruit and vegetables should be enormously increased in their place. Diversity right through the system is what is called for, both for our own nutritional health and for the health of the food production system. This would cut down on the waste material from the hugely intensive over-production of animals and reduce the need for fertilisers such as bonemeal. There would be a far smaller volume of waste products to flog off as fertilisers. In their place we should be making much more compost and using green manures, which are just as effective.

Gardening is a metaphor for how we live. It is a microcosm of agriculture, and the urban gardener is as bombarded with chemicals as the beleaguered farmer. Rather than falling into the trap that the agricultural industry has slumped into, gardeners should not be associating bigger with better, but going for a wide variety of plants, perhaps growing less well, content with each specimen being less productive. In fact I believe that we, the consuming (as opposed to the producing) public, have at last had enough of being lied to by shifty, biased, second-rate politicians of whatever political hue, [Obviously not. This was before Iraq, doctored

95

documents, invented weapons of mass destruction, the Hutton report, officially sanctioned torture and imprisonment without trial.] and are at last learning not to trust any of the food producers from farmer to fast food dealer.

There is an element of magic about sprinkling a handful of bonemeal or chemical fertiliser around a plant and expecting it to grow bigger, faster and 'better' as a result. How do we know that it has any effect at all? Why not simply prepare the soil well, keep it watered, weeded and mulched with compost and let it do its stuff?

I shall not be buying any more bonemeal, dried blood, or fish, blood and bone. Not because I think the manufacturers mean any ill, or because I think that I stand any serious chance of contracting Creutzfeldt-Jakob disease from using them, but because this whole issue has made me realise that they are part of wrong behaviour. I shall make my own fertilisers from compost and green manure. I shall grow a wider variety of foodstuffs. I shall eat less meat and dairy produce. I shall probably die young and soft in the head, but nevertheless, my garden and myself will be the better for it. [The BSE crisis instigated a much more militant attitude in me towards food production in particular and how we treat the land in general. I realised that our approach had become corrupt and that whereas most farmers were hopelessly compromised by subsidies and the long-standing culture of irresponsible production, gardeners were in a position to behave well.]

02.04.00 **My Roots**

All the seed potatoes are in the ground. The grass paths are firm and dry. All the soil is prepared or bearing seed. The sweet peas are planted and growing. The first asparagus appeared two weeks ago, the same day as the first tulip. The salad crops in the tunnel are growing faster than we can eat them. The hornbeams are racing into leaf. What a spring for gardeners it has been so far! The last time I can remember it being so dry in March was in 1976. I was working on a farm near Alton in Hampshire and we had all the spring barley drilled by mid March and were to make our first cut of the sileage at the end of April, which was unheard of.

An extended stretch of dry weather has built in the same sense of cocky confidence that I remember then. For you townies, insulated from the daily domination of the weather, this might not seem noteworthy but believe you me, this comes along but once every 25 years and I am making the most of it. I walk outside in my slippers and we have been eating regularly outside. Our gardening work is now being planned around what we feel like doing rather than grabbing opportunities to do what must be done whenever the weather allows us. I don't care about the odd cold day—dryness is everything in this sodden western side of the country.

There is, of course, still the real risk of frosts, and I am trying to hold back for another month before committing geraniums, citrus, dahlias, melianthus, cosmos and all the other tender perennials that we over-winter indoors. This means that all the cold frames, greenhouses and standing-out areas are completely clogged with pots.

We have been in this garden for seven years now and have reached the position where we have far too many plants. We have run out of space and will soon run out of storage space for the increasing number of pots that are holding plants that we want to accommodate but do not seem to have room for. It is rather like having the garage spilling over with much-loved furniture. Do you bring it into the house and spoil the effect that you enjoy and have carefully put together, or do you turn your back on things that are part of your history and have served you well? Also pots are expensive on compost and take an awful lot of watering. There is a temptation to start digging up the orchard to make new cultivated space, but that would spoil something that is slowly becoming magical. Actually, if I am honest, I think that this entire garden is becoming magical. Apart from my children, I am more proud of it than anything else I have been involved in, and I think that is as much because it has been a truly joint creation with Sarah. A solo garden must be tinged with loneliness. [This remark caused a huge flurry of indignant correspondence from solitary gardeners who took it as a belittling of their state. I still cannot see how one could read that into it and I still stand by the remark.]

11.04.04

I had a strict C of E upbringing, and its tenets, myths and rituals are tattooed indelibly into my psyche. For many years I read the Bible and Book of Common Prayer daily. I was kicked out of confirmation classes at fourteen for being 'a disruptive influence' (I asked questions), but got myself confirmed at the age of 22 because I wanted to experience communion. I have studied Buddhist, Sanskrit and Hindu texts and visited gurus. In other words I have tried. I have put in the spadework. But for the past 25 years I have neither a believer nor a practiser been.

However, I do believe in the spiritual essence in everything. I am happy to call this God. It doesn't seem to matter to me if others don't. But working with the soil, growing things, tending them on a daily basis, seems to have a strong element of ritual and celebration about it that goes beyond horticulture as a hobby or the chores of keeping the garden tidy. It is more than just the extra time created by a bank holiday that links Easter to the garden. All across the country, whether Christian, Muslim, Jew or any denomination you choose, we celebrate the rebirth of the year in our back gardens beyond any calendar measurement. Nothing lasts, nothing stays the same. Renewal seems to be the secret even if, as Beckett said, it is just to fail better.

For the gardening trade, free from such spiritual or philosophical niceties, this is the commercial high spot of the year, the equivalent of Christmas and January sales rolled into one. They have not created this but are merely responding to an overwhelming, instinctive demand to plant. The urge to instigate and celebrate regrowth and renewal is inarticulate and does not depend upon any religious framework, but is universal and irresistible.

I like the way that Easter falls on the Sunday after the first full moon after the spring equinox, which means that it floats in a four-week sea from around 23rd March (in 2008) to 24th April (2011). The connection between lunar phases, religious ritual and the evidence of our eyes all fuses into genuine significance for even the most stubbornly secular of us.

Since January the garden has been limbering up, catching the sun and resisting the snow, wind and rain. The flowers that sneak in ahead of the race, like snowdrops, hellebores, winter honeysuckle and all that kith and kin, merely confirm the impression that they are an exception to the evident rule: the garden is biding its time.

This time is not merely linear any more than Easter is. It is more a meeting of moments than a fixed destination that is arrived at. The light balances between night and day, the moon swings from phase to suitable phase, the evidence of life literally pushing up through the ground is there all around; and, lastly, we give ourselves the time to pay attention and it all comes together.

The herbaceous plants are entering that astonishing green phase where flowers would be a distraction. If ever anyone needed a sign or miracle to confirm their faith, then surely they need look no further than any border herbaceous perennial like delphinium, geranium, eryngium, oriental poppy or peony? How can anyone fail to feel more alive, more hopeful, when you come home in the evening with light still to see by and these plants have grown since you left in the morning? OK, so I know I am atypical in this. Most people do not walk round their gardens before work and rush back out again the minute that they get home. These things slip through the days. But they are there to be celebrated if you have a mind to do so.

And there are flowers, real flowers, that are starting to spill out over the garden. The early clematises—*armandii*, *alpina*, and *macropetala*—are all in bloom and will remain so for weeks. In my own garden I have not found a suitably sheltered spot for *armandii*, but the other two are vital for—well, you must be getting the drift by now. For eye, mind, heart, soul . . . Place well-being in whichever part of the anatomy suits you best. The fritillaries are all out and tall on their elegant stems, white and patchworked purple all mingled at the bottom of our spring garden. The imperial fritillaries have been stinking for weeks but are now producing the carnival flowers that justify that hot, feral odour. The primroses are becoming more leaf than flower, but the cowslips have taken over. In the borders they are at their best, and never better than in conjunction with the slim-hipped primrose-yellow tulip 'West Point' and the blue smattering of forget-me-not flowers. This is yellow of a different intensity from the luminous lime that will flush through the garden in a few weeks' time. This has a new-born softness that will gain an electric edge as the euphorbias, new leaves of box and lime start to grow.

101

The blossom started weeks ago (but still within rolling Easter-time) with the cherry family, which includes blackthorn, and moves through gean and damson wild in the hedgerows to the eminently garden-based Sato-Zakura Japanese cherries, which are starting to flower in gardens all over Britain and have a delicacy and freshness that makes a cold day sing. Equally at ease in icy Easter winds is the pear blossom that covers the espaliers now, the pure white flowers with curiously hard dots of brown anther hovering amongst the knobbly, leafless branches. Crab blossom, preceding most of the true apples in the orchard by weeks, is completely different, all pink and soft and coyly tucked in leaves, and hints at the billowy fullness that will characterise our gardens in a few weeks' time.

Finally there is a point that falls somewhere within the Easter catchment—it probably only lasts for a day or two—when the stems of the hornbeam hedges are still clearly visible but the space between them is filling with leaf. They never look anything like this at any other time of year. Just for a few days the regrowing hedge becomes as translucent and intense as a stained glass window and as heart-liftingly beautiful as anything you might imagine. At times this life is intolerable, but a few moments of hornbeam in the Easter sunshine do as much as anything I know to give one strength and reason to start again.

11.04.04 **My Roots**

I seem to have become overwhelmed by strawberry plants and the paraphernalia of strawberry growing, although only a minute percentage of them are mine. I did weed my own strawberries the other day, getting them ready for their spring growth to flower and then fruit. Because strawberries like rich soil they are prone to weeds, and a heavy mulch or even a weed-suppressing mat helps control them. When the first flowers appear I put cloches over a few rows to try to force them into fruiting a little earlier, although a late cold snap will defy this. The cloches only accentuate the heat that is already there.

The irony in all this activity is that down the road from here a monstrous three-hundred-acre strawberry farm has sprung up. [Since then this is set to increase to six hundred acres, and another unit of 150 acres has been established by the same crew a few miles away. It is a very visible example of factory farming and despoliation of the landscape to satisfy a desire for cheap, year-round food. Insane, immoral and another example of our crazy 'food' industry.] One might be surprised to find that strawberries can cause huge social unrest, but they certainly have in Herefordshire. In order to supply supermarkets with 'home-grown' strawberries they have covered hundreds of acres with black polythene, sterilised the soil to kill all earthworms and any form of life and then erected hundreds of acres of plastic tunnels over all this. Arguably this is no different from me and my cloches and hemp matting, but the scale is apocalyptic. Non-organic strawberries are amongst the most chemically polluted foods that you can eat, and everything about their production is a cynical million miles from the summer treat that strawberries should be. It also involves a labour camp for a thousand pickers, mainly from eastern Europe, plonked, poor things, into a field in a hamlet that previously had a population of 31. It is not your backyard, but the moral of the story is to grow or at least pick your own and do not buy them from these monstrous fruit-factories.

I also cloched the first shoots of asparagus that are just appearing. I am world-weary enough to suppose that there might be factory-farms producing asparagus, but I cling to the innocence of cutting my own spears in a week or two, rushing to the pan of already boiling water and tasting that astonishingly rich flavour again. I try to avoid asparagus of any kind out of season, because the standards of ones cut fresh from the garden are so much higher than anything that you can buy. Strawberries might have been perverted, but asparagus, surely, can be kept unsullied.

14.04.02

I would swap my garden, any garden ever made, for a decent piece of deciduous woodland. No habitat seems to me to be more congenial or rich in sensuous experience. It is partly the scale and relationships of objects to space, from the grandeur of a mature oak or beech to the intimacy of woodland flowers or even fallen leaves; partly the way that light constantly plays inside the trees, falling in beams and spangles or distant splashes; partly the sheer variety of flora and fauna that all coexist in a state of perpetual shifting poise, and partly the usefulness of a wood. A deciduous wood supports life as I want to know it. Woods are the best place to be busy; and if you want to be happy, be quietly busy.

My friend Henry has nearly two hundred acres of woods in Usk, South Wales, and I went there the other day to cut some hazel. 'You're a bit late' was the first thing Henry said. I was. I had meant to go in January but things got complicated. By the end of March the hazel is heavy with sap and this makes it last a lot less long when cut. No matter. I cut enough for bean, clematis and sweet pea tripods, which can all be replaced with more seasonally attuned sticks when they turn brittle and snap in the wind. In fact over the years I have used hundreds of hazel rods as supports for climbers, both decorative and edible (as though the two were mutually exclusive), and they do all eventually snap at the point where they meet the ground. This means that one is forever coming across hazel-henges in the ground, gently rotting relics of either sweet peas or unfathomable ritual. I usually get the sticks delivered, but that went badly wrong this year, so I was forced to face Henry's gentle scorn and spend a day in the woods in radiant spring sunshine.

In my romanticism I see them as fences, handles,

charcoal, bean sticks or whatever else man can devise, but Henry gets more for it as pulp than anything else. *The Woodlanders* it is not. But the plant does not mind. There is no natural hierarchy of usage. Once cut, they are all eventually pulp, either rotting below ground in my borders or processed by vast machines. This harvest happens every seven or eight years with hazel, ten to twenty years with ash and thirty years with oak. No sooner are you done than it's back in a flash. But if you have more than an acre—and according to our local estate agents, who regularly deal in such things, less than forty acres of wood is 'amenity' land, i.e. a playground for people like me, and more amounts to serious stuff; so a 'decent piece' is thus defined as 41 acres or more—then you will coppice as much as you can manage every year, and traditionally this is two acres for a full-time woodman. So 24 acres of hazel would, at any one time, provide full-time employment in perpetuity (certainly for five hundred years) for a woodman and have twelve different stages of growth accompanied by twelve different stages of shade, ranging from the wholly open to almost complete summer cover. The net effect of this is to create a finely tuned, very varied micro environment where plants, insects and animals can live in very tightly defined habitats with exactly the right amount of shade and cover that is sustainable for centuries as well as changing every year.

Henry's woods were thickly speckled with wood anemone (*Anemone nemorosa*). I have got it in our little coppice at home and it is slowly spreading, but in Usk they were there by the tens of thousand. If any plant can be compared to stars in a dark sky it is the anemone in April. Despite the sheer mass of them, each flower was somehow articulated and separate. They grow from a rhizome that creeps underground and, like primroses, do best in areas that are only lightly shaded, surviving the last few years of the coppice growth but bursting out in the years following a cut, providing pollen and nectar for bumble- and honey-bees as well as voles and mice.

However efficient the anemone is at using the conditions of coppiced woods, it is an easily bruised thing set against the two real bruisers of woodland, the bluebell and wild garlic. The leaves of both were swarming over the woodland floor when I was there, the garlic consisting of fat spathes and the bluebell more finely splayed, with not a flower in sight, although I would expect the first bluebells to appear around the time you read this.

I had an astonishing encounter with wild garlic in the middle of May last year at the Nine Stones, just outside Winterbourne Abbas in Dorset. The stones are hard on the A35 but backed by a small wood, which was filled, crammed, with wild garlic, *Allium ursinum*, or, to use their vernacular, ramsoms. Despite the fumes of the lorries thundering by, the air was heavy with that curious sharp sweetness that garlic has, and the ground completely white with the flowers. They go well with ancient sites, because they are rooted in British place names, the word ramsoms coming from the Old English root *hrmsa*, giving a whole number of place names beginning in 'Ram'. Because they are so invasive it is probably a mistake to plant ramsoms in the garden, but tempting, as they are wildly decorative. They are also very edible, the strap-shaped leaves being a perfectly good substitute for 'real' garlic, both cooked and raw, with a much milder flavour than the smell might suggest. They will take a lot of shade, but need the open light of a deciduous winter, so could go in a corner where not much else would thrive.

Although bluebells and ramsoms share a preference for exactly the same conditions—light deciduous woodland with damp, preferably alkaline soil—they hardly ever grow together. Once one has a hold the other surrenders completely. So although we have our small bit of coppice, where the bluebells are beginning to take off (and perhaps take over), and which would be ideal for the garlic too, I think the choice has already been made.

Bluebells (*Hyacinthoides non-scripta*) actually need more light than wild garlic to really take hold, and as long as the soil is sufficiently damp (but not boggy) can quite often be seen growing in fields or verges right away from a wood. My own most unlikely bluebell sighting is on the cliffs on Sark, in the Channel Islands, where the bracken provided the necessary deciduous summer cover. Sometimes scattered woodland flowers in a meadow are the last vestiges of ancient woodland that might have been cleared centuries previously, but I cannot believe that this was the case on these Atlantic cliffs. The cover is necessary to stop grass establishing, which would push the bluebells—or wild garlic for that matter—out. They survive the deep shade of the end of the coppice cycle in an attenuated form, flowering modestly where grass gives up the ghost and then, when a coppice is cut, the bluebells go berserk and spread themselves wildly before the grass gets a look in. In the garden it makes sense to grow bluebells in a situation that mimics coppicing, but it is a hopeless plant for any kind of border as it will completely take it over once established, and the only thing that will suppress them will do in anything else growing there as well. So it is all or nothing.

You can buy the Spanish bluebell (*Hyacinthoides hispanica*), which is less invasive, less slender and less pointed. It has the futility of soya sausages or caffeine-free coffee. Far better to go with the real thing or go without. It also hybridises with our native bluebell, so never grow the two together or else you will end up with the sum of the worst parts: an invasive, squat, less delicate flower.

Bluebells have been the subject of much research into their chemistry because they seem to possess toxins that protect them—and therefore potentially us—from serious infections and diseases such as HIV and cancer. They also produce a toxin that the plant uses to fight off potential pests such as nematodes that would otherwise eat the bulbs, and attempts are being made to extract this for commercial use as a natural pesticide. In fact nothing will eat bluebells because of their toxicity, which explains why you find them growing in great lakes in woods where all other undergrowth has been grazed off by deer or even cattle and sheep.

Gerard Manley Hopkins talks of 'the sweet gum when you bite them', so although I have not tasted them myself, they will not kill you if you have a quiet nibble, or lick your fingers after picking the strangely juicy stems. But it's best not to pick, save for the gesture (and there are certainly times when only an impetuous gesture will suffice), as they do not last well in water and never look quite as good as you think they will. Best to take yourself to a wood and just look. And look and look and look.

22.04.01 **My Roots**

Howard is out on the JCB. I'm anxious, mainly because he is petrified. Howard dug our septic tank ten years ago, when the garden was no more than a gleam in my eye and a series of strings and bamboo canes in a field. It was the first and last time he had ever operated a digger. It will take a couple of days, I think, Howard, I say. And more than a couple of Valium, he mutters. I haven't slept all weekend. It's a bit tricky . . . You may remember that we flooded last autumn and our septic tank was out of commission for three weeks. So we have arranged for another one to be put in, which means digging up a large piece of the garden. To be honest I had almost forgotten about it, but they turned up yesterday with JCB, dumper and a lorryload of stone. It was like knowing that you had a nagging tooth and coming down to breakfast to find the dentist hovering over your kitchen chair, drill already whirring. Did I say that it has rained all week? That the garden is like slurry? That even a wheelbarrow is almost impossible to manoeuvre on the grass? So a JCB . . . Never mind. It must be done.

The new bench for the greenhouse got

delivered. It is all aluminium and stainless steel. We are now seriously smart in the greenhouse department. We don't *need* this, of course. It is a way of pretending to be more professional and grown-up than we ever are, and the trick works every time. I walk in there, in the same way that this lovely Apple Cube tricks me every day into thinking I need it to get the words out just so. Every inch is now laden with seedlings (bench, not Cube). I made some soil blocks the other day, sowed them with 'Little Gem' lettuce and mizuna, and went off to Birmingham the next morning to spend a few days filming. I swear that by the time I came home all had germinated and were sprigged with leaf. Magic.

Rather grudgingly I tackled the lesser celandine in the spring garden. There is no joy in this kind of weeding, because it resists being pulled up and has infiltrated nooks and crannies so thoroughly that precious hellebore seedlings are inevitably taken up as you fork, however carefully you do it. It is a real object lesson in weed control, as it should have been tackled properly last year, but as it wasn't too bad then I let it go. Fatal. Apart from anything else, lesser celandine is voracious in taking nutrients out of the soil, so everything suffers. It has got much worse this year, as has the creeping buttercup. It is the wetness in the spring garden from global warming that has ruined the drainage system, which has meant digging new drains and has upset Howard so much. It's all that George Dubya Bush's fault. I'd get him to come over and remove the celandines and send him penitent back to Kyoto, but Howard says he'd have to do the JCB stuff first. That would sort him.

23.04.00

Blossom works on us in a way that few other flowers do. It is partly sheer joy—that froth of flower is as life-confirming as anything your eyes will set on for another year; partly surprise—trees in flower are scarce in this country, and it continues to amaze us that it happens at all; partly sheer beauty—I still find the combination of May blossom and cow parsley on a lovely spring day the most achingly beautiful thing in the world; and partly the hint towards fecundity, because all blossom is merely a precursor to possible fruit. So many different messages riding on little white or pink flowers! But all arriving at the same place: that heart-lurch when you come across the first blossom of the year in the sunshine—what Dennis Potter, dying in front of our eyes and swigging morphine from a hip flask, [In a wonderful TV interview with Melvyn Bragg.] called 'the blossomest blossom'. What was really remarkable about that remark was not just the blithe courage or the glimpse of the daily world made infinitely precious in the jaws of death, but that each of us experiences this arching intensity daily for perhaps a week a year, courtesy of blossom.

All roses are blossom and all blossom are roses, sap-brothers under the bark. The Rosaceae family includes all our blossoming trees. It explains a lot. If you see a cross-section of an apple, a plum and a dog-rose flower they all look remarkably similar,

112

with the fruit waiting to swell just behind the petals. For years the appearance of fat apples or swollen-hipped pears from these flowers seemed to me to have an element of transmutation about it rather than being just stages along the same journey. The flowers are the fruit becoming.

In this part of the world the becoming happens as a procession, moving slowly through the countryside like the gorgeous retinue of a benign emperor. First is the blackthorn, *Prunus spinosa*, more often playing a minor role in a roadside or field hedge than planted in a garden, although it is a plum of sorts. The tiny white flowers convert into sloes, that wither the inside of your mouth with their astringency, but they make sloe gin, which is the best winter-warming drink that there is. When it flowered, my grandmother—whose entire speech was a series of saws and homilies strung together on a thread of bony rebuke—used always to murmur forebodingly, 'Blackthorn winter', and it does often seem to coincide with a sharp spell of icy weather. It has the wickedest thorns to be found in this country and, if trimmed, makes an impenetrable hedge. Just after the blackthorn comes the damson blossom, also pure white, sitting on scruffy little trees dotted along the hedgerows between the cathedral cities of Hereford and Worcester like crenellations. The other day I was driving by and I thought it had begun to hail before realising that in fact it was thousands of damson flowers swept off the branches by the wind.

As a plant the damson is not worth its place in any garden. But as a flower and fruit no sane gardener should be without it. So the answer is to put it in a hedge or orchard, to scramble honeysuckle, clematis and perhaps a small rose up it, and to relish the blossom for a week or so at the end of March and the fruit in September. The plums follow just after damson, overlapping by a few days, the baton passing from hedgerow to orchard, just as the fruit is changed from strong and small to full and sweet by the process of breeding and hybridisation. Plum blossom sits on the trees thinly, measured as much by the sky between the flowers as the massing of the blooms themselves. It is too late to check this now, but have a look again in eleven months' time.

Not long after is the wild cherry, the gean, *Prunus avium*. This is often found in numbers at the edge of a wood, creating a wall of blossom set against the unleaved branches of the trees behind it. They make large trees (up to seventy foot), so are not terribly suitable for a small garden, but they look incredibly decorative at every stage of the year. The bark is almost as good as the Tibetan cherry, and I remember a friend's father making his pipes from wild cherry wood, polishing the bark to a patent-leather shine on the side of his nose. *Prunus avium* 'Plena' is much heavier with flower and probably the one to plant in your garden. It also flowers a month later than the fully wild version, along with the sweet cherries. Ornamental cherries are the most popular of all flowering trees on account of their range of blossom, from the almond-like *Prunus subhirtella* to the hanging white flower-bells of 'Taihaku', but for me they do not fit the emotional bill of blossom because they are not producing any edible fruit. For the same reason I would not include hawthorn in this list, [This seems bonkers to me now, but I was on a roll or—more

114

likely—running short of space.] despite the power it has to jumble up my heart like an emotional spin-dryer. But the sweet cherries get a look-in, flowering like candyfloss (and almost as overpoweringly saccharine to the eye) at the end of this month. Then the flowers drop and blow around like brown litter for days.

Morello cherries (*Prunus cerasus*), crab apples (*Malus pumila*), quinces (*Cydonia oblonga*) and pears (*Pyrus communis*) all come into flower at around the same time, according to variety. Certainly they always precede the earliest apple blossom. Quince blossom is one of my favourites, having flowers with a delicacy and sublime fragrance. Quinces had a bad time of it last year, suffering from a fungal disease that browned and withered their leaves, but mine seem to have recovered. Incidentally, I have four varieties of quince, all planted near each other, and 'Lescovac' proved to be entirely resistant to this fungus. Crab apples are also wonderful in a much more cheeky chappy kind of way. I don't know quite how they create that effect, as they have perfect pink and white flowers that can fill the air with their scent, but compared to the bone-china refinement of quince or the purity of pear blossom, that is the result for me. Pear is my favourite blossom of all, either in a great tree with the blossom piled up cumulus-like, or stretched out along espaliers.

The main problem with these early blossoms, as with peaches and apricots, is that they are prone to damage by late frosts (just such as there was today—the ground absolutely white at seven o'clock in the morning, and the sky absolutely blue). The answer is to plant them either against a

115

west-facing wall or shaded from the early morning sun, as it is not in fact the frost itself that does the damage but the bright morning sunshine causing rapid thawing of the frozen cells.

The first apples, like 'Gravenstein', which has magnolia-pink flowers, start in mid April, and the last, like the very old variety 'Court Pendu Plat', finish a month later. This is an indication of their harvesting time, although unfortunately the fruit do not ripen exactly in the same sequential order that they flower. Thus in Roseanne Saunders's wonderful book *The English Apple* the earliest apple to ripen is 'Emneth Early', which is group three, and the last is 'Granny Smith', which is in the same group. The real difference between pear and apple blossom, other than the pure whiteness of pear and the strawberries and cream pink of most apples, is that apple blossom is borne as the leaves start to emerge, whereas pear adorns naked branches. This gives apple a fullness and softness that epitomises the fecundity of blossom-time. Also, by the time that the last apple blossom is coming out, the grass is growing strongly, the buttercups are out and the swallows are turning around the sky. Go and find an orchard of old standard apple trees sometime in the coming week and lose yourself beneath the branches. You will then know that we have arrived at the best of times at last. There is no going back.

That, above all else, is why you plant blossom in the garden.

23.04.00 **My Roots**

The hyacinths are all coming up, even though they were all put in ridiculously late (beginning of February) which proves that all rules are made to be broken. But at this time of year everything is just shooting up. You go indoors to make a cup of tea, and when you come out the entire garden is an inch taller.

And every spring there is a day like today when tiredness bleaches out all enthusiasm and energy from me. I have nothing to give and, worse, nothing to take. The garden is a beautiful stranger. I loathe this and deeply resent the slog that builds up such a weight of exhaustion. On such evenings I stumble round the garden, clumsy and stupid, not doing half a dozen different things before giving up. I suppose this is not what I should be writing here—but it is a reality of this place and this pace and is a reminder—as if I needed one—of how precious the good times in this garden are.

20.04.03 [I wrote this piece in response to a request from the editor for 'something for ordinary gardeners—dealing with pests and diseases'. It turned out to be a short manifesto of what I believe to be good principles of gardening.]

It is Easter again, comfortably straddling pagan and Christian ritual, flitting between March and

April as though, heaven forfend, there was more than one way of doing something right. There is a genuine sense of holiday despite this being, in that silly expression that one of the fatter cabinet ministers keeps using on the radio, a '24/7 world'. It is incumbent on gardening columnists to lay out projects for Easter, the jobs that need more than a weekend to get done, although I suspect that it is only people like me who regard the prospect of four unbroken days outside in the garden as a gift. And we don't need me to tell us what is what. So here is a change of attack. Here are, in my very 'umble opinion, the ten biggest problems that the average gardener has to face over the course of a year, and how you might deal with them. It is ten, by the way, not because they were brought down from the mountain on stone, but because that's the way we journalists do things in this 24/7 world we live in.

1. Slugs and snails.
2. All fungal problems (mould/blight/blackspot/wilt/honey fungus etc)
3. Vine weevils
4. Aphids
5. Weather (frost/drought/wind/rain)
6. Caterpillars
7. Mammals (cats/rabbits/foxes/moles/rats/mice/voles/deer)
8. Moss
9. Birds
10. Lack of flowering

To be honest I was scratching around after the ninth, but I do often get people complaining that their seemingly healthy plant (usually, in this instance, a shrub) refuses to flower. Number three, vine weevils, is not something that I have ever come across, so I cannot begin to speak of it from experience, but the source is nearly always plants bought from garden centres and it does seem to be becoming disastrously endemic in town gardens. Number seven on the other hand is likely to affect people in the suburbs and countryside more, although cats and urban foxes are a pest pretty much everywhere. There is not space to do justice to all these, as each one would and probably will provide the material for a full column, but here are some general rules that will help create a healthy garden.

Most disease in gardens is fungal. This often results from over-feeding, over-crowding and over-watering. We all deliberately cram plants into a small space, feed them extra goodness and water and expect each one to be perfect all the time. Global warming is not helping. The combination of warm, moist air and dry soil around the roots is particularly bad. Sustained periods of cold in winter are the best antidote to this, but these are becoming increasingly hard to come by. We tend not to value the existence of a healthy mould being cultured by our glorious garden.

Good drainage is always important in the prevention of disease. The only way to get the right balance between the seemingly mutually exclusive combination of drainage and water retention is by adding plenty of organic matter to the soil on a regular basis. Sometimes it is necessary to add grit or sand or even lay drains, which can seem a heavy-handed way to deal with mould or moss, but works.

A range of animals want to live off and in your garden. The extent to which they can healthily do this will be determined by the food supply and the levels of predation. These two factors are inextricably linked. In the natural scheme of things the food supply will fluctuate according to season and the amount of mouths it is feeding. Where there are seasonal gluts of food, the breeding cycle will be one of boom and bust, as the population will multiply rapidly and then eat itself out of house and home. At this point they will either move on to another source of the same food supply, eat something else or die. Part of the 'dying' process involves a rapid reduction in breeding in an effort to ration the available food.

Where you have a boom of one predator you will inevitably have a parallel increase in the creatures that predate on them, and so it will go right up the food chain. By definition it is self-limiting. Gardeners often react immediately to a sudden increase in pests, but their actions are rarely very successful. It is often better to wait a while and let the natural predatory balance assert itself without human interference—and whilst it might look disastrous for a few days, my experience is that surprisingly little damage is done to plants. A case in point is blackfly (the black aphid *Aphis fabae*) on broad beans: they look bad, but do little or nothing to reduce the crop and provide a meal for the aphid-eating population. The problem is caused by the soft new growth being available at that point in the breeding cycle. It is pointless to spray. Simply remove the growth by pinching out the tops of the plants and the problem is solved.

Any garden will always invite in animals of one

kind or another to prey upon the plants that we grow. Song thrushes eat snails, ground beetles eat the eggs of root flies, rove beetles eat aphids, as do hoverfly and lacewing larvae. Damsel bugs eat caterpillars. The numbers will reach saturation point within a year or two and then a predatory balance will be established. Healthy plants will cope with this.

Occasionally there is a plague of pests where, either because of circumstances beyond the garden, like exceptional rain or drought, or because of the life-cycle of a particular animal, like that of the field vole, there can be a huge increase in one particular problem. Beyond short-term expediency, I tend not to take this personally and to accept that it is beyond my control.

Forcing any plant into quick growth is disastrous, as it causes fast, sappy growth that is choice food for predators, prone to attack by fungus and disease, and weak to recover. It is always good to grow plants 'hard', which means not feeding or watering any more than is necessary, not giving too much protection from the cold or wind and making sure that they are properly hardened off before planting them. Be patient. It is a long game. It is a temptation to push right up against the edge of hardiness in a plant in spring, putting it outside as soon as possible so that it will flower or crop a few weeks early, but this never pays off. We often have very cold nights in April and May, and the key is to sow or plant out any but the hardiest plants only when the nights have warmed up so that the minimum temperature is five degrees. Extreme fluctuations in temperature will weaken any young plant and make it more susceptible to damage by predation. Sometimes this will mean ditching plants that you would love to grow. Better to get real or get a conservatory.

Part of getting real is to avoid monoculture wherever possible and to accept the limitations of your soil, climate and aspect. Grow as many indigenous plants as possible. These will have evolved defence mechanisms against local pests as well as being an integral part of the local micro food chain. The greater the variety of plants, the less chance of a visiting pest finding a host. In a small garden this is not so much of a problem, particularly if you have neighbours on either side with their own diverse mix of plants, but even within small areas of the garden, it is a good idea to break up blocks of plants. Alternate rows of unrelated vegetables and use annual companion plants amongst soft fruit. Feed the soil, not the plant. If your soil is in good heart the plant will grow at the rate it can cope with. A healthy plant is one that has fully adapted to the conditions that it finds itself growing in. This means that you can have plants that are perfectly healthy even in poor soil as long as you accept that they might be smaller and slower growing. A robust plant will not be weakened by the odd nibble by a slug or caterpillar or having sap sucked by an aphid. It will heal itself faster than the predator can cause permanent damage.

Also basic 'housekeeping' can go a long way to keeping the garden healthy. Pruning properly at the right time will promote good ventilation and discourage fungi, as well as removing any diseased or weakened plant that will attract predators. Tying climbers securely will stop branches rocking and fraying against each other and cut down on wounds that are the first entrance point for disease. Refreshing the compost in containers once a year will stop otherwise healthy plants getting root-bound and losing the vigour to resist attack. Keeping on top of watering and weeding will mean that your garden plants receive a steady supply of liquid and are not having to compete with weeds for nutrition.

Finally, it is important to remember that for plants, as for humans, it is the ability to resist and heal yourself from damage or disease, rather than the absence of such problems, that indicates true health.

25.04.99 My Roots

The other day a van drew up outside our house full of plants—1,123 of them to be precise. Sarah and I and three of the builders working on the barns unloaded them, us with a slightly embarrassed and hysterical grin and them with incredulity. They filled our yard, tray upon tray of them. This was the first wholesale plant order that we have ever made and it is utterly thrilling. There is a local wholesaler, Pottingers at Ledbury, that supplies many large gardens hereabouts. Typically we have been slow to find out about it and have almost seen it as immoral to buy in what we could produce ourselves from seed and cuttings. But friends of ours, with less money than ourselves to spend, persuaded us that it was no more expensive than doing it yourself if you

123

included the time saved, and produced a wonderful instant hit of planting. This is, of course, a very different kettle of fish from an instant garden. The plants are mostly small, in nine-centimetre pots, and will take a while to establish, but being small will grow the better for it. The main thing is that everything is delivered in batches of twenty for the smaller-growing plants and eight for the larger perennials, so you can establish really good groups in one go.

I planted fritillaries, white *Pulmonaria* and *Dicentra spectabilis* 'Alba' in the spring garden, and Sarah planted digitalis (Excelsior hybrids), echinops, echinacea and *Acanthus spinosus* in the bouncing garden. Both of us finished surrounded by dozens of empty pots, but we had made no impression whatsoever on the sea of trays. I am not sure if this is encouraging or not.

Sarah and I had one of those 4 am garden conversations that most gardening couples will be familiar with, redesigning the garden with the added insight of insomnia. We decided to put in a box hedge around each of the borders in the jewel garden. Should we use our own cuttings, adding to them each year, knowing that in five or six years' time they will have done the job at almost no cost, or, in the flush of our wholesale buying, do the main outlines in one fell swoop? Even if we could afford the latter (we can't), when would we have time to plant two hundred box? But common sense never came between us and our garden before, so we have gone ahead and ordered the plants.

The best thing about this time of year is that even when it is pouring with rain, there is loads to do in the greenhouse and potting-shed, and my main drive this year is to keep up with the pricking and planting out. It is always better to move a plant on than to let it sit in too confined a pot or seed tray.

The weather has been stunning, if in short doses. I love the way that the hedges in April are translucent and the tiny emerging leaves hold the light like a million fairy lights—only infinitely more magical. No experience or cynicism jades the pleasure of this newness, especially as it is mixed with familiarity at seeing old friends reborn. It is as though we have all travelled thousands of miles together, plants, birds and us human caretakers, across our own private oceans to arrive at a predetermined meeting.

May

02.05.04

Gardening is an odd thing. For a start it is immensely popular—according to a recent poll only 'listening to music' and DIY can claim more active participants across the whole range of leisure activities. More people garden regularly than go fishing, to football matches, church or the gym. And yet these comparisons all involve going out or joining others in an organised fashion. Gardening is introverted and domestic and woven into the weft of our daily lives in the same way that cooking is—except that fewer and fewer people are cooking anything at all.

The truth remains that the British are obsessed with gardens. Whilst there are just as good gardeners and gardens right across the world, no other country has the same intensity of feelings about them. It is a completely classless, democratised phenomenon. Very few people, given the choice, do not eventually want their own patch of land, even if it is initially to watch someone else tend it for them.

Historically we have had gardens to grow food, feel safe from uncontrollable nature, and provide aesthetic pleasure. Whilst all of these factors are still important, I also think that gardens are where we feel most free. Modern life is, for most of us, a kind of serfdom to mortgage, job and the constant assault to consume. Although we have more time and money than ever before, most of us have little sense of control over our own lives. It is all connected to the apathy that means fewer and fewer people vote. Politicians don't listen to us anyway. Big business has all the power; religious extremism all the fear.

But in the garden or allotment we are king or queen. It is our piece of outdoors that lays a real stake to the planet. The garden is not just the grass to be mown and the straggle of weeds to be pulled from between the paving, but the sky and the rain and the birds singing in the bushes—our bushes.

Gardens are places where we can connect with the weather, the seasons and the natural rhythms of plants and animals. We all lead such hermetic lives, wrapped in central heating, air-conditioning, cars, trains, neon offices, streetlights and a constant supply of cheap gratification that it is possible not to experience anything at all directly. It is Living Lite. A garden—however small—is the objective correlative to this ersatz existence. Gardens are wet and cold and bathed in sun and, despite all our worst endeavours, continue to obey the cycles of nature. To be out there and doing something is deeply empowering because you then become part of that rhythm. You don't need to pass an exam or register. It only works if it is personal and completely honest. Visiting a garden should be like having a meal in someone's house rather than going to a restaurant, and you can spot phoneyness in a garden as soon as you step into it. All you need is to put some seeds or plants in the ground and care for them. That's gardening.

This is highfalutin stuff. Sometimes it is a patch of grass and a bit of colour. Somewhere for the kids to muck about and the dog to scratch its arse. Somewhere to catch the odd moment of northern sun. But all gardens have the potential to be sensuous, poetic places, feeding the soul as well as letting us spread beyond the house. A window box can be a shrine, and I have visited scores of small back gardens that are brilliantly and reverently tended. There is something happening there that goes beyond horticulture just as a superb loaf of bread or bottle of wine goes beyond nutrition. In a world of terror and anxiety this is art in a million backyards. There is a real sense that in making your garden 'better' according to your own taste, then you are doing more than outdoor decorating. I absolutely believe that you are making the world a better place for everyone else as well.

This is why I have little time for gardens that are merely a collection of plants, however rare or exotic. This reduces gardens to filing systems. An overgrown lawn with a winding path trodden through it is likely to be more beautiful and rewarding. For a while British horticulture was hijacked by collectors, bringing back trophies from the Empire as a piece of one-upmanship. A culture of technique—almost always male-dominated— where the garden almost became a laboratory superseded the true spirit of gardens which is feminine, intuitive and full of guile. Gardening is no more a science than cooking is. This does not mean that science has no place in the garden. Gardeners are at the cutting edge of GMO, pesticides, fungicides, earth sciences and the whole intricate balance of maintaining our ecosystem whilst trying to contain nature in what is always an unnatural corset of horticulture. But the goddess of the garden is Gaia, which, of course, connects every weekend mower with the future—the real, political, breathing future—of this earth. Perhaps

131

every politician should be forced to do a month's gardening leave every year.

No other domestic activity combines the public with the private so completely. This is why I garden organically. It seems to me to be an absolute moral imperative to try and do as I would be done by. If I want less junk food in the supermarkets then I must grow some proper organic vegetables in my plot. If I don't want pesticides sprayed over every inch of the countryside then my inner-city backyard should be clean of them too. In the garden I can practise being good, make somewhere I think beautiful and be master of my scrap of outdoors.

07.05.00 **My Roots**

In a way I like a wet day at this time of year because when it is dry I always feel driven to get on outside. It is as though I wake up to see a day-glass in front of me and the sand already slipping remorselessly down. All gardening at this time of year becomes a race. But when it is wet our clay soil becomes immediately out of bounds. Nothing can be planted or sown, grass cannot be cut, and hardly any weeding can happen because the weeds come up all slicked with soil, filling the wheelbarrow with a congealed lump of weedy earth that will sprout yet more vigorously healthy weeds if dumped. Yet, having been away from home so much over the past two months, I have to do something in the garden, and now the potting-shed and greenhouse come into their own. Our potting-shed is an unreconstructed stable, and the first thing I did when we took it over five years ago was to muck out three foot of manure. But it is dry and reasonably warm and I can happily spend all day there. I have the radio on (always Radio 4 on long wave—can't stand FM), frequent cups of tea and am completely absorbed. Pots have to be organised and washed, and compost mixed for various purposes. Wet weather means that I often sow many more seeds than we need just because . . . well, just because it is there. Everything edible is sown in plugs, two seeds to a plug, so that they can grow fast in a slug-free environment before transplanting outside, although it is a battle trying to keep the slimy little bastards out of the greenhouse. I reorganise the greenhouse to fit new stuff and play in there happily for at least an hour, moving A to B and then outside to C, which are the cold frames. I suppose this is a man thing and a shed thing and is, viewed in this light, a little sad. I'll catch myself smoking a pipe next.

We have replaced all the six-foot hazel hurdles that we have around the outside of our front garden (with a yew hedge slowly growing inside them). They are a direct link with the Hampshire village I grew up in, where a hurdle-maker worked up the hill at Herriard. That hurdle-making yard has long stopped working, but I still have to go back to Hampshire to get them made despite strenuous attempts to get local ones. Perhaps because these pieces of Hampshire coppice are outsiders, I put an aesthetic and emotional value on these bits of fence above many of our plants, and in many ways they are a stronger aesthetic influence on that part of the garden than any plant.

The first swallows arrived this week and the sky will be full of them by the time you read this. One swallow may not make a summer, but it damn sure made my day.

11.05.03

When I was a child I would walk a great deal, often with a friend, often alone but always with a dog or two. The dog was essential because somehow, in the rather odd scheme of things in the Don household, taking the dogs for a walk was classed as a 'job' in the same way as washing up, chopping wood or weeding the paths was. If a job had pleasure attached to it then it meant that you were not doing it properly. So I was sure that as soon as anyone realised that this walking job was an unalloyed pleasure, then it would be rationed and balanced with an appropriate amount of drudgery. But it never happened. Taking the dogs for a walk ensured a couple of hours of happy freedom as well as counting in the balance of soul-saving labour. Maybe my parents were more benign than I suspected and gave me this task as an act of generosity.

The upshot was that I spent years mooching along tracks, fields and woods of a smallish area around my north Hampshire home. It is a countryside of hedged lanes and coppices, gently curving downland and beech woods. Thirty years ago it was rare to see another person, except for the gamekeepers patrolling the shoots like security guards and a lone tractor driver working a field. While I walked it was my land, my hedgerows and fields. I got to know its face in every season, every weather.

As I write this, I realise that I garden now in exactly the same spirit that I walked then. It was walking as work but also walking as play, walking as celebration, walking whilst scarcely able to believe that this much pleasure was officially sanctioned. Flowers decked the way. I knew exactly which bank sheltered the first primrose, where the bluebells misted best through the beech shade, which field had the best cowslips for miles. Cornflowers, chicory and poppies, now wiped from the cornfields by ever-increasing use of herbicides, fringed the headlands, and cow parsley lined the lanes like an ecstatic choir. These were as familiar to me as my family, yet I hardly knew their names and certainly had no more botany than a bird. I never really articulated it, but I think I thought that studying them would break the magic and reduce this intense, private world to the foolishness of rational intelligence. It was the difference between watching a butterfly bob and float until it disappeared and scrutinising the same specimen pinned to a block.

Here we are, in May again, with the same ecstasy and the same confusion. I have come to learn about plants and their names as part of the process of articulating and sharing their magic, but I am still wary of those who categorise and measure with botanical fervour. You can know everything *about* something without really knowing anything at all of its essence. The poetry slips through these cracks, and without poetry gardens and plants are reduced to something between a specimen and another chore to measure the day. The light does not get in.

But even the driest horticulturist must see the way that every growing thing, named or not, blazes with an inner glow at the moment. There is no colour so redolent of light and life and hope as the new green of early May. I probably say that in these pages every year but I experience it anew every single year as a blinding revelation. In my travels around the world I have never seen anything as lovely as the British countryside in May. Our gardens are, at this time of year, a touch of this, a walking memory, the spray from the green waves rolling in. As such it is almost enough just to bathe in that generalised sense of green wonder, letting light and growth wash over and through you. But in amongst the overall splendour there are touches of individual prettiness that are worth stooping to peer at and name and know in more than ecstatic communion.

Prettiness is something I value enormously, mainly because I feel clumsy and gauche with it. It is, I suppose, a fear of toppling from pretty to twee. But in spring there is scope for unrestrained, rampant prettiness. All 'cottage' gardening pays homage to this, and there are cottagey plants that manage to decorate and embellish the green power of spring without diluting it. One of the first flowers I ever 'learned' was *Dicentra spectabilis*, the bleeding heart or lady's locket. The bleeding hearts have been gently dropping their sanguine pink flowers for a few weeks now. In fact it is quite wrong to paint a bloody picture of them because no pink was ever pinker nor more sugary, hanging in rows from each stem in every stage of their development from the initial missile into the perfect heart shape to the final opening flower with the hanging rocket head folded back to make a bonnet above the gleaming white sheath containing the stamen. Look up into it, or gently pull it apart, and it is tender origami.

09.05.04 **My Roots**

I work to the soundtrack of cuckoo and curlew call and the chatter of swallows. The garden, especially at this time of year, belongs as much to the birds as it does to us. That is why it is so important not to cut any hedges between February and the end of July. The birds need them, not just for nest building but also for the young to have cover whilst they learn to fly and look after themselves. The hedges in this garden serve as crowded streets which the birds run busily through. Mind you, our two cats do their best to destroy any avian life that they can get their horrid claws on. We tried putting bells round their necks and they simply scratched themselves raw attempting to take them off. The truth is that cats do terrible damage to birds. A year or so ago I watched the swallows return here, flying precisely to our eaves from Africa, and as they swooped to scoop up insects one of the cats rather lazily flicked up into the air and pulled a bird out of the sky, killed it, then walked slowly off. One beautiful creature pointlessly killing another.

The asparagus is in full throttle, shooting up spears overnight. So far we can keep up with it, still relishing the luxury of eating it within minutes of cutting, but I know that in a week or so it will feel rather a tyranny. To waste it seems criminal, and yet the thought of the fifth dish in five days can feel a trifle too much. But having fresh, organic, seasonal food from the garden is so life-enhancing and such a vital corrective to the tasteless, seasonless mush that is pumped out of the agri-factories masquerading as 'farms'. In this way gardens and allotments remain a vital yardstick for those of us who care about what we eat. Whether it is asparagus or plain old lettuce, I always grow too much fruit and veg and yet long to grow even more. It is an attempt to make the most of the astonishing fecundity of the season—not to fill every spare inch with food that we want to eat seems a missed opportunity. Yes, there is excess—even waste—but at least it all goes on the compost heap and the goodness is returned to the soil.

14.05.00

So much of gardening is bound up in ritual and every garden has its own liturgy. The seasons impose a rhythmic observance of custom, which then in turn becomes customised by every gardener. This is all part of the shoring up of ruins that shadows the making of any garden, the sense that if it is not dealing with real life (it is, it is) then at least it is keeping real life at bay and there is a sure and certain comfort in denial.

One of my own favourite gardening rituals is the

annual laying out of seeds that we have ordered by mail, shuffling the pack on to the kitchen table to create an embryonic map of the garden. We pretend that it is an important 'job'—that it needs to be done sometime in January so that we can plan and organise the pattern of seed sowing. Utter nonsense, of course. We do it because it makes us feel good, because all those packets of flat paper envelopes look good. When the game is done they all go back into the box and the seed is sown as randomly and impulsively as horticultural sense will allow. But the ritual pleasure of relishing the seed packets themselves never wanes.

I learned this by chance long before I ever sowed a seed. Nearly forty years ago I marched into a neighbour's cottage unannounced—as we all seemed to do in those days—to find them standing back and silently admiring their seed delivery spread out on the table like a feast. I did not know what the individual seeds were—although with hindsight they would have been nearly all 'essential' vegetables—but I could tell that the table was almost glowing with richness and promise.

Thinking back on it, they had probably pored over the catalogue for weeks despite the fact that they bought exactly the same year after year. That spread of seed packets represented real investment and expectation. They would hardly have starved if all the harvests had failed, but certainly the quality of their lives would have been lower. Those packets were precious. [The introduction of the deep freeze around 1968 radically transformed our lives. Until then we ate only the vegetables that we grew, mostly fresh in season. This was healthy but, to the modern pampered palate at least, very dull.]

One of the ironies of this is that very few seeds are remotely precious. Most plants produce the things effortlessly, in huge quantities, for free. This raw material needs no working by expensive machinery, no human skill to make it useful or transformation of any kind at all. The costs are tiny. Just collect it, sort out the chaff, keep it cool and dry and pack it. It is the packing that is the key. In practice we buy the packet as much as the seeds inside it. It acts as much as a marketing device as a container. A poster or TV advertising campaign for seeds would be stupid—they are a poster campaign in themselves. You can chart cultural and aesthetic values through the changing designs in seed packets, from the surreally garish, the hand-painted, the coyly kitsch promising flowers as wholesome as apple pie to the rigorously brown-paper plain of the organic movement. You can even collect antique seed packets—the Richter Gallery (www.sover.net/oldlabel/seeds) will sell you framed pre-First World War packets on the net.

I had always thought of seeds as being predominantly a mail order business. I have been involved in mail order in the past and know that it can be a nightmare on the production side. Inevitably 20 per cent of the range provides 80 per cent of the sales, although you never know which 20 per cent it will be. So the vast majority of a catalogue simply makes no money at all. But seeds are the perfect candidate for mail order. They take up hardly any space, will store for years, cost practically nothing to produce and have a steady source of supply. They are very light, therefore cheap to deliver and are unlikely to be damaged in transit. There is huge profit to be made from them.

However, the vast majority—some 90 per cent—of all seeds are sold retail. One of the side-effects of these huge profit margins is that the larger seed companies wage fierce discount wars to get retailers to stock their range and give it pride of place. Although seeds are a fantastically cheap way to fill the garden, most people prefer to get an instant plant rather than nurture one from a seed.

Seed packets are like book covers. We browse through them and buy on visual whim—so that a shopper for a tray of petunias will see a packet of lettuce seed, buy it and in the process pick up half a dozen other packets as well. Most of these will never get sown. Seed companies, like mustard manufacturers, happily make money from their product being wasted.

And, like book covers, the quality varies from the charmingly kitsch to the annoyingly kitsch. Very few seed packets are actually beautiful. Thompson & Morgan told me that changing the photograph on the packet can transform sales overnight. But printing good quality colour pictures is expensive—much more expensive than the seeds they illustrate—and only viable on huge print runs. Inevitably this counts against the small, specialist producer. But niche marketing is probably the future of seed selling. Every producer is now packaging mixtures of seed, either in the same packet or as a set of packets, be it for a herb garden, summer salad, Intimate Salad with a few Chosen and Stylish Friends, hanging basket, spring window box or oriental greens. For the most part each 'collection' (pass the sick-bag) has an artful but unstylish photo. The result is probably very popular and successful but it has all the style of a 1950s girdle ad. [Since this was written, seed packets have dramatically improved their art work thanks in large measure to the introduction of beautiful packets by Franchi. Their seeds were initially sold through delicatessens, thus appealing to a very different, much more visually sophisticated market.]

At Sarah Raven's Cutting Garden—a small producer of specialist seeds primarily for producing plants for flower arranging—they have turned this on its head by using transparent packets, so you can see the seeds inside, and colour-coded, stylishly printed labels with one picture per group of seeds. The result is glamorous and distinctly up-market. Chase Organics (The Organic Gardening Catalogue) sells all its seeds in brown paper bags with green (geddit?) lettering. Predictable, even depressingly so, but certainly clear branding. It is a very competitive market and one that is not increasing. More and more people are buying their bedding plants in trays from a garden centre for hundreds of times what it would cost to grow them from seed. But we are a rich society. We can afford it. The fact is that most people with a garden would not dream of ever growing anything from seed. I think that sowing a few seeds is probably the most significant shift from 'doing the garden' to becoming 'a gardener'. At a stroke you are going beyond the kick of instant, easy gratification and bringing time into the equation: and time always makes gardening so much more interesting than 'make-overs' or any kind of quick fix.

16.05.04 **My Roots**

At this time of year I wake early, slip out of bed and dress, trying to wake as few people as possible, make a cup of tea and go straight outside to the garden. It is the best time of day. I set no alarm and follow no routine beyond the discipline of getting up as soon as I wake. Sometimes I am out by five, other days not until six thirty. Sometimes I hoe or sow seeds in the veg garden, sometimes I just take photographs. More often than not I work in the potting-shed, listening to the radio and pricking out or sowing seeds. This morning I sowed purple sprouting broccoli, cavolo nero and red kale, all into coir. Anything that can possibly be transplanted is sown under cover, pricked out and potted on as necessary before finally planting out, as a (very effective) anti-slug measure. None of them will be tasted before November and the broccoli not until April. It seems a long way ahead. I feel uncomfortable with most modern psychobabble, but this feels like my time. It sets me up for the day ahead and is well worth the loss of an hour's sleep.

There are too many days when I get to do no other gardening, at least not in this garden. This is a problem, as for this month Sarah and I have no help in the garden. The care of two intensive acres has to be squeezed in around the rest of our absurdly busy lives. I can hardly expect sympathy as this is precisely what most people have to do, but it does make me think hard about what my own garden is for.

Clearly it works fine as a private, domestic garden. But equally clearly, thanks to these pages and my work on television, it is a bit more than that. It is not open to the public but feels as though it is. We have photographers here fairly often, and all visitors judge it with an eye that is rather more critical than the one they cast on most gardens. It works as a laboratory, research ground and yardstick that I relate all my work to. It means that we feel that we can never let any part slip in any way—even though the reality is that I could probably write this column and not do any gardening for weeks on end. But not live happily.

19.05.02

Last week we became a wrist short of a good garden. Also a wrist short of a mother, wife, driver, cook, writer, manager, designer, washer, cleaner— it is surprising what you need two working wrists for. Sarah fell, put her hand out on to the stone flags to break her fall and broke the wrist instead. It is not a real disaster—could've been a whole lot worse, bones heal, think how lucky we are—but for the next month or so everything is tricky. She can't hold anything at all in her right hand, which means that I have to do all the driving, cooking, washing and home stuff as well as trying to write these damn words every day. [The damn words in question were my various regular journalism, but mainly the book *The Complete Gardener*, which I wrote over most of 2002.] Sarah, in full frustrated health, is educating her left hand fast, but the limitations are on the level of a bad joke. She can't sign a cheque or a credit card slip. Can't type. Can't do up her shoes. In terms of the garden it is a catastrophe.

Whatever impression I give through these pages, this garden is *ours*. It was made by us and is gardened by us. Neither of us plants or removes anything without consultation with the other. Neither of us does anything at all in the garden without the agreement of the other. Sarah has proudly refrained from cutting a blade of grass, and does not have a lot to do with the plant-raising side of things (although, come to think of it, she does nearly all the direct sowing of annuals), but in every other way she is as essential to this garden as I am. She weeds, plants, prunes, tidies, fine-tunes incessantly. She prepares for every photo shoot— and we seem to have a lot of those nowadays. She grows everything that we have in containers. To forgo that throughout the month of May can only mean that either I double my own output to cover or that things will go to the bad.

If you make a garden with someone else, it is partly a celebration of your sameness, just in the way you enjoy the same food or laugh at the same things, but it is equally a celebration of your difference. It is only by allowing the other to take you where you would not have gone yourself that the garden becomes greater than the sum of its parts. In practice this means that although we never impose our horticultural wills on each other, we often profoundly disagree over what we should do and plant. I am by nature impetuous and impatient and like to execute an idea while it is still warm. Sarah would rather think through all possibilities and come to a conclusion that she is sure is right. She would rather do nothing than the wrong thing. I would rather do something than nothing. We appal and admire each other in equal measure. But it is a good mix and—you've guessed this already—an important part of our marriage.

Which brings me to the damp garden. Sarah keeps returning there and thinking that it is lovely. When I am told this kind of thing I know that there is trouble brewing. It means: it is good enough to see the possibilities of how it might be *really* good. It means changes. It means upping the ante and trying harder.

The damp garden is a bit at the bottom of the garden that is the first to flood and the last to drain. The soil is as rich as fruitcake and it never truly dries out. It has led an uncertain existence, never quite establishing an identity until a couple of years ago when I moved all the hostas and ligularias in the garden down to that spot. The hostas had been mainly in the spring garden and the ligularias in the jewel garden, and both were unhappy by the end of summer. Funnily enough the ligularias were suffering most from drought, whilst hostas simply prefer the wet rather than need it. To these two wet-lovers I added in the royal fern *Osmunda regalis*. This has started seeding itself all over the place, much to my pleasure. There is a small quince tree and two bamboos, *Phyllostachys nigra* and *P. aurea*. Self-sown honesty (an escapee from a compost heap that used to be on the site) has filigreed itself into the area; and it is all set against a backdrop of hornbeam hedges and prolific weeds as the boundary of our garden dips

146

into the water meadows. Last year we turfed a sort of path along the back of one of the borders, and put a seat there. No one walked down the path. No one sat on the seat. Sarah hated it.

This spring the grass has all been lifted—having had a year in which to get good and established— the seat has been shunted away, and a mass of comfrey has been dug up and taken to a strip by the tunnel to provide a supply of leaves for nourishment. I cannot be doing with making comfrey juice or tea or whatever the liquor is called. I know I should, but it is too much of a faff to sustain interest. [I have since got in the habit of making it regularly, as it is particularly good for tomatoes, chillies and aubergines grown in pots. It is no more of a faff than making a cup of tea, but it certainly smells like dog's breath.] It is also foul-smelling. But it does work wonders as an activator on the compost heap and if used as a mulch. Comfrey is very rich in potash and a good way of taking trace minerals, which it absorbs particularly effectively, and transferring them to the roots of other plants. I just cut the whole plant to the ground and lay the leaves like a poultice under roses, tomatoes, gooseberries and redcurrants. In rich soil it will give three or four cuttings a year.

In the newly cleared space at the back of the damp garden I have planted seven *Stipa gigantea*s, which have been dug up from the jewel garden. Stipas do not like being moved much—they have rather pathetic roots, given how big they become— but they will survive and thrive. The idea is that they will provide the perfect link between garden and countryside. It is a good idea. An idea I wish I had had. An idea that took one wrist to

147

conceive and two to execute.

20.05.01 **My Roots**

Real sun. From dawn (too early, but there you go, I will catch up on my sleep in winter) to last night's ridiculous dusk, we have had baking, brilliant sunshine. The best sequence of weather for at least eighteen months. Everything, of course, is easy. You forget how much effort goes into keeping warm, keeping dry, dealing with mud. It is surprising how slowly plants respond to the weather. Just because I immediately slough off the winter creakiness (actually not, as I hurt my back taking down the chicken fence. I am a physical wreck and I accept it, but a happy one), I expect everything to grow visibly before my eyes. It is all about night-time temperature, of course, and the clear skies have meant cold nights, so everything is holding its fire a while longer. But the pleached limes are all sprouting leaves from their knobbles and the apple blossom, having held back at least a fortnight past its normal start, is getting good. I planted out lettuce, spinach and 'Primo' cabbage grown in soil blocks and took a risk with French beans, also in blocks. In my experience you gain nothing by trying to hurry beans along, as even if the frost does not get them, they do not grow at all if the night-time temperature drops below 5 degrees. So as a general rule I plant them out in June, having hardened them off in a cold frame. But I have experimented with planting them out under closed cloches—effectively little tunnels—hoping that the high daytime temperature will be stored overnight. We shall see. In the meantime I have sown another batch in blocks.

I transplanted a quince, 'Lescovac', from the pot where it has been sitting for the past eighteen months to the new wet garden in the hope that it will appreciate the inevitable winter flooding it will get. Because of our septic tank upheaval we have had to move all the stuff that we had been keeping in pots and have tried to plant or ditch everything older than a year rather than move it all back again. We ought to do this every spring. I also moved a couple of royal ferns from the jewel garden to this new site and found that they had multiplied themselves tenfold by runners in just a year. At least something has appreciated the wet of the past twelve months. Not much has. A lot of things in the jewel garden have been lost, with corresponding holes to be filled. This is, of course, merely an opportunity to get new plants and to sort things out, but even in the sunshine that is a bit gung-ho.

And why the ridiculous dusk? Because at nine the moon suddenly poked its head above the horizon, as orange as a Californian poppy and as big as a beach ball, turning the night into fancy dress. I have lived more than half my life and seem to know less and less as it goes on, but I have learnt this much: nothing gets any better than this.

31.05.98 [It is normal for a column to take an entire day's research and writing, but this piece was written almost without pause between 5 and 7 am when I was filming Chelsea Flower Show and had no other way of reaching the deadline. Look carefully and you will see that there is no research needed at all.]

Chelsea '98. Two members of the gardening sorority meet. Darling! Mwhoa Mwhoa! My God I just love that little sweater! Thankyou! (Slight pause for the smile to develop fully and the pay-off to have its full import.) It's Prada—my absolute favourite sweater of all time.

Well, it would be. The fact that it was 80 degrees in the non-existent shade and little rivulets of sweat were glistening on the skin of her back between favourite sweater and the top of favourite trousers —no matter. We gardeners are earthy types. In the muddy, sweaty, exhausting build-up to Chelsea Flower Show all flesh was equal. But now the build-up was effectively over, the judges had been and left prizes like schoolmasterly Father Christmases. It was Press Day. The build-up was all about cranes and fork-lifts, teams of young underpaid people working eighteen hours a day for weeks and sleeping in tents in Battersea Park. This is for the foot soldiers, you understand. The RHS officer class wandered round in shirt and tie, 'Everything all right? Jolly good.' At ease, everyone. Stand easy.

Except that preparing a show garden is never remotely easy. Take the Chanel garden, handily titled 'Le Bosquet de Chanel'. ('Darling,' I overheard from the crowd, 'what does that mean?' 'It's another word for baroque, darling—you know, twiddly bits.') This began two years ago, planned with the precision and guile of Normandy landings or Paris collections. The rumour is that it cost a million pounds. Huge beeches were selected to be grown into arching frames surrounding the garden and trained in pots for over eighteen months, prepared for Chelsea long before Chelsea knew that they were coming. The planting—exquisite, all in white, as honed as a supermodel's cheekbones—was chosen at and before birth, bred for exhibition and performance like an East German swimmer. The parterre and surrounding hedges were grown in boxes and pots in polytunnels in segments by the contractors Waterers, clipped for months so that on arrival at Chelsea they only had to be fitted together like a jigsaw.

Such precision and attention to detail is everything at Chelsea. Nothing, but absolutely nothing is left to chance. Even the real stroke of genius of the Chanel garden—the fact that the beech hedges were left unclipped and slightly shaggy—was as accurately measured as the deshabille of the catwalk.

Oh, all right. I'm straining the image. Royal Chelsea Flower Show is so British and uptight, so formal and staid, so reassuringly predictable and magnificent that it does not at first seem an easy bedfellow with fashion and all its fickle foreignness. Chelsea is a trooping of the floral colour, a chance to show the world that when it comes to doing things proper, we Brits do it more proper than anyone else. But in fashion the British are the grit in the oyster. Maverick British fashion designers are underfunded and unregarded and yet feed the world with ideas and energy which then get appropriated and manufactured into fashion's stylish pearls. French designers look first to London for inspiration and it is now almost obligatory for Paris fashion houses to have a Brit as head designer.

I spent ten absurd years of my life designing jewellery, living my life to fashion's rhythm, and even in the early 1980s Karl Lagerfeld was as hot as it gets. We awaited each of his collections with the same anticipation that you wait for your favourite band's new record, inspected and devoured it from the pages of glossy mags and hated the bastard for being so consistently one step ahead. So what was he doing at Chelsea?

If you want to speak to the best-known gardeners in Britain you look in the phone book and ring them up. To speak to Karl involves an audience at his court and weeks of negotiations with his people. It is a big deal. Consequently I was told that I only had fifteen minutes with him, 11.15 to 11.30, and I must be there at 11 sharp. And that he would be late. And, as a final reminder, that if I didn't know my stuff he would be difficult. What stuff? Gardening stuff or fashion stuff? Anyway, if someone says something like that you instantly forget any stuff you might have known.

The night before Press Day I was still at the showground late, waiting for a friend. The foot soldiers slogged slowly back to their billets, horribly anxious and exhausted, no time left to do any more before the next day's judging. Walking past the Chanel garden, I noticed three men in immaculate designer jackets and white shirts with those sticky-up collars that don't turn down, and with huge shoulders and necks. Designer bodyguards. Inside the garden, which in correct baroque, bosquet fashion was an ordered patch of controlled horticulture surrounded by woodland, was a man with a grey ponytail, white jacket and stubby legs who was photographing the garden's designer Tom Stuart-Smith nestling up to the golden statue of Venus de Medici that was the garden's focal point. Tom is a tall, serious man with beetling brows and an academic's gravitas, and he posed with all the ease of a man embracing an angry porcupine. As I left the showground I noticed two stretched Mercedes parked confidently in the no-parking spot by the gates.

On the big day, gardeners turn out in their best bib and tucker, which rarely encompasses Chanel, Prada or anything much beyond hats and sensible shoes on women and awkward suits and ties on men. The atmosphere is grimly festive. The PRs bustle about with bossy offers of hospitality, a corporate charm offensive that is more offensive than it is charming. I turn up at the Chanel garden, film crew in tow. It has—unsurprisingly—won a much coveted gold medal. A crowd of photographers and crew are already there, literally queuing for their slot with Karl, who is sitting hidden in a leafy alcove. Every other second I see a black fan flicker out of the shade like a snake's tongue. His press dominatrix is in a fluster. Film crews with an official appointment have clout, but she clearly hates us. She and her assistants are all French and dressed from head to toe in Chanel. The labels are hidden but I know my stuff enough to notice and feel smug and impressed and ashamed of being impressed all at once. Mr Lagerfeld will see you in just one minute, she tells us, without the faintest attempt at conviction.

The interior of the bosquet is almost filled with a complex parterre in box, and there is only room to stand in single file around its outside. Karl is still hiding round the corner. We wait politely. I notice two girls standing, waiting rather shyly in the corner. They are both transfixingly beautiful and dressed in what looks like a very loosely woven check from raw silk or perhaps the finest wool—cockateels amongst the hedge sparrows. Their jackets flop to reveal naked breasts which they seem wholly unconcerned about. More and more women of a certain age step into the garden and walk straight across the box parterre, oblivious to the plants they crush beneath their expensive shoes. Mark Fane from Waterers follows them with a trowel, smoothing the gravel behind each footstep. He looks as though he is about to burst into tears. We wait, inches from our interviewee, ignored.

Half an hour goes by. In the middle of an interview, Karl leaps up, walks round the parterre and pays obeisance to a very thin lady with a bob and dark glasses. 'Ah,' says our PR lady, her voice softening in admiration, 'Anna Wintour, she is so beautiful.' Anna Wintour is editor of American *Vogue*. So beautiful and so powerful. Suzy Menkes comes by. Sarah Jane Hoare joins the party. These *grandes dames* of fashion are doing Chelsea like Fashion Week, their clothes pitched in that narrowest arc of perfection that will impress each other, Karl and a few others in the know and yet not scare off the horny-handed Chelsea gardeners. After 45 minutes of standing in the boiling sun, only able to move from foot to foot, a mass of photographers are suddenly spilt into the garden from a side entrance. Perhaps twenty squeeze in, taking shots of the models against the statue, gilded as shiny as a chocolate wrapper, with Karl looking proudly on. Tom Stuart-Smith watches from the back, unnoticed.

Finally my turn comes. We have five minutes and the interview must be done in the shade. I sit on the little seat next to Karl, chummying up. His skin has the pallor of a man living under artificial light. The black fan swooshes past my nose. Time for a few insightful, radically original questions. 'Hot, isn't it?' I hear myself ask.

'Yes,' he says, 'and I am not one who seeks out the sunshine.'

'That must make gardening a bit tricky, then.' (Was this friendly chat or not knowing my stuff?)

'Oh, I love gardening, only I don't like to do it, cannot stand getting my hands dirty, so I get other people to do it for me. But gardens I love.' The words flap from his full lips as fast as they will spill, eyes hidden behind dark glasses.

I ask about Coco Chanel's love for camellias, because the garden features white camellias, impossibly flowering in this garden (courtesy of a cold store). His reply is fluent and articulate. 'Chanel was French so I made a French garden—I am not a Frenchman, you know [I know that stuff]—and she loved the eighteenth century, so I make a bosquet, you know?' He is really asking. 'A bosquet is a kind of room in the wood where ladies can sit perhaps in the shade. Perhaps they can take

155

a little tea. And Chanel loved the white camellias so we must have camellias and everything in white too. Simple and formal because I do not want to bring an English style garden to England. This is French, you know.' He was not asking.

I thought of French seventeenth- and eighteenth-century gardens with their rigid lines and manicured formality pierced with high kitsch. It was Chelsea to a T. Clever Karl had not just paid homage to Chanel but had also worked out exactly what was required for this particular collection to be a success. He had Chelsea sussed.

How was gardening like fashion? Fashion is about new things and change. Change is always interesting. Gardens change all the time. I am always trying out new ideas in my various gardens.

So why had he done such a formal, retrospective garden? He did falter for a moment. The past was an inspiration and it was a homage to Chanel.

Of course.

Was the finished garden as he envisaged it? 'Yes. It is exactly as my original drawing. You must have seen this.' This was clearly testing my stuff, but the answer was both disingenuous and immensely proprietorial. It was actually much, much nicer than his drawing. That difference was almost all down to Tom Stuart-Smith. The minder moved in. That was it. Our director persuaded her to let us have one more wide shot from the other side. Whilst they did it I asked Karl what he thought of Chelsea Flower Show. Nine people out of ten in his position would have made some fatuous comment designed to offend no one, and provide enough lip synch for the camera but Karl answered simply that he could not possibly answer because he had not properly looked around.

The truth is that fashion talks city talk and gardening is rooted in the country. Chelsea Flower Show longs for the sponsorship and associated glamour of the big fashion names, and the corporations want the cachet of a social event locked into the Season, but Chelsea is too fixed and stuffy to adapt or learn and fashion too knowing to tolerate it for long. I can't see Karl Lagerfeld coming back. However, the spirit of the fashion business, with its collective studios and savvy, would do the world of British horticulture a power of good. It would gain enormously from the association.

Chelsea is hardly a gardening show. At best it is pure theatre, using plants as principal players. There is not a shred of wit or irony and very little humanity. Fashion understands this language of display with the added factor that the best fashion reels with wit and, for all the talk of homosexual designers not understanding 'real' women, is intimate with real lives, real bodies. Lagerfeld is a great designer because he is driven by what is new and by what he does not yet know. Chelsea is a great show because it is part of that British tradition that makes people feel proud of their past and, anyway, no one does those great state occasions like the British, do they?

June

01.06.97

Rousham is a garden preserved in amber, a 250-year-old dinosaur containing the DNA of what gardening might be if it had managed to avoid the prissy, lace-doily obsession with collections of plants that started last century and continues apace today. Gardens that have not been altered in anything but the minutest detail over hundreds of years bring the past alive in the most vivid way possible because, unlike a building or a painting, the components are always in the intense present. The scents, sounds of leaves jostling, water falling, and tastes from the original eighteenth-century kitchen garden are as transitory as the moments in the car driving to the place. So all the history is in the human connections that you inevitably make. This, the Rousham that you today are seeing, is what William Kent envisaged: this is where ladies with pannier skirts and piled, powdered wigs sat; this is where men in tricorn hats and brocaded waistcoats trod and shared their present with yours.

I love the shock of the new and the genuine creativity that it generates as much as I loathe the nostalgic sentimentality of the 'heritage' mentality with its fake 'period' homes and 'historic houses'. A craven worship of an ignorantly recreated past is manifested in gardens all over Britain, aided and abetted by the horticultural establishment, to which the majority of show gardens at Chelsea will be a depressingly predictable witness. [Readers will notice a recurring theme—or at least a bugbear—about Chelsea gardens. It has always seemed odd

161

and depressing that so much energy, skill and funding goes into recreating pastiches of existing gardens. There is little culture in modern Britain of celebrating new and innovative garden design. There are complicated and interesting reasons for this—mostly sociological rather than horticultural —beyond the scope of a footnote.] We make bad, phoney 'old' gardens and let good gardens that have a real identity with a certain time and place go to seed. This is why gardens such as Rousham are so special.

William Kent is the genius responsible for Rousham. In 1738 he was hired by the owner, General Dormer (the Dormer-Cottrell family still own and live there), to vamp up the designs of the royal gardener, Charles Bridgeman, who had laid out gardens in the 1720s in the new, landscaped style that was beginning to emerge as a contrast to the severely formal Dutch and French influence of the late seventeenth century. Of Bridgeman's garden Alexander Pope said that Rousham was 'the prettiest place for water-falls, jetts, ponds, inclosed with beautiful scenes of green and hanging wood that I ever saw'.

Kent's brilliance was to take an established garden and transform it into greatness with a relatively light hand. He was at the centre of the Picturesque movement, which in the second quarter of the eighteenth century established a revolutionary style of garden design that placed classical scenes within the English landscape. Whereas we are largely ignorant of classical mythology, the meaning of such scenes was intensely vivid to those contemporaries for whom the gardens were made, creating an intellectual

162

subtext to the gardens. Classical allusion indicated by a statue or style of garden building would inform and enrich the experience of the visitor in the same way as a modern garden thematically dedicated to a soap opera would be able to use visual references to characters and events that would have added meaning for aficionados.

But whether or not we now understand or even spot the classical references, what remains is more than the sum of most gardens. The house itself, worked on and added to by Kent at the same time that he did the garden, is impressive rather than beautiful, although the honey-yellow stables and car park are entrancingly informal and un-National-Trusty. While Rousham is one of the nation's most precious horticultural treasures, it is still a private home. You come as a guest rather than a customer.

Although it has been calculated that there are over a thousand circuits that you can take round the garden, which is an extraordinary tribute to the way that so much has been fitted into a relatively small site, you are likely to take a route which starts by going round the back of the house across the bowling green. Most owners would have succumbed at some stage in the past two hundred years to cluttering this with a cedar of Lebanon, wellingtonia or, worse, stolidly pretty herbaceous borders. Mercifully it has been left as a monumental open space of grass with wide surrounding paths and an enormous flanking hedge. A single statue stands at the end against the skyline. This zen-like emptiness clears the mind-clutter before you turn on to a small path down the hillside. Immediately you are aware that the garden is a journey, with intervals of contemplation rather than a series of pleasant images.

The first thing that strikes you and which will be reinforced throughout is the absence of flowers. The overwhelming impression is of green in every shade from the lime yellow of new leaves on box and lime trees to the blue green of ivy underneath the yew trees. The sophistication and delicate beauty of this is anything but drab: rather than reducing the picture it intensifies it. Green light spatters through the trees on to ivy, wild garlic, herb Robert, holly and tightly cropped laurel. The yews hold dark. The mind is open and clear, garden-ready.

As a startling touch of colour you look down on to vermilion fish in a brown pool. This is fed by a rill that snakes down the centre of a path through the trees. A thread-like canal no more than a foot wide and a few inches deep, the rill is still shockingly modern and inspiring. It is a sinuous intruder that snakes the curves of the landscape right into the heart of the classical order and references. It is as minimalist as the bowling green but, like all good minimalism, liberates the essence from clutter so that it can fill a space, endorsing Wittgenstein's sentiment that 'the bad architect succumbs to every detail'. So many gardens, from Repton to the present day, succumb to an accumulation of pointless detail.

One particular of the garden that must be modern is the use of laurel as ground cover. Laurel is, in general, a horrible plant, heavy with the dreariness of Sunday afternoons in middle England, but here it works well, given a flat-top cut so that it creates boxy planes of green on steep, shaded slopes. Practical too, as Rousham only has two full-time gardeners and the laurel would need just one hard cut a year.

William Kent was no gardener. [I increasingly feel that good garden design is perhaps incompatible with horticulture.] He saw the garden as a medium to create a series of living stage sets, and at Rousham every path and ride through the trees culminates in a statue or building, creating a sequence of tableaux. What makes them exceptional is that they need humans to make the pictures exist.

Kent included people in the same spirit that he made buildings, paths or planted trees. So, as you drift round Rousham, entranced by the way that it uses the physical here-and-nowness of the landscape to transport you into a dream, there is this extraordinary sensation of making it happen, of your presence being the vital ingredient that brings the buildings, trees, ground cover, even the water of the River Cherwell and the sky into being. This is enormously flattering, which is hardly something that you expect from a garden.

The severely classical buildings include the seven-arched portico Praeneste, Townsend's Building (a temple with, very charmingly, a distinctly unclassical sash window in the side), and rusticated arches gushing water in the Vale of Venus. They are constructed entirely from vernacular materials, which is an important factor in the integration of very English countryside with filtered images of ancient Rome. It is fortunate that the local stone is a beautiful ochre limestone which makes any building look good, but it is also used on the paths through the grass and woods, unifying

165

the picture.

After all this the huge walled garden is an anticlimax, too conventional and unworked. Whereas the emptiness of the bowling green makes clarity, the lack of human business in the walled garden is an absence. But it leads to another, half its size but still bigger than an estate of modern houses, every inch of which is cultivated and used for vegetables, fruit and cut flowers. The church leads off it in one direction and a superb working dovecote dated 1685, rich with the tang of guano, dominates a linking section of the garden made up of an elaborate and exquisite box parterre. This is the kind of formality that Kent and his subsequent followers such as Capability Brown swept away, and which represented the Old when he was the New. It is beautiful. So is the landscape garden Kent made. If only we could maintain the tradition of allying the radically modern with the established order.

03.06.01 My Roots

All my gardening has been squeezed into a day during the last fortnight. What happens, as anyone in a similar position will know, is that initially I rush around like a bare-arsed fly, creating more heat than light. I spent an hour or so staking in the jewel garden, trying to practise what I have often preached: getting the supports in before anything needs it. I planted out a couple of dozen cardoons grown from seed to complete the cardoon walk. They will sit and not do much this year, as is their wont, but should really take off next year. Talking of taking off, the quince blossom is extraordinary—a really sugary pink which would be offensive if it were not sitting on the particular shade of light green of the leaves. The result is pretty without a hint of saccharine.

If it were not for eggs, the chickens would be stock by now (too tough to eat). They found a couple of rows of lettuce early this morning and proceeded to strip the lot within an hour. Our lot are voracious, rushing at you every time you appear and attacking anything that is valued. I hate them, but would miss them terribly if we did not have them.

The best thing of all this weekend was that my son Adam cut all the grass—three hours' solid mowing after school before I came home on Friday night. A major act of love this, as he hates gardening and has always avoided anything to do with it. It meant that he missed *The Simpsons* . . . These are the things that break and make an absent parent's heart.

10.06.01

Twenty-two years ago I eloped with my wife. Actually she was someone else's wife. Hence the elopement, which, according to the OED, is the action of a wife running away from her husband with her paramour. I would be a liar if I did not admit to a hint of a boast in this—after all, I wanted and still want nothing more than to be her paramour—but it was a time of high and anxiety-ridden drama. Everybody gets hit by the shrapnel from broken marriages. Nevertheless, we ran up the A1 to the North Yorkshire moors, which was completely foreign territory to both of us. We had been lent a house on the edge of Glaisdale Moor for the winter, the rent being that I exercise the owners' horse, riding it occasionally to hounds, and that I paint all the exterior windows. I had done some window painting (although the Yorkshire winter meant that I had to tie the brush to my hand to hold it) but had never been on a horse in my life. This one was a seventeen-hand Cleveland bay with a spectacularly bad temper. But I learned, first to master and then to enjoy her. I went hunting a few times and enjoyed the experience, although I found it much less exciting than riding on my own across the moors, mainly because we hardly ever saw a fox, let alone caught one. I was a long-haired vegetarian, passionately socialist, with earrings and eye-liner, coming into a tight-knit, isolated community and was treated with nothing but hospitality and kindness by the hunt members. Ever since then I have had no tolerance at all for the fluffy sentimentality and ignorance of the anti-hunting lobby.

Occasionally the owners—who were distant cousins I had known since childhood—would ring up and ask us to do some little job as part of the maintenance. One phone call requested that we prune the raspberries. No problem. Consider it done. In fact I had never pruned a raspberry in my life. But I did have *The Fruit Garden Displayed* and I have that same copy before me now, the new and revised edition of 1965. It has a wonderful photograph of a man in an overcoat and what look like motorbike gauntlets gently snipping off the top of a raspberry cane with the caption 'Canes being tipped'. So, coated but gauntletless, I tipped the canes. It didn't look like much at all. Same as before but a bit less so. Then I turned the page and saw that autumn-fruiting raspberries had to be cut right to the ground. Perhaps these were autumn-fruiting? It was, after all, September, and there were signs of a few fruit. So, not wanting to shirk, I carefully cut all the raspberry canes to the ground, tidied and weeded. Which would have been fine if it had been January and they had been the autumn-fruiting type. But they were summer-fruiting and should have had the fruiting canes removed and the new ones tied in and (the photographic bit) tipped off. This was Yorkshire, where summer comes to the moors like a Great Western train, irregular but always late. September was summer and, I was to learn, October was winter. To this day I don't think I have ever really been forgiven for brutalising the raspberries.

That was about the extent of my gardening in Yorkshire, although I helped with the potato harvest on the neighbouring farm, picking up the potatoes by hand into baskets from a ten-acre field. City people will not know what that means, but take it from me, it is an awful lot of baskets. The farmer, a man named Robert Foord, was the reason I went back as part of this travelogue around Britain that I am currently filming for Channel 4. [*Don Roaming*. I squirm at the title but it had its moments.] He was an enormous influence on me and Sarah, being one of the wisest, nicest, most inquisitive, mischievous, fully alive people that I have met. He was seventy back then but still running the farm like a man half his age, and now at ninety is hardly changed at all: a little deaf, a little slower, but still out on the farm in his wellies with bright, hungry eyes.

Robert used to take us on trips around the moors with days in Farndale, Rosedale, Staithes, Hutton le Hole, everywhere peopled with a hundred ghosts, each with a story, going back to his days before the last war as a delivery boy for a grocer. Despite all the stories that belonged to every stone wall, every tree and granite gatepost, Robert lived intensely in the present. I remember sitting in the lee of a wall during a fine October day's potato picking, eating the tea that Mary his wife carried across the fields (half a dozen high-tailed cats in tow) and Robert pointing at the racing sky. 'It's an amazing thing, but there is a man in London who thinks that he owns this land. He's got a piece of paper like, which says as much, but he doesn't own this land any more than you or I own that sky.' And with a typically impish grin he added, 'Which we do.' For a moment, sharing the sky was more generous than legacies of land, stocks or shares. Only if you really know an area and are intimate with it can you have this sense of absolute and careless possession. For most of us the nearest we come to any real stake in the land is the intimacy we develop with our gardens.

I went back on the first day of May, a day so gloriously clear and bright that the moors rolled out to a blue infinity, quite unlike mountain clarity, unlike the lowlands, comparable perhaps only to the sea. In the dales and road edges the daffodils were at their northern best. Just before going up to see Robert and his son Martin, who now runs the farm, I learned that Martin's daughter, Joanna, had died suddenly just before Christmas, aged nineteen. My own nephew died a few years ago, aged twenty, and I know that when a child dies there is a lonely wound that never heals. There are no words of comfort, but I said that I was sorry. 'Aye,' said Robert, 'it's a strange thing.' He pointed to a tiny clump of daffodils in the hedge opposite the farm. 'See them daffodils on yon bank? Well, one day about ten years back I took Joanna and said come on, let's be planting some bulbs, you and I. I said that when I was in the sky she could think of me looking down at her when she saw the daffodils flowering. Little did I think that it would be her looking down on me.'

What is this to you? Why is this creeping into a gardening column? Because this is why I garden. If gardening were simply an extension of the Best Kept Village competition or a make-over programme, then I would stop today. It would be meaningless. Anyone who loves gardening does so because in doing it we are making up our lives, with all the poetry, all the sorrow and all the hope that this entails. Gardening is about all us flawed, ridiculous people. We are buying into the future and hoping against hope that it is our children and grandchildren looking at the flowers when we are in the sky.

10.06.01 **My Roots**

The garden is looking very good. While I was away in Dorset, Sarah and Gareth [Gareth Lorman, who worked for us in the garden from 1998 to 2002.] put in days of real slog to push it round the corner. You would think that a garden would slide effortlessly from early spring into late May and June, but every year we have to do this—only this year 'we' has excluded me. Some of the work was making good JCB damage, but most of it is that instinctive fine-tuning that is hard to prescribe but which real gardeners know and see absolutely clearly. Weeds get cleared before they seed. Ground that is developing a crusty veneer of capping soil gets broken up. Tender annuals are planted out and the herbaceous plants get staked before they flop rather than as repair work after a storm. The garden repays this tenfold. As I write, the combination of alliums, irises, laburnum, euphorbia, cardoons, geraniums, anchusa and oriental poppies are doing the sort of stuff that justifies cold and grey winters. We have arrived.

But not without mishap. I now realise that it is impossible to have topiary—especially in yew—anywhere near to leafy plants and especially edible leafy plants. The snails love the topiary as it provides the perfect dry cover from which to sneak out in the dark to strip the soft foliage nearby. For some reason they adore the pink celery and have devastated the first planting. The solid white next door to it is untouched. Odd. The

French beans that I planted out early (under cloches) have survived the cold but are made all but useless by the slugs and snails. Perhaps that is the price of trying to force them, as if I had held back a bit they might well have grown fast enough to outreach the reachers. If they are not hiding in the recesses of the yew then the snails seem to love the leaves of cardoon, allium and lovage to rest up on during the day. This makes them easy to pick, I suppose, but that is a dispiriting business.

But I cannot get too bothered by slugs and snails. They are part of the system and there's an end to it. Talking of which, I went to a talk by James Lovelock at the Hay Festival the other day. If you do not know, Lovelock invented the Gaia principle, which, very crudely, states that the physical planet itself, rocks, waters and gases, is evolving and adapting to survive, just as its creatures evolve and adapt. The implications of this are hugely important. He considers global warming to be a catastrophe greater than any other factor in our current civilisation and, when questioned on a possible solution to this, reckoned that individual morality was the best answer. I like this. It squares with my take on the garden as a metaphor for the planet. We should do in the garden as we would be done by on earth, slugs and snails and all. These bigger issues all make this near-perfect spring the more lovely for its fragility and do nothing to lessen my pleasure from it.

20.06.04

We have all sneered at Americans for being stupid and fat, but where America leads we wobble after. Of course none of the politicians, film stars or food industry execs are corpulent. They are all lean and glossy and rich. You have to be poor to do fat really properly but it certainly helps to be stupid. And boy, are we stupid! Cramming disgusting 'food products' into our mouths that are making us ill whilst as we do so 850 million people suffer from malnutrition.

Something has to give. The irony is that it seems that it is likely to be us. We will gorge ourselves to an unhealthy life and early death. Last month I shared a platform at the Hay Literary Festival with Colin Tudge and Felicity Lawrence, both of whom have written really important books on our food production. Felicity's new book *Not on the Label* is a brilliant exposé of the appalling politics of food, and Colin Tudge's *So Shall We Reap* is, I believe, a masterpiece. Tudge's arguments are complex and detailed, but at their heart is his assessment that food production based upon natural, local husbandry tends to be sustainable and effective. Obesity, famine and malnutrition stem primarily from the fact that the entire system of production and consumption has been perverted. The concept of husbandry—of caring for your animals, land and environment as partners in the process of providing good food—is alien to almost all food production in the west. The global food companies, who have power far in excess of any politician, are motivated only by short-term profit. As a result we have a highly processed, bland, unhealthy diet that is intensely wasteful to produce.

We are in deep trouble. But I believe that if everyone with a garden made a point of growing something that they liked to eat, that would be a start. Our gardens are a retreat from the problems of daily life. One of the best things about them is that we can go outside, step under the sky and shut the door on the pressing clutter that makes modern life so stressful. Consequently any reasonable person wants to fill their garden with soothing green and flowers and peace and harmony. (That, by the way, is my main objection to some contemporary garden design. Creating too harsh a jangle either of form or colour is like serving up blue food. Interesting, but missing the point.) So to become involved in the ethics of food production can seem like too heavy a burden for any garden to bear. But an allotment can provide a huge range of vegetables as well as being a life-enhancing place. A window box or a couple of pots can make a significant difference, if not to your diet—although it is extraordinary how much can be produced from a very small space—then to your whole attitude towards food. [Re-reading this, I find myself cheering. I cannot tell you how strongly I believe every word of this.]

By sowing the seeds, getting your hands dirty and relating the soil to the plant, by having to find out the best season to plant and harvest, having to water or worry about the weather, you connect to the real production of food and understanding husbandry. As a rule, the less food is processed, the higher the nutritional value. By cooking something yourself and not wasting the fruits of your hard work, you start to treat food as something valuable and not as disposable.

We are being told to eat five fruit or vegetable portions a day, which is clearly a good idea. But if you buy these from a supermarket many of the nutrients will have been lost in the processing. If they are a uniform size, colour and shape they will undoubtedly have been sorted and selected according to appearance rather than taste. If they are sold as 'British' then they will almost certainly have involved migrant labour working under appalling Dickensian conditions. If they are out of season then they will have been grown under artificial cover, defacing the countryside. If they are not loudly proclaiming themselves to be organic you can be sure that they have been produced under a chemical regime that you would never use in your own garden.

But it doesn't take much to connect yourself to the cycle of what and why we eat. Farming has become impossibly remote from most people's lives. Even in the countryside over 90 per cent of people have nothing to do with agriculture whatsoever. But I believe that gardens and allotments have taken their place. They are real and dynamic and integrated into our domestic world. Lots of us with a garden grow herbs, fruit and vegetables, but we are still a minority. [A MORI poll commissioned by the RHS in June 2004 showed that 38 per cent of households with children grew 'some vegetables or fruit in the past two years', whereas 43 per cent of households without children did so.] If more gardeners were to grow something edible it could make a huge difference to the way that we look at our global supply of food.

You simply clear a piece of ground, dig it over, buy some seeds and it starts to happen. Even at this time of year there is still lots of time to grow vegetables. The soil is warm and, critically, so are the nights, which means that everything will grow very fast.

It is not a good time to be planting onions, garlic, parsnips, broad beans, peas, tomatoes or potatoes, but if you start today there is a great deal that will grow and provide good food by the end of summer and on through winter into next spring. Any lettuce will thrive if kept reasonably cool and 'Little Gem' is the best for small spaces. Try a 'saladini' or 'saladesi' type, which is a mixture that you broadcast and cut with a knife as you need it. Over the coming weeks I shall be sowing corn salad, rocket, mizuna, mibuna, 'Winter Density', 'Rouge d'Hiver' and 'Winter Purslane', all for harvesting over winter. Rather than lamenting the lack of immediacy of results, this is all part of celebrating the real ebb and flow of the seasons.

Midsummer is the ideal time to sow all chicories, of which 'Red Treviso', curly endive and radicchio 'Palla Rossa' are invaluable for winter salads. Sow now for spring greens next March and April. These are unglamorous vegetables but genuinely delicious. French beans will grow fast and well, as will beetroot and chard, turnips and carrots. I would give courgettes a go and hope for a hot autumn. You have got to start somewhere. Now is as good a time as any.

20.06.04 My Roots [This is—to date—the last 'My Roots', as the page was redesigned and this part of the column lost.]

I don't feel smug about any of this. My own garden totters on the edge of anarchy and hypocrisy. It is certainly full of delicious vegetables and fruits, but our biggest problem is the time to consume or store them. Growing your own takes more time than nipping into a supermarket and bunging a ready meal into a microwave. I have rows of lettuce going to seed, broad beans that have become too big and leathery, strawberries being eaten by slugs and blackbirds because they have not been picked over enough, and we missed at least ten days of the asparagus season because they grew out and feathery. But I cannot pretend to feel too bad about any of this. The excess goes on to the compost heap and I, my family and friends have still had masses of fresh, tasty food from this garden, even in a frenetic year like this one. I suppose that the compost heap is the greatest healer in all this. It means that there is no such thing as waste. What does not get eaten is returned to the garden as goodness six months or so later to enrich another round of growth. But I have had to turn it, and that is sweaty, hard work, and as good as any session in the gym.

It is hard to beat oneself up at this time of year. The garden, although unruly, is basking in these weeks of long, long days. It is light by four thirty in the morning and on a cloudless evening you could still read a book after 10 pm. Even though my working days are exhausting and very long, there seems to be enough time left over to enjoy the garden perform. I have been in this garden long enough now to put myself in the right place at the right time for certain precious moments. So I know that the eremurus catches the sun for just a week at seven in the morning. The *Stipa giganteas* in the jewel garden positively burn with light between 8.45 and 9.15 in the evening. A splash of light falls down the little woodland path at midday. Just after lunch one half of the damp garden is in deep shade and the other—just across a narrow path—is in bright sun. This intimacy is a form of love.

08.06.03 [Most of this was cut to make room for a description of that year's Chelsea Flower Show. I liked the cut bits better, so here they are for the first time.]

There is usually that lovely moment when you realise that the doors and windows have been open for days and you have not even thought about changing shoes as you go in and out of the house. Instead of the bottled-up indoor life our climate forces us to lead for most of the year, there is that liberation out into the weather that, unless you are a farmer, fisherman or serious gardener, is denied most people except in high summer. And any sensate person wants sunshine on a pillow of dry green, strawberries and summer pudding, and the evening slipping slowly down the sky past bedtime with the swifts screaming round church towers and the air feeling exactly like the smell of warm earth after rain. We want to walk on the lawn in our bare feet and feel the dry blades of grass wispily between our toes; we want abundance and warmth on our skin, and gardens that do not tax or expose us to the chill winds of horticulture, just gardens soft and florid, full of flowers like roses, delphiniums and poppies, that the least horticulturally-minded of us can recognise.

My earliest memories of summer are of waking to the sound of wood pigeons calling in waves of soft, throaty seduction, getting up and wriggling into a pair of shorts and an aertex shirt and sockless plimsoles and slipping downstairs and out into the garden. It was clearly too early to be permissible, given that the household was all asleep and I was too young to do anything much without express permission, but also inevitable. The call was irresistible. Everything good in summer happens outside. The summer garden, then and now, is liberation into light, that sense of being where the action really is.

It took me ages to realise that I was more or less alone in feeling this. When I went away to boarding school, in April 1963, I left home with spring still struggling into being. When I next came home, I saw the beech in full leaf and the white alyssums planted in front of the house and the pelargoniums barrowed up from the greenhouse to be planted by the front door, and I crumpled. Summer had come without me. I can remember the intensity of that small grief as though it was yesterday. Summer holidays were never taken abroad or even away, but always spent in the garden. I remember being confused when, as an undergraduate, someone asked me where I was 'going' that summer. Going? Home, of course. That's where summer was. And if I was not there it might happen without me.

Now that I have children and am officially a gardener (although all my gardening pleasures and instincts are exactly as they were as a boy scarcely old enough to dress himself), the best thing about summer is the garden littered with the detritus of children's play. It still annoys me constantly that they never clear up behind them, that everything is just flung down and abandoned, and yet, and yet . . . to step outside when the rest of the household is asleep and see a pair of shoes, a jersey, a ball, a copy of the *Beano* and a half-full glass in the dew gives me as much pleasure as the first sliced-off flowers of the rose 'Charles de Mills' or the blue spires of the delphiniums. It is not until June that the privations of an indoor life really make themselves known.

But we take what we get and know that it is the only reality. It is an odd thing: wholly different summers can exist side by side within the same household. If you get up and go to work in the usual train or bus, earn money indoors under artificial light and entertain yourself of an evening indoors, after dark, after weather, then summer happens at weekends. One wet Saturday makes a wet week. Two wet weekends were a dreadful month. But for those of us who live as much of our lives as we can out of doors, summer drifts through the days shaping itself hourly. And summer rain is a lovely thing, feeding, healing and soothing the land and everything in it. But summer rain is too loaded with disappointment for most people. The thing that makes summer really beautiful, that gives it its fullness and green abundance, is lovely rain.

This is a cheat really, because it is rain like shade, tempered and measured by sunshine and heat. Rain that breaks days of sullen weather and rain that puckers the dust without making mud. I want an inch of rain every week, preferably all in one go after dark. But most of us want summer dry and clear all day and every day. I suppose I have rain on the brain because summer, for me, is what happens after Chelsea Flower Show. And a wet week we had of it there. Before Chelsea it is all expectation and swelling growth, and after Chelsea we have arrived. Not necessarily where we want to be, of course, but, like it or not, we are Here.

24.06.01 My Roots

So we arrive at midsummer.[One of the facts of a regular column, especially one that is tied so closely to the seasons, is that the same points come round year after year. My own responses tend to be almost identical—and yet I am surprised and taken aback by them. Either this is part of the human condition or I am simply more foolish than most.] It is as much a place as midwinter or Manchester, a port of call on the journey. It is loaded with every kind of significance, not least the shortening of the days and the slide towards winter. But it takes a hardened depressive to really go down that road at this time of year. Most of us take what we can get from the light and warmth and try and charge the batteries. But there is just an edge of preciousness running with the days, whereas May is always careless. In order to grab the light we have dug up part of the herb garden and laid a square of old red sandstone flags, so that we can sit and admire the falling sun. Sunshine only hits this bit of the garden after six o'clock and only between the months of April and October, so it seems crazy not to make the most of it.

In digging out the marjoram, lovage, rosemary, lemon balm *et al*, I noticed that the ground was bone dry. As dry as I have ever seen it at any time of year, let alone at the beginning of June. I know I have said this almost every week, but it is worth celebrating again and again—it has so far been an astonishingly sunny and dry spring and summer. The Mediterranean plants don't mind this in summer at all, of course, but it is a curious combination with the winter saturation. I can see this becoming a problem as the months go by.

One of the curious side-effects of the dryness is that the birds (including our horrible chickens that fly fatly over the fence) are using the potato patch as a dustbath and serrating the ridges with their wallowings and in some places uncovering the growing tubers. This is actually as much a product of the lateness of their planting as of the drought. They should be up by now and the earth, dry or not, covered.

So far I have not done any outdoor watering at all, save for when things are newly planted, but I might have to begin soon. I do not have any kind of irrigation system, and standing with a hose feels excruciatingly wasteful of my precious time.

Putting a sprinkler on is equally wasteful of water. But the effects are showing. The spinach has suddenly bolted and the lettuces are sitting ready for less long before stretching into bolt. This year I am going to leave something of everything to set good seed and collect it for next season. This is not to say that there are not very good and wholly ethical seed suppliers, but I have been too lazy about collecting my own veg seed (although we do this a lot with flower seed) as part of the drive to keep the genetic stock as broad-based as possible and to stick two fingers up at the globally dominating plant breeders and genetic manipulators. Grow your own everything if you can.

25.06.00

I was handed a script for *Real Gardens* [A weekly garden series I presented for Channel 4 between spring 1998 and autumn 2000.] on Friday night and the opening bit was written something along the lines of 'Welcome to *Real Gardens*—Monty this is a chance to say something personal about the season or something you love but no more than ten to fifteen seconds please.'

OK. In ten seconds I shall tell how there is this rolling midsummer fever inside my veins, made of light falling through the leaves, made of the smell of the first roses and the lilies that begin to flower in midsummer and honeysuckle and musky tobacco plants in the dusk, made of the richness of this earth that astonishes me more every year, made of the thinnest of skies at five in the morning drawn up like a wispy tent by half a dozen larks singing as high as sound will take them, made of the patient husbanding of the vegetable garden, bringing food to the table with all the skill and care I can muster, made of the evenings that stay alive till past ten, the sky turning Prussian blue but still lit enough from inside itself to walk torchless at midnight.

Is that OK? Did it fit? These are just hints, just pointers at what is going on, no time to explain, no time to dwell on any wherefores and whys.

It doesn't work. You get nowhere near it and yet not to attempt to explain, not tell everybody, is a dereliction of duty. This, if anyone cares, is why I garden. All the sensations and ancillary emotions towing along with them bundled into moments of perfection. This really is as good as it gets.

Midsummer is not the only still point. It is not necessarily the high spot. It seems to me to be a measure of success to find those justifying moments in a hundred days, but in practice there are weeks and sometimes months when only memory and anticipation sustain you. But midsummer is a cairn on top of the year and there is a view to be taken from here.

For a start there are all the temporal measurements that place this weekend on the pinnacle of the year—summer solstice, longest days, middle of the calendar—as though we reach this peak, take a breather and then slowly trudge down the other side to the unrelieved gloom of the winter solstice. But it is as likely to be a grey, rainy solstice when the grate yearns for a fire in the evening as 21st December is to be dazzling with hoar frost. It is not the garden's summit. That

185

comes later—in this garden perhaps as late as September, when the vegetable garden is spilling over with its harvest and the borders have that rich, late-season intensity. But because there is this sensation of so much more to come, coupled with maximum light, maximum time and freshness it is probably the best of the garden's time and should be celebrated as such.

Intimacy is at the centre of all good gardening, so your own backyard is always the most interesting garden, or at least it should be. Broad horticultural sweeps of the brush make for dull pictures. For a start, you inevitably load certain plants with significance that the casual eye does not share. For me those plants at this time of year are the roses. If you don't like roses then you are simply growing the wrong ones. I adore old roses and they never fail to repay that adoration, even in a mildewy, blackspotty, aphid-coated season. Is there anything in the garden more beautiful than the rich pink buds of 'Chapeau de Napoléon' opening from its frilly bright green tricorne? If there is, it is probably the sliced-off flowers of the gallica 'Charles de Mills', the white flowers with green eye of the damask 'Madame Hardy', the intensity of the gallica 'Tuscany Superb', the alba 'Celestial', the incredible velvety cherry red of 'Scharlachglut' before they bleach pink in the sun . . . and fifty more. Every day in June, when I am at home, I go and cut a selection of about a dozen different roses and put them in small vases—just the flowers—on the kitchen table, our desks, bedside tables.

Sweet peas have to be cut too. The sweet pea season has begun, although it will not hit maximum intensity for another month. We grow ours on

186

wigwams of six hazel bean sticks, planting a four-inch pot with two sweet peas in it to each stick, so each wigwam has twelve plants of the same type. The jewel garden has sweet peas with rich single colours like 'Black Knight', 'Violet Queen' and 'Hannah Dale', and the walled garden, which is a much softer, gentle place and has most of the old roses, has Spencer varieties with good scent, like 'Cream Southborne', 'Lovejoy' and 'Gipsy Queen' as well as the original 'Cupani'. I have written about sweet peas before, but suffice to say that I cannot imagine midsummer without sweet peas. A bunch of sweet peas has an incredible healing power, [Healing what? I do think that gardens function as much to repair the damage of life as anything else. They exist to make the gardener survive better.] and seems to combine the inevitable components of nostalgia with a life-affirming intensity of the moment.

The third component of the midsummer flower garden that seems to make a trinity in my association are the poppies. The oriental poppies are pretty much done, but the opium, field and Shirley poppies are at their best. Field poppies, *Papaver rhoeas*, need disturbed ground to germinate but will lie patiently waiting for their moment for a remarkably long time. Each flower will produce around seventeen thousand seeds, of which around three thousand will remain viable and dormant in untilled ground for at least a century before bursting into flower when the ground is disturbed and the seeds are exposed to light.

We let these flourish wherever they appear—and they appear everywhere, from cracks in brick paths to the middle of the onion bed. They usually get it wrong, poor dolts, but they somehow get an exemption from the degree of colour ruthlessness we try to apply. Not solemn enough for heavy August and too fulsome for spring, the frilly silliness of opium poppies against their dusty glaucal leaves—also frilled like a 1970s dress shirt—is exactly in the spirit of midsummer. There is a particular batch of 'black paeony' opium poppy, *Papaver somniferum*, that has been popping up in the vegetable garden for the past few years and would be fabulous in the jewel garden. Poppies hate being moved once they have got any size at all, but you can take a clump of seedlings in wet soil and move them without them noticing the change in scenery. But the only time I did move some seedlings of opium poppies from the kitchen garden they turned out to be an unacceptably anodyne pink—which would have been fine where they were, in amongst some maincrop potatoes, but hopelessly jarring amongst the purples, crimsons and oranges where I had put them.

The jewel garden arrives at this end of June at a good point of intensity without heaviness—a memorable lunch rather than a heavy dinner. It is held together by the combination of, amongst other things, delphiniums, roses, sweet Williams—of which we have 'Nigricans' and one with the most intense, shimmering magenta of any plant I have ever seen and whose seed packet I have lost. Geums, the ligularias [I moved all the ligularias later that year to a damper part of the garden, where they have thrived.] 'The Rocket', 'Desdemona' and the unpronounceable *L. przewalskii*, the last of the June flowering

188

clematises, the first of the dahlia 'Bishop of Llandaff' (setting a benchmark for red amongst all the is-it-red-is-it-pinks?) all lit by the great tracer sprays of *Stipa gigantea*.

The spring garden has gone dormant and I suppose I only walk through there about once a week, but that's fine. It needs the rest. Only a hedge-width away the white foxgloves all along the pleached lime walk are perhaps past their true best but have another week in them. By which time we shall be in July and, somehow, another season.

July

01.07.01

Here we are, on the year's pivot, six months in and six months to go, and by far the most dominant factor shaping this garden is not me or Sarah or Gareth but global warming. One of the ironies of being a gardener, that most domestic of activities, is that we are in the front line of the single most important issue facing this planet simply by virtue of the fact that we get outside. We live the changes. This prissy government is too scared to do anything about it, and anyway no government ever sees beyond its nose because they never get out. And the changes are certainly happening.

I remember that a few years ago there was a plethora of books about gardening in drought, because that is how we thought global warming would manifest itself. Then we had our run of wet summers and we got used to the idea that global warming was manifesting itself in cool wet summers and mild wet winters. I don't think that anyone reckoned that we would have to deal with both the extremes of hot dry summers and warm wet winters.

Last autumn was the wettest ever and the garden drowned. The Mediterranean plants in particular suffered and a lot of the larger bulbs rotted off. We lost practically all of our *Allium giganteum* and our agapanthuses in this way. Throughout the late winter and early spring this wetness was so close in the memory and the ground was so saturated that I almost did not notice that we were getting very little rain. But throughout April, May and the first half of June we had practically no rainfall at all—in this the wet western half of England. The upshot is that the ground is incredibly dry. In a normal year—i.e. drier than it has been for the past three summers—you can dig down a few inches in September/October and the ground will be rock hard, dried out completely. That is how it is now.

Any discussion of global warming cannot be based just on empirical evidence. The weather has always varied from year to year and place to place. That is the whole point of the British climate. It is variable. But only up to a point. I have kept a weather diary for the past ten years and can remember pretty well the weather in broad terms for the previous twenty and the astonishing thing is not how much it changes but how incredibly consistent it is. I stress that this is only in my own personal experience. But whenever I have raised this point with anyone else who shows any interest—usually farmers, milkmen, postmen—people who are outside and affected by the weather day in day out, they all agree. Until recently. In the past five years or so the weather has not just become less predictable, it has noticeably changed.

The point of real conviction for me came exactly two months ago when I was up in Yorkshire filming my old friend Robert Foord and visiting my cousins down the road from him. Both independently and unprompted raised the issue. Robert said that in his ninety years the weather had followed a steady pattern. Spring was wet, summer was warm—and sometimes wet, autumn was often dry and winter was cold. The implications of this were entirely agricultural: spring rain made the grass grow; summer sun ripened the corn and made good hay;

a good autumn meant that the harvest could be brought in and the grass grew back after haymaking, and a cold winter meant that the ground was in general hard enough for the cattle to stay outside. But he pointed out that in the past five years the ground was so wet in winter that the cattle could never lie down—for the mud—and tractors could not get to them to take them hay. So they have to be kept indoors. Which is bad husbandry. My cousin is considering giving up his small herd of cattle for precisely the same reason. Winter wet makes them unmanageable outside.

The summer effect of global warming has not really hit us until this year. But we are now having to deal with winter flooding and summer drought. As gardeners we need as much cold weather as possible in December and January to kill off the bugs and diseases that proliferate in warmth—especially wet warmth. Warmth, in winter terms, is when the night-time temperature is above 5 degrees. Even the tenderest plant can survive this, so it is luxury for your average slug or fungal spore. But we need some rain in summer to give us growth. What we have now is a Mediterranean dryness (although as I write these words the rain starts to fall for the first time in weeks. Ha!).

So we have three problems. How to cope with too much wet, how to cope with too much dry and—this is the really interesting one—how to cope with both within the same year as a matter of course. I suspect that the secret is to survive the wet of winter in order to make the most of summer dryness. This might seem barmy following recent summers, but my hunch is that this year is more in tune with the trend. This means gearing the garden

195

for drought and taking extraordinary measures to cope with regular winter monsoons.

Take drought first. Commercial growers estimate that full irrigation in a truly Mediterranean climate needs 50,000 litres per hectare per day. For a garden 50 foot by 25 foot that translates into roughly 2000 litres or 500 gallons a day—or about four hours with a hose. Scale that down to a very hot, dry, British, globally warmed summer and you are still going to need hours of watering every day. It is a non-starter, even if we have the water to do so. But there are two absolute rules of watering that can be applied to any garden in any situation:

1. Enrich the soil with plenty of compost and other organic material. This will help the soil retain water as well as provide a good medium for strong and healthy root development—enabling the plant to reach for water deeper in the soil. This will also have the advantage in the winter wet season of draining the water a fair bit deeper, so that the roots do not sit in puddles of wet just below the surface. This miraculous combination of soil that drains well whilst simultaneously retaining moisture is one of the wonders of compost. One word of caution, though: do not dig too much manure or compost into the soil at any one time. This will cause very lush growth that will be the first to droop in a drought. It is better to add a middling amount, well mixed in, and then to top it up at least once a year in the form of a good mulch.

2. Water more less often. The latter is vital. Watering lightly every day will actually cause plants to be damaged in hot weather. This is because the roots will go where the water is. A light watering

never sinks much below the first few inches of the topsoil, so this is where the strongest root formation will be. As long as that supply is constant, the plant will be fine. But if it is irregular—and this can be caused by extra sun and especially wind as much as by a break in the supply—then the roots at the surface will be the first to dry out—and as these are the main feeding root system, the plant will suffer immediately.

If, however, you water very thoroughly once a week, the ground will get really wet to a good depth. The roots will then grow downwards to this water source and, if it dries up, they will not be affected so quickly.

There is perhaps a third rule of watering, which is to direct the water at the roots whenever possible. Sprinklers are incredibly inefficient on anything but lawns and very young seedlings, because most of the water lands on foliage and then evaporates in sun and wind before it can reach the ground. On larger plants and shrubs the leaf canopy acts as an umbrella, cleverly deflecting the water from the roots below. It is far better to direct a hose at the ground around the plants or to use a leaky pipe or similar irrigation system.

On top of this it is essential to mulch any bare soil around plants to reduce evaporation. Stones and gravel can do this as effectively as an organic material, but it does seem better to kill two birds with one pile of compost and mulch thickly every spring to feed and protect the soil.

Finally there is the question of how our Mediterranean plants cope with winter wet. Any plant that is adapted to surviving shortage of water hates sitting in water, and mix the wet with cold (i.e. below 5 degrees) and you have real problems. Perhaps physical protection is the answer. Last year I put a cloche over a row of thyme in the vegetable garden in October and left it there until a week or so ago. I left the ends open for ventilation but it received not a drop of direct water in that period. It has turned out to be the healthiest, most vigorous, least woody thyme I have ever grown. Who knows—maybe we shall be cloching and protecting all our Mediterranean plants like rosemary, thyme, cistus or lavender with winter hats as a matter of course, to protect them from the rain rather than the cold.

06.07.03 **My Roots**

I have been filming or writing every day for weeks now without break. It is work I love, but work all the same and I grow homesick for some unhurried hours in the garden. When I do get outside—usually between 8 and 10 pm—it is to try and get done as much as light and weariness will allow. This is not good gardening. Too much bustling about gives a sense of industry, but the easy joy and poetry gets trampled on if you are not careful. Last night, as the light collapsed, drawing shapes in, I just walked this ground for half an hour, looking at what was becoming harder to see with every minute. It was a lovely time. England, in the country, at midsummer, in a garden, is as good as it will ever be. What amazes me most is the maturity of this garden now. Because it has grown from an empty field and because I have busied so much, head down, on always to the next thing, I had not really noticed how much it has grown up. This is not to say that this garden, or any garden, is anything other than a continuous process, but somehow, after ten years, it has reached a kind of adulthood. For years it has been something that Sarah and I have nurtured and helped along, but now the relationship has changed. It could exist pretty much as it is without us. For a moment or two, beneath the navy blue sky of the midsummer night, this was a letting go of sorts and with it a kind of freedom.

And of course with daylight there is unavoidable business. Sarah has been thinning the poppies, orache, bronze fennel (which has gone berserk) and calendula from the jewel garden. In the end she removed eleven barrow-loads of these self-seeded annuals, enough to fill a large compost heap. Even after this, the beds seem very full, although there was just enough room created to plant out the dahlias and chocolate cosmos. It is rather later than normal for this, but it has not been a normal year. I also put in *Salvia elegans* and *guaranitica* and some *Angelica gigas*. The jewel garden has to be constantly cleared out and re-stocked like this if it is to look as untouched as possible. In the pursuit of the effortlessly natural, artifice is everything.

09.07.00

What are gardening make-overs for? [When I wrote this it was contentious stuff. Television gardeners tend not to criticise each other for fear of rocking the boat carrying the happy gardening fraternity. In reality they are as friendly, bitchy, sullen and delightful as any other group of people sharing the same profession. But attacking 'make-overs' was seen as a personal attack on the individuals that featured in the enormously popular make-over programmes. One of the great weaknesses in British gardening is that it is without enough good, serious critics. Criticising a garden—even one devised solely for television—is seen as below the belt, rather like criticising a home-cooked dinner.] Not for gardening obviously. A good garden must have humanity and that can only come through personality, dedication, a sure sense of place and love. The last is a difficult deal—awkward and fumbly on the modern tongue—but unequivocal. There are gardens made with dedicated work and skill of an extraordinary level but from a loveless household, and the result is sterile and unlovely.

Make-overs are horticultural muzak. They fill a space entertainingly. Obviously that is their function and, as such, they are a resounding success. But you get up from the table hungry. They do not nourish. Good gardens have soul and I am sure that the reason for gardening is to make something beautiful and to nourish the soul. You need both. Opinion might divide on the measure of the former but not on the latter. A garden with no soul is empty. Gardens must have personality and style and should never be formulaic or predictable.

I think that this is why most professionally 'designed' gardens are no good. It is incredibly difficult to make a good garden for someone else. I have tried and given it up as a hopeless job. (Yeah, yeah, I know, it could be just that *my* designed gardens were hopeless. No, they weren't. They were good—but not good enough for me, which is exactly how I feel about nine out of ten of the professionally designed gardens I see.) It either takes genius—which, happily, does exist—or else a sense of *possessing* the garden. But chucking money at a piece of outdoors will merely decorate it and that is somehow depressing. It results in gardens like hotel foyers. Perhaps the lesson of this is that public spaces are more amenable to being designed than private ones. The impersonality suits them. Come to think of it, that is what make-overs are: public spaces. They belong to the audience, not to the household. Bland, easy, quick and chirpy. Junk gardening.

Only people who are not interested in gardening or just lazy want someone to make over their garden. If you want to change your garden, then get on with it. Nothing beyond the limitations of health, time and money is stopping you. But I know wonderful gardeners with severe disability or rotten health, hardly any spare time and no spare money. The truth is that if you are lazy then you will never garden. Gardening is hard work. Gardening can be difficult, confusing and frustrating. It demands a commitment and a desire to learn and to keep learning. You have to accept that you will get wet and cold, hot and sweaty, sore, tired and depressed. It will cost you money and will take up more time than you have to spare. And this will make you feel, at times, as fully alive and as content as body and mind can be. That's the deal. Everybody who gardens knows that, as deals go, it is a pretty good one.

If you pay someone to come in and 'do' your garden for you, it will not be true, and you can spot a phoney garden the minute you set eyes on it. Anyway, 'doing' a garden is like shovelling the tide, because a garden is never 'done' any more than a river or the breeze is done. Gardening is something you do privately and without inverted commas.

I write as someone who has done garden make-overs in the past for television and is part of a television culture that manipulates events in order to suit the truth it wants to present within the context of a particular programme. But however you dress them up, other people's gardens are like other people's dreams—so much less interesting than one's own. (By the same token, other people's lives are so much more interesting than their gardens.) Anyone who has been reading this column regularly over the years will know that just as I prefer to work in my own garden more than anyone else's, so I like writing about my own garden best. I like the way that intimacy with a garden only grows with hundreds and hundreds of hours of acquaintance, of seasonal, even daily, change and of knowledge of your plants from seed or tiny potted thing to its maturity. Anyone with children will know that the child is invariably the father of the man and this is always true of a garden. The layout that seemed to be the guide for the future garden—a kind of trail chalked on to the ground that the garden could follow—is the thing itself. Your garden is defined on its own terms from the first day.

This is not all bad news. Gardens run along a dozen different time-lines simultaneously. Obviously there are the seasonal and plant-driven timescales ranging from the emergence of seedlings a few days after sowing, to the gradual (but always astonishingly dramatic) growth of a large hardwood tree like an oak or a beech. But there is also the human factor. As you grow and change, so too does your relationship with a garden. I am not sure if living with the same garden all your life does not mean outstaying your welcome. Mind you, there are few enough people who ever do that. I suspect that ten to fifteen years is needed to see your garden grow, and at the end of that time almost anything that you have planted, other than the aforesaid hardwood trees, is either fully grown or establishing well. Perhaps thirty years would confirm real maturity. Apparently this is how long it took for Levens Hall—which dates back to the 1690s, making it the oldest garden in Britain surviving in its original form—to reach its current maturity. Which means that all of the past 280 years have been spent containing and restraining its growth. It is an astonishing thought. But I like the idea of the garden, like Michelangelo's slaves, struggling to free themselves from the marble, and doing so amazingly fast.

In making up gardens we are harnessing that almost uncontrollable growth for a few years. The whole place crackles with energy. Yet it is entirely benign, entirely at ease with itself and the rhythm of things. One of the things that is apparent in restoring abandoned gardens is how important are the roles of straight lines and clumps or abstract curves. We clearly impose straight lines on to the landscape to mark it out and restrict it, just as clearly as we mark out a street plan on a virgin site. Yet these are the first to show signs of freedom if they are let loose. At Levens Hall there are two huge beech hedges flanking the central path down from the topiary garden. During the Second World War, when there was not the manpower to keep them trimmed, in just a few years the hedges grew across to form one impenetrable barrier, that had to be hacked back like a jungle.

When nature was regarded as fundamentally hostile the lines were straighter and more tightly maintained. As we got bolder we grew to trust in a less autocratic dominion of nature. I used to think that Capability Brown was a vandal for replacing the highly formal seventeenth-century gardens with his looser landscapes, but now suspect that he, like the American Thomas Church two centuries later, was tapping into a wiser, more integrated relationship between the garden and nature. Brown's work was all on a grand, public scale— which makes him one of the first make-over artistes, although his gardens took dozens of men years to create and he never saw any of them in their maturity. But then, for all his huge transforming schemes, he was a true gardener and knew that you cannot pull gardens, like a rabbit, out of a hat. The excitement is all in the growing.

08.07.01 **My Roots**

For the past fortnight I have been gardening by phone. Sarah has been telling me about the garden in bulletins dictated by the ability of my mobile to break the signal code. I am writing this in Forres, on the Moray Firth, where the North Sea breaks upon the jut of Scotland. It is a long way from home. It is my birthday. I say I don't care. I do. Down the phone Sarah tells me that the sun has been incessant and unyielding and she has spent hours in the jewel garden weeding in a bikini, while I listen huddled in a thick coat that is not really sufficient to stop the rain soaking through nor the wind cutting this cloth. Two worlds. I have a file of pictures of the garden stored in this laptop and I set the alarm each morning for six, wondering which way to walk through them today, tracing ten thousand steps. The dog features heavily. Everything is skewed to sentiment. It is like being back at school.

And in my absence they have put up another greenhouse ('How does it look?' 'Great.' 'What sort of great?') and cleared the yard. I live this in full widescreen in Aberdeen, the yard that has been filled with cobbles and slate and builders' sand and piles of timber for over a year now, and rising above the admiration and enthusiasm feel the gagging taste of naked, shameful jealousy. All reason dictates that it is a fantastic piece of generosity for Sarah to organise this to be done by others in my absence. It waits for me, the clear yard, like a gift for homecoming. And I can only resent it for not happening with me—ungenerous and ungrateful to the end. But if I do not hear of news, of progress, albeit of single plants moved and a patch of weeds cleared, then I grow anxious and feel further excluded. Although the party swings along fine without me, I long for a running update on each and every dance. And the garden in late June and early July is a dance before the grass fades and the early bloom shrivels. I have never been a dancer, never known what foot should fall where, but can see it clearly in every leaf and bend of flower head. Sarah's commentary is the beat and rhythm of the song. Before I left, the roses were all rising to the moment and are now at their best, the oriental poppies were just slowing down and are now gone. The lilies are flowering without me. While I struggle with late-night Scottish pub food, at home lettuce, broad beans, peas, artichokes and gooseberries exceed the mouths to eat them. We talk of food parcels at midnight. And the consolation prize is these wide, wide mountains ringed with curlews, an adder curled in the sun amongst a clump of tiny violas in the heather and the sea as unhorticultural and unmeasured as my yard is clear.

21.07.02

Although I have been an organic gardener for about seven years now, I had not explored the reaches of biodynamics. I knew that it was a step further down the organic road. It is veganism to organic growing's vegetarianism. I also knew that the waxing and waning of the moon and the use of concoctions came into the growing process at some stage, but no more than that. Then a reader sent me *Working with the Stars*, which turned out to be a 'biodynamic sowing and planting calendar' rather than a guide to working in Hollywood. Written by a German couple, it is studded with nuggets of advice that unfortunately have not always had the advantages of perfect translation. The result is a literary style akin to a set of instructions for assembling a bookcase translated drunkenly from Taiwanese by a Finnish prankster. So for July, we have: 'Burn crickets, grasshoppers and locusts on July 9th and 10th. For snails and slugs use Leaf days between July 9 and Aug 9. It is particularly effective on the July 11 not later than 04h.' And in October: 'In the past it was common practise to burn the dried potato leaves. However, if there are seeds on the potato leaf it is better to put it on the compost instead, because the nonsense of burning has caused a severe degeneration and bad health of the potato.'

Stunned by this information, I thought it time to learn more about biodynamics. I started with the basic historical facts. In 1924 Rudolf Steiner gave a series of eight lectures to a group of farmers which were eventually published in English as *An Agricultural Course*. It took as its premise that the farm should be viewed holistically, integrating crops and livestock, the soil, recycling and the relationship of the farmer and the workers to the land. The environmental, social and financial aspects of the farm were all wholly interactive. Clearly, all this would apply to gardening as much

207

as farming.

In 1928, an organisation called Demeter was established as a certification programme for biodynamically grown foods. The argument was that all foods grown under this regime tasted better and did you more good and made you a better person than alternatives. It also was better for those that grew it and—not least—for the land and environment. If there was only a whiff of truth about this then it deserved to be taken seriously.

But there is an aspect of biodynamics that needs a dumper truck of salt to retain credibility. This is the essential tenet that cosmic and terrestrial forces can be harnessed for the benefit of soil and plants by the mixing of certain preparations. These preparations range from oak bark buried overwinter in the skull of a domestic animal to valerian flowers buried inside a stag's bladder. This is very hard to take seriously, but I persevered. The preparations are used in minute quantities—such as a level teaspoon to ten tons of compost. Crazy stuff.

While much of Steiner's approach seems common sense and intuitively right, some seems completely barking. But before I dismissed it as irrelevant to me and the righteous, perfectly oiled organic machine that is the Don garden, I wanted to see biodynamics in action. I heard of a farm on the Welsh borders with the lovely name of Fern Varrow, that was growing biodynamic vegetables that were apparently fabulous and much in demand by such places as Neal's Yard and St John in Clerkenwell. So I rang the farmer, Andy Trim, and arranged a visit.

Fern Varrow is set in the least spoilt part of

England, in the eastern lee of the Black Mountains, which is a heart-stopping maze of tiny steep-banked lanes, brooks and small fields. It is countryside that would bring the hippy out in the crustiest old colonel (me). It is biodynamic country.

Andy and his wife Jane are not locals. Their own links to farming were tenuous. They moved to Fern Varrow from London ten years ago, buying a smallholding with a few barns and less than ten acres. Andy had been in the building trade and Jane was a cheese buyer. She had come across biodynamic cheese-makers and they had heard chefs say that biodynamic vegetables were the best—but they couldn't get hold of them. This was enough to set them going. But the initial signs were not good. The government advisory body, ADAS, came and went round the land with them and advised them not to grow vegetables because the soil was too poor. The Soil Association wanted money even to talk to them. [As a life member of the Soil Association it pains me to admit how often I have heard this.] Finally Demeter were positive, friendly and free. It was enough to confirm the decision to farm biodynamically. It meant signing up to using Steiner's 'preparations' at the stipulated times and 'to increasingly understand them', planting and harvesting according to various phases of the moon and integrating their entire lives with the rhythm of growing vegetables. Now there are those who might argue that any farmer has no damn choice but to be thus integrated, but the biodynamic option clearly involves more than a commitment to hard work.

When I arrived, on a sodden July day, it was time for the morning break and six workers, some foreign students on visits, some local labour, came in for their tea break in the farmhouse kitchen. Small children played around them and then accompanied the workers back out to the fields to help. The atmosphere was that of an extended family engaged on a communal project. Not glamorous work in the rain and mud, but there was plenty of laughter.

Andy, who radiated health and fitness, told me how the farm had grown. 'When we came here we had eight and three-quarter acres. We now farm 35 acres, of which ten acres are vegetables. These are grown non-intensively, exactly the same as in a garden. We have some Tamworth pigs and Dexter cattle, but the vegetables account for three-quarters of our income. They are not cheap but everything is picked when ready to eat (rather than when most fit to travel and be stored) and delivered the same day. The demand is growing all the time.' I saw some veg boxes (brown paper carrier bags actually) ready to be delivered—eggs, strawberries, chard, peas, onions, carrots, herbs—all looking as wholesome and attractive as any veg I have seen.

But what about the preparations? The mumbo-jumbo? Andy seemed such a down-to-earth sort of chap, and Jane, who is in charge of the marketing, is not just warm and friendly but clearly a shrewd, extremely competent woman. Surely they didn't entirely buy that stuff?

Andy gently picked me up on my sensationalism. 'It's complicated. When I started I was happy to go along with it all but thought it a bit. . .' He pulled a wry smile and chose the word carefully: '. . . cranky. Then I began to see that biodynamics added some heart and soul to the process of growing. Now I see

210

that there is a kind of alchemy. It works for sure. The results are there to be seen—and eaten.'

He showed me the preparations in their box in the cool store. 'You need minute quantities. The preparations needed for two hundred tons of composted cow manure would fit in a pint jug. They exist not to change the compost or plant but to make nutrients available. We have been educated to eat plants that are pumped up with water. But plants taste differently depending on their soil.' He unscrewed a mayonnaise jar and showed me the anonymously dark contents. 'This is oak bark that has been scraped gently from a tree with a knife, then buried in a pig's skull for six months. Oak has the highest concentration of calcium of any plant, and the skull is, of course, bone. Its effect is to get the calcium in the compost in balance.' There was camomile that had been buried in a small intestine and yarrow buried in the bladder of a horned stag—Andy's came from a roadkill. I must have looked cynical because he caught my eye. 'The preparations have to be taken in context. It is as much to do with timing as anything else. I was really converted when I found myself not using them because the timing didn't seem right. So I thought that it followed that there must be a "right" time. I was starting to think about these things, to feel them.'

He took me round. It had none of the clinical efficiency of a nursery and yet was more garden than farm. I asked him if he was a farmer or a gardener. 'A gardening farmer,' he said. We started in the propagating greenhouse, which was a large, home-made structure, filled with plants in plugs standing on home-made staging. My gardener's eye

211

hunted detail. I asked Andy what their compost mix was. 'Composted cow manure, molehills and screeding sand at a ratio of roughly 4-2-1. But nothing is measured.'

They pick most things smaller than a supermarket or even greengrocer would consider viable. This means that they are tastier. To deal with this they do repeated sowings and harvest right up till Christmas. This is a good lesson for the gardener. I have become stuck in my seasons, still trying to produce one or at most two 'good crops' instead of looking for three or even four smaller, faster harvests.

We went out to some of the vegetable fields, where everything is grown in narrow, informal raised beds. This is part of the biodynamic principle. 'If you raise the soil up you speed up the life process. Which is why we use molehills for the seed. The disadvantage of this is that you exhaust the vitality of the soil quicker. But we remake the beds after every harvest.' There were weeds everywhere but the vegetables were clearly thriving. This, remember, is the soil that the government advisory body said was certainly no good for growing vegetables. Either biodynamics is doing something that conventional farming could not, or the conventional approach is hidebound and hopelessly limited.

It is a huge amount of work. Organic growing is more work than conventional farming and biodynamics more work again. But Andy stressed that the high labour content was an important part. It contributed to local social and economic health. It made the farm healthier by anything other than purely economic standards. He refuses all subsidies for the same reason. Not that he does not need the money—there is clearly no spare cash about—but because he thinks that subsidies are one of the main problems in agriculture. 'So many farmers are being subsidised to grow the wrong thing at the wrong time in the wrong place. Nothing is left to their own judgment, experience or intuition.' For the organic certification they have to follow strict rotation guidelines. Andy feels uncomfortable with this imposition too. 'I think that a lot of the rules of rotation are received and not really necessary. If you have healthy ground and healthy seed then rotation is not really a problem. You have to relate its relevance to every separate piece of ground and not just do it by rote.'

I came away rethinking my own approach to gardening and organics. Andy and Jane are clearly producing first-class food in a happy, sustainable environment. [Andy is no longer living with Jane and she now runs the farm.] Conventional farmers and growers are in a mess. I suspect that the government is incapable of understanding the problem, let alone providing any kind of solution. The answer lies in us as individuals, gardeners with an allotment or scrap of ground or people brave enough to sell up and buy a patch of ground 'no good for growing vegetables'. And if that is accompanied by the burial of dandelions collected at dawn or a chart of the motion of the stars and phases of the moon, then is it any weirder than the hopelessly damaging incantations and potions of scientists, ministers and experts down the years, or indeed than the sincere prayers of a conventional farmer as he swallows the blood of Christ at communion in the local church?

20.07.03 **My Roots**

I've been ill and it's been raining and both things have done me and the garden a lot of good. There is, of course, ill and ill, and I wasn't ill. But for one to whom robust good health is axiomatic it was odd to drift around feeling sorry for myself and going back to bed in the afternoon. Odd and rather nice. I watched that appalling Henman person [This remark inspired more outraged mail than any other comment I have ever written.] do tennis (does anyone else think that he looks like a more athletic version of that appalling Blair person?) and drifted in and out of semi-feverish sleep whilst the birds and children filled the garden. When I was up I pottered. I want to do a lot of pottering at the best of times but don't give myself the permission. Must get on! Carpe diem! So much to do and so little time to do it in! But the delving and hewing was beyond me, so I tied up the tomatoes in the greenhouse and tunnel (try that on the hottest day of the year with a temperature), watered everything that needed watering, did a bit of mowing, pruned the various early clematis like *alpina* and *macropetala*, planted out chard, endive, cavolo nero, purple sprouting broccoli and January King cabbages and spent an entire afternoon cutting back the walled garden, stripping away layers, so that by the time Sarah and I had finished it was six barrow-loads lighter and looking like a duchess in Ascot hat and underwear—and as endearing. But all this was done at a dribble of a pace, with rests and stops and a lot of looking around. I noticed things in a completely passive way. The ligularias arrived. I heard the last of the cuckoo. The lovage has grown yellow flowers and must be cut back. The pears have gone from incipient to young in what seems like an afternoon. When you're not feeling well your knees hurt more. The seseli is twisting taller and I don't know whether this is a good or bad thing. But the zigzagged kinkiness of the bronze fennel is a wonder and the poppy petals catch on ruby thorns. The day goes by.

26.07.98

What would you think if you went to the Royal Academy Summer Exhibition (let alone a new exhibition by a recognised artist) and found that it was comprised only of copies and pastiches of old masters? Would it be post-modernist irony or depressingly uncreative hackwork? If you went to a first performance of a new play by a young author and found that it was 'new' only insofar as it was a skilfully assembled medley of scenes from Shakespeare, Marlowe and Kidd you might think it clever and probably instructive, yet surely not creative. However, this is exactly the way that most professional garden designers put their gardens together.

I was at Hampton Court Flower Show a couple of weeks ago and—as at Chelsea Flower Show—was amazed at the skills displayed in the show gardens. But for the most part these skills were those of set designers. This was brought home particularly clearly courtesy of the *Daily Mail*. They had employed professional film set designers to create a life-sized model of a seaside house in fibreglass and then surrounded that by a seaside quasi-horticultural theme park. Quite brilliant it was too, insomuch as it was convincingly realistic and awe-inspiringly dramatic in conception. Opposite was a show garden calling itself 'The Spirit of Heligan' that attempted, according to the official show catalogue, to 'skilfully transform a modern landscape into a glorious spectacle of the past . . . built using reclaimed materials . . . blended with modern technology and building practices, while not compromising the garden's authenticity'. This garden was divided into three sections, of which one showed the fallen state of chaos that Heligan was in when Tim Smit found it in 1990, another was a slice of vegetable garden and the third a small taste of the eighty acres of woodland garden. The chaos was cleverest, a lovingly assembled mass of bramble, broken glass and nettles utterly convincing in its verisimilitude. I found myself in the confusing position of liking what I saw very much but hating the fact that it was there to be seen. It was a brilliant piece of marketing for the real Heligan, but utterly irelevant to gardening as we approach the millennium.

It was hardly alone. Another show garden was the recreation of a Blitz garden, complete with bombed 'house' that was stocked with furniture of the period—all for sale. What other nation would celebrate being bombed with a garden and then queue round the block to be sold second-hand tat?

There are two situations here. The first is only about marketing. For the most part the show

216

gardens at Chelsea and Hampton Court are merely marketing vehicles. There is no such thing as a free garden. Chanel did not sponsor a garden at Chelsea through the love of gardens but to sell Chanel. Newspapers sponsor gardens solely to sell newspapers. Even the only truly innovative garden at Hampton Court, the Water Wise garden by Cleve West and Johnny Woodford, was sponsored by Thames Water not through enlightened patronage but from a shrewd assessment that being associated with something forward-looking will disassociate them from their own appalling public image. [I cannot remember why their public image was so appalling at that time—maybe such associations as show gardens have successfully blanked it from my mind.] The budgets for these show gardens are, in advertising terms, tiny, but in horticultural terms huge. Between £30,000 and £100,000 per garden is the norm. Unless the designer is supremely confident, that sort of money will paralyse innovation. Highly skilled and loving recreations are easier to justify financially than flights of creative fancy. It would be better to put a cap on all spending, limiting it to, say, £20,000. [Inflation and experience suggests that £50,000 might be more practical, but the principle holds.] The RHS does not feel equipped to judge the standard of design, feeling much more comfortable with the quality and condition of the plants included as part of the design. [There have been some real changes in this area. Seven years later, the RHS seems to be much more confident and comfortable with evaluating design per se.] This is like judging a building by the cut of its curtains but, to be fair, this did not stop them giving the Water Wise garden a gold and that was aggressively challenging to the 'heritage' status quo, although its planting was clearly superb.

Of course the RHS could include the likes of Dan Pearson, Christopher Bradley-Hole or Cleve West on its panel of judges for the show gardens— all gold medal winners and brilliant contemporary designers [They do precisely this now and Cleve West is an experienced judge.]—but I suspect that they would be too anxious about frightening their elderly membership to do this. Certainly until the RHS takes a view and positively discriminates in favour of innovation and contemporary design the show gardens at RHS shows will be driven by marketing departments rather than any desire for good design.

The second part of the problem is bigger and harder to deal with. Gardening has become part of the national heritage theme park culture. You have to wonder what is wrong with us. I include myself, because I am just as subject as the next person to the knee-jerk response to nostalgia and heritage. It is a comfort zone where a little knowledge replaces thought, and history is an opiate for the present. But here are we, a tiny, waning nation, systematically abusing and destroying our countryside whilst at the same time pathetically engaged in dubious recreations in our back gardens. It is pathetic. Clearly the urge to do that is a mixture of slavish adherence to social precept and a chronic lack of confidence. The British past is a country where the uncarcinogenic sun shone more brilliantly, where security and ease were spread like a rectory lawn. Make the past in your garden and you can step into it like a Tardis, flying for a few hours free of the tyranny of a hostile and uncertain present. We confuse the careful historical restoration of a garden—like the actual Heligan in Cornwall or the Privy Garden at Hampton Court—with the pastiche made on a virgin site. One is a labour of scholarship and love and the other a failure of nerve.

The energy that made all our great historic gardens was a rude and iconoclastic force that often brutally ravished the past. Capability Brown thought nothing of ripping apart the work of his predecessors to install a shockingly new landscape. That same energy needs to be harnessed to any genuinely creative project, because it has to have the arrogance to believe that this new thing that is being made is better than anything that preceded it. This confidence is what has been lost in modern British gardens.

So how does this relate to our private backyards? I think that it is a matter of playfulness. Gardening in Britain is bogged down in technique and procedure. It is all too serious by half. Far too much attention is given to how we grow plants rather than what, where or why we grow them. To experiment and play you have to take risks and accept failure, and for some reason a garden is not seen as a place to do this in. The countries that lead modern garden design are arguably America and Australia, and they have much less historical baggage to weigh them down. They feel free to make themselves up in the garden just as children make up a world with camps and games outside.

We can do this, you and I. We are as good as we need be. I would suggest that there is no other area of life where the ordinary person can make up their own brave new world than in the garden. That world can be informed by a deep and loving knowledge of the past, just as the best abstract painters have a great draughtsman's skills, but it cannot *be* the past. Your garden is your link to the soil, your source of the freshest food available, your solace from the grind of the over-compromised day, and—the big, vital and—it is also the made-up living future. No one in their right minds wants children to be carbon copies of their parents or grandparents. They astonish us by becoming people we only partially know. So it must be with gardens. We control and tweak and fiddle with them obsessively, but if they are worth half that attention then they must become something not yet known.

23.07.00 **My Roots**

The rain has given the snails a second wind and they have wiped out my first planting of French beans and are doing their best to eat through the third wave of lettuces before they get big enough for us. I cut comfrey to seduce them and perhaps it works, but I never know how you measure the success of these things. The potatoes got blight at the end of the first week in July, just as they have done for the past three years. I cut the tops off and then used the flame thrower to burn off the haulms and—hopefully—kill the fungal spores. The idea is that the potatoes remain safe under ground until one digs them up. Potato blight is the indicator of a real turning point in the year.

By the beginning of July the vegetable garden is becoming rich and full, the borders are sliding into sumptuousness and a fat softness takes over. Then it seems to become dissolute almost overnight. The potatoes are hacked back. The hedges are cut, delphiniums cut back and roses over. What is left is sharper, harder, experienced. It is not worse but it is certainly something else. One of the areas of the garden that is affected most dramatically is the herb garden, which looks positively tatty if it is not cropped right back by now. It comes again, but looks like a fleeced sheep for a few weeks.

For my birthday the other day my eldest son Adam gave me *Smiling in Slow Motion* by Derek Jarman (Tom gave me a box for my sox—the spelling comes with the present—and Freya two bunches of sweet peas she had grown herself.) Jarman has long been my favourite garden writer and *Derek Jarman's Garden* my favourite gardening book. Howard Sooley's photographs seem exactly in tune with the subject, and it ecstatically transcends the bleedin' obvious that dogs so much of what is written about gardens and gardening. Jarman's gayness and illness (he died of AIDS in February 1994) are central to the book, but the garden on the beach at Dungeness runs through it like a flowering thread.

I suppose a 'gardening' book is one that is about gardens, but gardens are enriched beyond all horticulture by the lives that pass through them. What do they know of gardens who only gardens know? I am ashamed to say that I have never been to see Prospect Cottage, ashamed because I have long wanted to and nothing has stopped me except my own indolence. I wonder how it is, now that Jarman has been dead these six years. Gardens move cruelly on, as indifferent to human sentiment as a crow alighting on an injured lamb. I finished the book terribly sad that we have lost a thoroughly good and heroic human being, and very angry at the sexual bigotry and hypocrisy that still demeans our society. But above all, it makes me glad to be a gardener. So, inarticulate and very moved, I went into the garden and picked a bunch of flowers for Derek Jarman.

29.07.01

It is always hard to know how honest to be. At the beginning of this year the editor of this magazine and I talked about the structure of these pages and agreed that I should do an expanded 'My Roots' once every month or so. This seemed like a very good idea to me, for the purely selfish reason that I have always been more interested in my own garden than anybody else's. But inevitably I would collate and expand the events of the previous month, so as not to repeat myself and perhaps to anticipate and cover the time between writing and publication. There has been some omission, some wishful thinking and even some invention, but on the whole I have tried to stay honest. But it has been hard. Not because the temptation to embroider has been greater than usual, but because I have been here so little.

I have been told that some people take a

vicarious pleasure in reading about this garden, projecting their own fantasies on to this couple of acres. I usually try and provide that envy fodder, playing up the bucolic pleasures that are certainly there to be relished and playing down the ceaseless grind of a life driven by work and endless demands. But honesty insists that I put this garden in some kind of proper perspective. I love it. It feeds me with more happiness than anything other than Sarah and the children. But this life I am currently leading is unfaithful and truncated. Head, heart and body are flying in different directions, and if they do not regularly fuse in this patch of private outside then I am lost. I considered abandoning these monthly pieces because of the paucity of material, but two things give it some kind of credibility.

The first is that, for the first time for many years, I am in the same boat as most gardeners, snatching time in the garden from the unyielding demands of work, children and the fragments of a social life that come my way. Since 1988, when we left London, I have been gardening with a focused application that most people's lives could not accommodate. There are really very few things in this world that I want to do more. So this enforced period of abstention at least adds a level of empathy to those of you whose lives are not so completely dominated by your garden as I want mine to be.

The second reason is that I know that a lot of people return from holidays or trips away to tackle the wasteland of the garden. It is completely daunting at the best of times, but it is time to get stuck in. The end of July produces a weary shagginess in most gardens that is a stage beyond the lush charm of June. To get back on even terms with the garden and to get the most from it in September and August, now is the time to cut back, clear, weed, be ruthless.

And here is the honesty. I did set out yesterday—having got back at two in the morning from a disastrous week on a boat off the Turkish coast—to cut back, clear, all that. I loaded the wheelbarrow with cutters and clearers and strode manfully towards the shagginess and . . . picked at it in a half-hearted, rather hopeless manner. My own brand of muscular gardening failed me. There was so much to do. The hedges—miles of hornbeam, box and hawthorn—had grown yards, and the pleached limes, which now surround the veg garden and form a pair of flanking avenues at either side, have developed sprouting wands of whippy growth as long as the span of a man's arms, laden with outsized leaves—a textbook example of the result of hard pruning but wrong! The wrong thing in the wrong place! Pleached limes only get the treatment to provide a grid as constraining as a corset and—at best—just as sexy. So these must be cut back, and the cuttings must be collected and shredded, which means hiring a shredder and . . . Jesus. No time. A hard week would be a good start and a fortnight would get really on top of things. I have about two hours.

So I picked raspberries for supper. Now this is fine in a cosmic way. A raspberry slid easily from its naked white plug and slowly crushed between tongue and palate is gardening enough. It is a good year for fruit of all kinds. Last year we lost all our blackcurrants to birds that stripped the bushes

224

almost overnight. This was my fault. I had originally chosen a site for the cage and planted raspberries, cordon and bush gooseberries, white, red- and blackcurrants, starting at one end and plodding methodically over to the other. When the fruit cage arrived, all aluminium tubing and a mysterious inequality of net, it was fixed over the top. Everybody stood back and admired it and themselves. But the black- and redcurrant end was both too shaded and too protected from wind. This meant that the fruit were not ripening properly and—more seriously—that sawfly became a huge problem on the gooseberries and redcurrants. So I moved all the bushes, leaving just raspberries and cordon gooseberries protected. After being moved they grew well, bore lots of fruit which, unprotected, was promptly wiped out by birds. So the fruit cage was dismantled and reassembled around the currants, and the raspberries seem to be fine without protection. The birds have their fill and so do we. The only raspberry problem that we have this year is that I did not tie in all the canes to the top wire, nor prune off the tips (or alternatively loop them over back to the wire) and the upshot is that a number of stems are bent right over under the weight of fruit. Next year I will have a tying-in session around the end of May, [Actually I simply now cut the tops back to the height of the top wire. We still get more raspberries than we and the birds can possibly eat.] and I must tie in and tidy up the autumn raspberries very soon.

This is actually pretty much what all our gardening is like here—lots of trying things out, failing, and trying something different until it seems to work. Of course this is based upon a lot of

225

reading and listening, but every garden is different. Whenever people ask me for sure-fire ways of growing anything I always know that they have not quite got it. All successful gardening involves tuning in subtly and intimately to your own absolutely specific conditions and circumstances. The process of doing that is where the centre of pleasure lies.

To finish on a high, the best thing about being away so much is coming back and seeing changes like a blow to the head. While we were in Turkey the roses all went, blown apart by wind and rain, but all the crocosmias came. 'Lucifer' is a cliché, but its fantastic flat fishtails of crimson are none the worse for that. The clematis in the jewel garden are growing up tripods, although the *viticellas* have already completely outreached theirs and are still growing. This is the first year that we have not also had masses of sweet peas growing up tripods, and although I love them, I had hardly noticed their absence. But my daughter Freya brought in an exquisite little bunch of 'Cupani's originals' that are growing almost as an afterthought on a solitary tripod, and their fragrance carried an immediate clutch of regret like seeing a face across a crowded room that you thought you had learned to forget. Next year there shall be sweet peas again by the score, growing up the hazel wigwams. And next year, come what may, I shall spend more time with my garden. [I did, taking a year off from television to write and spending practically every single day at home. Bliss.]

August

10.08.03

Due to interminable delays on a couple of flights, I read three books in 24 hours the other day. I had chosen them at random, but all three homed in on the same theme. There was Milan Kundera's *Ignorance*, which is all about the ambiguity of an exile's relationship with the home country and the impossibility of memory to be truthful or even available unless constantly exercised—which in itself is destructive to any kind of forward-looking life. There was Geoff Dyer's *Yoga for People Who Can't Be Bothered to Do It*, which, although brilliant, shares almost nothing of my own life or attitude towards it. Dyer prefaces the book with 'Home . . . is the place where least has happened. For the last dozen or so years, in fact, the idea of "home" has felt peripheral and, as a consequence, more than a little blurred.' The final one was William Fiennes's superb *The Snow Geese*, which takes as its leitmotif the migratory bird's instinctive and irresistible movement home. Pages of the Fiennes and Kundera on nostalgia—the suffering caused by the unappeased yearning to return— overlap, and Dyer's restless, directionless travelling of body and mind was the necessary counterbalance to fill out the theme in my mind. I even did not mind sitting in Birmingham and Belfast airports and almost resented the final appearances of the planes.

Fancy books don't butter no parsnips nor dig any weeds, but gardeners cannot live by earth alone and I have been thinking about scent and plants and what it is that is triggered by them. It is not just lovely fragrance, although heaven knows that would be justification enough to sow and plant, weed, stake, water and generally nurture a plant of any kind. Scent is atavistic and primitive and trips wires in the brain that only certain passages—even single notes—of music can finger. And there is almost always an undertone of sorrow or at least regret.

Scent invariably works with memory. You walk round the corner and brush against a box bush or a pot of scented leaf geraniums, or the rain dampens hot summer dust, and as soon as the nose registers these things you are flooded with how, when and where it was that you first registered these scents. Nothing provokes the yearning to return home more than the flowery musk of childhood. It is like listening to Beethoven quartets or children singing Christmas carols—the celebration of what you hear (or smell) involves some necessary mourning to appreciate the experience fully.

And yet. A late summer garden planted with flowers that release their fragrance as the light falls acts like constellations or magnetic earth lines do to a snow goose. They will guide you home, the real home plangent with memory, conflated from a lifetime of similar revelatory experiences to a moment of recognition of 'the centre where three or four things/that happen to a man do happen' (which is the quote from Auden that provoked Geoff Dyer to feel blurred about home).

I suppose the summer plant that evokes most for me with its scent is the annual *Nicotiana sylvestris* with its six-foot flower spikes and the white tubes of flower hanging off them like floral dreadlocks, the whole thing rising up from great fleshy leaves. I first smelt them in the greenhouse of a childhood friend where we used to change into our swimming trunks. Not just the swimming pool, but that earthy greenhouse warmth, tomato and tobacco plants and a fridge stocked with fizzy drinks and chocolate digestives all seemed to combine into the most luxurious mix on this planet. Since then I have been round the world and stayed in a lot of fancy places and never yet found better. *N. sylvestris* don't need a greenhouse to grow in and actually do well in slight shade. The flowers will shrink and close in bright sunshine and then open in the evening, releasing scent as they do so. They will also open on a cloudy day, but the hotter the daytime sun the stronger the fragrance will be in the evening, as the air cools. *N. alata* are easier to get hold of but are not as dramatic—reaching perhaps three feet and with flowers less trumpet-like than *N. sylvestris*, but they too smell wonderful and are easier for all but the biggest container.

Lonicera periclymenum 'Belgica' is ubiquitous but a wonderful plant for evening scent. In fact it likes the cool of either morning or evening for the scent to be at its best. I remember we had one by the kitchen door in our garden in Hackney and its fruity fragrance smelt heavenly at breakfast. *L.* x *americana* has a distinct scent of cloves and *L. japonica* 'Halliana' is especially good for a shady, even north, wall.

Brugmansia suaveolens has huge white His Master's Voice trumpets of flower that are sweetly fragrant at night. These enormous flowers only last for a day before twisting into soggy used tissues, but they compensate for this by producing them continuously from July right through to October. They are not hardy, so I grow them in the greenhouse until June when I bring the pots out into a sunny corner, putting them back before the first frosts of autumn. They need a rich compost and lots and lots of water as well as a weekly feed of seaweed or home-made comfrey elixir. But they are worth the trouble.

Night-scented stock (*Matthiola*) has a scent that is sweet and honeyed and is really the only justification for the plant, because during the day it does not amount to much. They are best grown from seed, sown directly where you want them—which will inevitably be near where you sit of an evening. Evening primrose (*Oenothera biennis*) is a plant which it seems inconceivable to sow once you have it in the garden, for it springs up everywhere unbidden. At times and in the wrong place it is just another weed, but for adding a touch of sweet lemon fragrance to the scented medley of an evening sitting area it is worth its place in the sinking sun.

05.08.01 My Roots

The wetness of July provided a necessary kick up the backside. For a week the garden became increasingly ravaged and wrecked, exposing anything that was not really well staked. Weeds romped. The peas and broad beans, such a visual mainstay of the early summer garden, both went over together, practically overnight. The party became the morning after in the blink of an eye. So we all cut back, weeded, did the necessary and everything looks better than ever. Cutting and weeding gets you back to the ground, gets you looking at detail again rather than basking in a vague overall effect. Not all of this is floral or colourful. For instance I have been getting as much pleasure from the newly revealed trunks of the limes set against a backdrop of dark green hornbeam leaves as from any flowers. It also sets up the new season of late summer which is what we are entering. The *Verbena bonariensis* is popping up all over the place—it loves the shelter of the young box hedging and I have removed every single plant from here this year. Along with the nasturtiums, annual salvias, euphorbias and sweet Williams that all draped over the young box plants. Last year we lost a couple of dozen of the same through being blanketed and I have learned my lesson.

I have harvested all the onions now, 'Turbo', 'Sturon', 'Setton' and 'Brunswick', and they are drying on racks in the greenhouse. I cut the hedges behind these plots in the veg garden, weeded them thoroughly, dug them over and planted three smaller squares out with red drumhead cabbage, chard and radicchio, each crop taking up a bed three yards by four. The other onion plots will be sown with annual rye-grass as a green manure in a week or two.

The major battle in the vegetable garden at this time of year is with cabbage white butterflies. The secret of all good brassica crops is to give them a good start with a constant supply of water and heat; once established, they pretty much look after themselves (although everything other than the curly kale was wiped out by our minus 14 frost at the very end of last year). An attack by cabbage white caterpillars weakens them a lot and they never really recover. The only successful solution against the butterflies laying their eggs on the young plants is to cover all the young brassica plants with fleece or fine netting, which looks horrid but nothing else works.

Finally, it is funny the places that happiness strikes. Last night Sarah and I were sweeping the paths in the jewel garden—eight o'clock, supper not cooked, tired, sun beginning to sink, just filling the last couple of barrows before going indoors—when I was overwhelmed with a sense of joy. There was nothing else in the world I would rather have been doing, nowhere else I would rather have been and no one I would rather have been with.

13.08.00

The Bang has a spring in it. Whoosh Ka-bang Boing. Then, as the sound lands, Thump. For two teenage boys this is a good noise, a sound rich with all the corollaries of pleasure. For the two adults weeding over the wall it is almost torture, almost bloody intolerable. But not quite. It shatters the peace that the garden so carefully laces around itself and is an assault of a kind, but one thing saves it. After each elastic, clattering crash is a whoop of laughter—of triumph or derision depending upon the success of the noisemaker. That raucous, pubescent addition to the general row clears and legitimises everything else.

Adam and Josh are having fun.

I got a nice letter today from a reader of this column asking me to drop by and see the letter-writer's garden in passing, asking me to bring the children too 'as it is a great place for playing hide and seek'. Whilst it is a charming image (and invitation) it presupposes that my children are locked between the ages of about four and eight. The truth is that gardens are dangerous places for unsupervised toddlers and dead boring for any child much over seven. Popular garden lore can accommodate toddlers and young children and there are a number of books that explore all the delightful ways that small children can enjoy your garden. Whatever the book is called there is always an unwritten subtext—Children Enjoying the Garden Without Trashing It Too Badly. But trashing things is inevitable if you are having the right kind of fun. Football and cricket ruin lawns, flowerbeds and greenhouses. (This summer Adam hit a cricket ball through the open door of the greenhouse, and it bounced once on the path, miraculously went through an opened window and out the other side—straight on to a pile of spare panes resting against the fence. Six sheets of glass smashed. That'll teach me to bowl gentle half-volleys outside the off stump.) Tree houses are most fun, with six-inch nails, scaffolding planks and rope, and with plenty of branches sawn off to fit them in and get a view. Bicycles make good muddy ruts in paths and, anyway, seem to spend most of their lives thrown down on the ground blocking a doorway or at the narrowest point of a path.

My children are all heavily into blading [This seems an age ago. The blades have long been left in an abandoned corner.] (or is it skates? The wrong terminology in front of their friends is met with eye-rolling contempt)—hence the half-pipe. This consists of three pieces of 8 x 4 marine ply coaxed into curves to make an enormous ramped semicircle, so they can swoop down one side, up the other, jump and twist in mid-air and either whizz back down again or fall tumbling on to their backsides. Hoots of triumph, hoots of derision. It is brilliant and took the two boys a whole afternoon to make. It took a variety of tools (No, you *cannot* use the chainsaw), and the principal ingredient, other than the ply, assorted blocks of wood, concrete blocks, four milk crates, all my nails and a mysterious quantity of rope, is the courtyard garden. This is a minimalist area, refined down just to an exquisite harmony in stone and wood, the yard paved in York stone, the walls of ancient red sandstone and a square of river-washed pebbles in the centre. Around the perimeter are nine cubes of green oak, now weathering into a silvery cracked maturity. It is the children's best bit of the garden at the moment because it is brilliant for blading. Unfortunately the half-pipe blocks the only entrance to the walled garden, which is where we eat whenever we can in summer. (Have you blocked the entrance to the walled garden? 'Er, not really. . .')

The walled garden was completely revamped last year for the children. They wanted a lawn near the house. Sarah and I wanted a hard surface and abundance near the house. There was a huge open space down the end of the garden, but children like popping in and out. They like the garden as an extension of their bedrooms, and after a day at home the two look pretty indistinguishable. So we cleared the four big borders, moving them to the perimeter and made a lawn in the centre. The trampoline sits in the middle of that patch of grass. Trampolines are just another piece of the affluent family's kit nowadays. Boasting of having a trampoline is dead uncool, and I'm the only one in our household who does it. But the children use it all the time. From the landing window I can watch my lovely daughter Freya leaping and flying, headphones on, crazy auburn corkscrew hair shooting out, eyes closed as she dances to the rhythm of her CD walkman. Actually it is mine and was a birthday present but she has nabbed it. Nine-year-old Tom goes and jumps when he is angry, and it soothes him. Ten minutes later he gets off, jumped easy in himself again. Adam and his friends Josh and George, all fourteen, fight and laugh and swear in that hoarse, shouty way fourteen-year-olds do, like boisterous, awkward, lovely cubs.

The funny thing is that Sarah and I ignore the presence of the trampoline—which totally dominates the space—in the same way that they ignore the subtleties of the planting—all pastels and whites—around their leaping selves. We accommodate each other's needs by pretending that they are temporary.

And of course, on every level, they are. The children grow as fast as the garden does and they change their demands on the garden almost daily. Certainly by the time you have established any kind of specific set-up for them they have moved on to something else. What children beyond the hide-

and-seek age want is a kind of loosely equipped playground with enough familiarity so that they can loaf comfortably but enough novelty to make the world up afresh as the spirit takes them.

Horticultural doesn't come into it. My daughter made a garden this year and did it carefully and well. But once made—which took her perhaps three sessions of an hour spread over a week—it was forgotten. Everything was in the doing. In fact it has thrived and her sweet peas are every bit as good as ours despite total neglect. Tom periodically makes camps and tree houses, but his are all essentially hiding places. One was elaborately dug out and then camouflaged to look like a stack of brashings (sweet that he does not think I know every stick and leaf of this garden), and he has a series of flower pots sunk in the ground, covered over with a tile and then hidden by soil. Each contains an emblematic piece of him, like a key or a sweet. He roams this garden like a member of the Resistance, seemingly compliant to its strict regulations and adult, horticultural tyranny, but really possessing it as fully as anyone.

And there is his shed. This is strictly private and entrance is by invitation only. There are a series of notices to that effect, the latest of which reads 'BUGER OF, I LIVE HEAR'. His shed is a serious workshop and much more highly sophisticated than anything I possess or am able to employ. At the age of nine he can make almost anything that he sets his mind to, copying things seen on television or in magazines or making up inventions. He makes things all day. Nothing is more admirable. Yet his mess spreads like a dervish workshop ripple from his shed to the farthest reaches of the garden, with saws, power drills, hammers, endless bits of wood, plastic, metal and string put down and abandoned wherever the fancy has taken him. And he bangs an awful lot. Boys in the garden always equal noise. Tom seems to foray out from his shed with the tools of the moment and to work wherever the action is. This is not just limited to the garden but has now gone quietly out into cyberspace. I got a bill the other day for a domain name registered as 'www.tomshed.com' which he had gone and done entirely on his own. I think perhaps that tomshed.com is the most accurate metaphor for a growing child's garden—a mental space of limitless imagination founded on the comfort of an actual, utterly safe haven. Inevitably the real garden with a growing family of children will be untidy, messy even, noisy and often destructive. It drives arch control freaks like myself mad. But I hate it when they are not there. [Predictably my children have grown up and are rapidly becoming young adults rather than children. Re-reading this makes me extremely nostalgic for their careless youth. Mind you, Tom is as untidy as ever and his shed empire has spread to a current count of three. Also Adam is a huge help in the garden, which is a completely unexpected bonus as he showed no interest of any kind for the first eighteen years of his life.]

12.08.01 My Roots

I spent yesterday in a peat bog in Westmeath, Ireland, and one of the things that was thought to be a good idea was to go bog snorkelling. This involves jumping into a man-made wallow or pond with wet suit and snorkelling paraphernalia. Ha ha, such larks! In fact it is a disgusting experience, on a par with taking a dip in the local cesspit. The water is pitch black and filled with solids of various consistencies. I also talked to a herbalist promoting the healing powers of peat. These seem extensive, ranging from an effective treatment for arthritis and rheumatism to the removal of heavy metals in your skin (for 46 years I have been irresponsibly unaware of the heavy metals in my skin). I don't feel sceptical of this. The Germans, apparently, have been using peat medicinally for years. It is only us Brits that are backwards in the ways of peat. The most beneficial peat is the oldest and they use black peat about five thousand years old for preference. I also visited a man who extracted peat for fuel, using a great digger and a machine that converted it into blocks. This was shown me as an example of small-scale, sustainable peat use. Even so, his site, about two acres big, was six feet below the level of the true bog surface with its heather and curlews.

It was a moral dilemma. He was a nice man, who worked hard for not much money and was only applying technology, albeit crude, to the ancient practice of cutting turves. But there is a wetlands crisis. Gardeners and nurserymen are the worst culprits, encouraging large multinational companies to strip out thousands of acres of peat every year. The truth is that the only sustainable use of peat is dictated by the method of extraction—anything bigger than a spade is going to worsen the already bad situation. I have spoken to many nurserymen who say that they would like not to use peat—but that there is no viable alternative. This is simply untrue and irresponsible. If we are to do something about improving the quality of our environment then it cannot be left to other people. There is coir— with real questions about travel miles—crushed bark, garden compost and loam. All are viable horticulturally and economically and all are readily to hand in enormous quantities. The Americans claim that their use of horticultural peat is less than the rate at which new bogs are forming—which sounds dubious but may be so. It certainly is not so in Britain and Ireland and there is a huge backlog to replace that will take thousands of years.

There is only one solution. Do not buy any peat products for the garden. Keep peat for removing the heavy metals or your arthritis or, if you really must, snorkel in it.

17.08.97

There are many yardsticks of manliness, ranging from the ability to drink enough beer to fill a water butt, to strong-but-tender muscular competence. But for me it has long been the ability to use a scythe. The man that went to mow, went to mow a meadow, always seemed to be the real, defining thing. This is partly bound up with an absurd private glamorisation of a Hardyesque rural world, and partly based upon my own acquaintance with scythes. In the tool shed at home one hung from the wall with a curving handle of silvery ash and a yard-long, oiled blade thrillingly sharp to touch. I would look at it with saucer eyes, marvelling at the blade that could, I was told with finger-wagging certainty, cut my leg off with one clean swing, and also at the curve of the ash handle that was unambiguously womanly and voluptuous. More than anything I wanted to hold that handle and swing that blade. Unable to find anyone to teach me how to use one, [I have since come across *The Scythe Book* by David Tresemer. It is American and, to my British sensibility, very ponderous, but very helpful in the art of using and maintaining a scythe.] I would study pictures of haymakers and note tiny details of grip, angle and lift. I have five scythes now, each with a past much longer than mine, each with a character of its own.

I would like to say that I have mastered the art of scything but it would be an untruth too far. I do not use one often enough to develop the necessary easy familiarity. It was certainly a quarter of a century old when I first knew it, forty years ago, and for the past five years I have used it annually to mow a certain piece of long grass. The cutting movement is a slow side-to side swing with each pace forward, drawing it back as the right leg leads and cutting with the left. It should look lazy and yet metronomically efficient, the cut grass flopping aside against the sinuous curve of the handle that perfectly wraps around your body whilst the great blade twists on its wider curve.

A scythe will not hang easily on the wall, will not stand alone on the ground, will not lie balanced on the floor. But take it in your hands and hold it as intended and immediately it falls into balanced

242

place. The curving snaithe, or handle, has been steamed into shape from lengths of ash, cleft down the grain for strength, allowing exactly for the twist of the body as the hands swing, the blade almost parallel to the ground, tilting slightly forward on the downswing and up and away as it crosses the legs. It is a tool perfectly evolved, and the various modern versions that I have seen and tried are futile reductions. It would be like redesigning a shark.

Although its use should look effortless, it is shockingly hard work. I am fit and experienced yet am reduced to a trembling lather after ten minutes. [This is actually a measure of how badly I handle it. Used properly, it is tiring but not exhausting work. However, this does not in any way devalue the labour of those that scythed all day, day after day.] An hour exhausts me. In the pre-tractor age, when men were real men, mowers would work for twelve hours a day for weeks at a time during haymaking. All this was done with skill and as a natural part of their day for a wage of around 75 pence a week—perhaps twenty pounds in modern money. It reduces the preening gym culture to effete inadequacy.

The skill is in getting the blade to swing evenly so that it shaves the ground without the tip digging in, which has a disastrous effect, rather like catching a crab in rowing, as well as buckling and blunting the blade, which has to be kept razor sharp—a skill of its own.

If you can sharpen it and are prepared to sweat, a scythe is wonderfully efficient at cutting the long dried grass of high summer. And if you don't use one, what else will do the job? Wild-flower meadows are all very well, ['Wild-flower meadows' were all the rage back then. They were no such thing of course, merely patches and pastiches of the rare real thing, and most came to grief after a few years due to the over-fertility of the soil.] but to make them perform at all the grass must be cut in high summer when it is least amenable to cutting. The best mechanical alternative is an Allen scythe, which is fundamentally a straight cutter bar with powered reciprocating blades—exactly like a hedge trimmer—but they are expensive and hard to find now. A rotary mower has to be enormously powerful to tackle dried, tall grasses and almost all ordinary garden versions are not, appropriately, man enough. If they will cut the grass at all—and most dribble to a halt within yards, they soon clog. A strimmer is not designed for the task, although a brush-cutter head with nylon blades will work, but it is no faster than a scythe and much noisier. Although it could be considered more butch than a scythe, what with the engine and natty orange protective gear, it has none of the sinuous poetry and is therefore devoid of the finer qualities of true manliness. Case rejected.

Of course gardeners have been using scythes even more than farmers for centuries. It is incredible to think that all grass was cut by scythe and shears before the invention of the lawn mower in 1830, which was in principle identical to the modern cylinder mower and based upon existing machines used to cut the pile on various cloths. And until the rotary mower became commonplace after the last war, all grass above lawn length and all but the gentlest banks and slopes had to be cut with a scythe. There are those—with more expertise than I can muster—who claim to be able to cut to a finer finish with a scythe than any machine, and there is no reason to suppose that the lawns of two hundred years ago were any less perfect than ours. Until the bowling green became a popular play area in Tudor times there is no reason to suppose that the lawn as we know it existed. But bowls demanded a short, smooth surface that needed frequent cutting, and it is significant that the French word for a grassy plot is *boulingrin* (bowling green). The landscape movement of the mid-eighteenth century meant that grass around great houses was grazed by flocks of sheep that cropped, compacted and manured the grass—just as they still do in the orchards here in Herefordshire, leaving a lawn-like sward under the trees.

What is amazing is the amount of grass that was cut and manicured in the great houses. In 1874 Blenheim Palace had 160 acres of grass 'under the machine and scythe', and Drumlanrig Castle had forty miles of 'soft silent carriage drives . . . kept like lawns'. Until around the middle of the last century (i.e. the 1850s), when the mowing machine became universally used, the gardeners would rise before dawn to scythe the grass, which cut to a finer finish when still wet with dew. Even after the mower, the bents were trimmed off by hand with a scythe. Mowing machines were, of course, not powered and were either pushed or pulled by a donkey or pony—wearing leather shoes over its hooves to stop it pocking the ground with hoofprints.

The mowing machine created a tyranny of grass cutting that still controls all gardeners today. I think that urban gardeners do best to free themselves of that cycle by avoiding lawns altogether and replacing them with a paved area to sit on. In the country we have the chance of converting stripy lawn into meadow billowing with wild flowers, although this takes great skill and quite different soil conditions than that which suits a good lawn. It is certainly a myth to think that an uncut lawn becomes a wild-flower meadow. Instead it converts to a hayfield, which can be lovely but its beauty is agricultural rather than floral. Hay has to be collected once cut and the process of raking and gathering into heaps is laborious. The advantage that a rotary mower does have is that it chops the grass up and thus renders it compostable, whereas the long strands of scythed grass take years to rot down. Cut hay is also full of grass seed, and when one eventually does use it as a mulch, it inevitably throws up a bright green rash of grass.

Although it is extraordinary how precise an expert with a scythe can be, there are always margins where it cannot safely operate. This is where shears came in. They were the bane of my childhood, being a suitably boring, unskilled job to dish out to a sulky child on a long hot summer's afternoon. Steep and awkward banks, areas beneath shrubs and along stone or brick verges were only coped with by clipping with shears. It is horrible work, crawling on your knees for hours at a time, cutting a pitifully small area of grass. The invention of the strimmer in 1975 made shears all but redundant for anything but topiary and any house sale has dozens of them going for a song. And, the final condemnation for me, shears were not manly. [Eight years on I disagree with this and

246

am now a fan of shears for their low-tech simplicity and silence.]

17.08.03 **My Roots**

At this time of year the maturity of the garden is best appreciated and because this is a novel thing—I reckon maturity has only hit us in the last year or so—I am seeing it with rather surprised eyes, like looking into a mirror and seeing to one's astonishment that there is, to all intents and appearances, a grown-up looking back.

It works best now because the hedges are all cut and yet big, and we have been trying hard to tidy the garden for the next book photo shoot (coming to a good bookshop near you sometime next year), with the result that it is as smart as a judge in a three-piece suit. How I love a big hedge. I honestly think that it can be the finest thing that any garden can offer, a kind of triumph of order and restraint without it becoming petty reductiveness. They need nothing but grass between them although almost everything looks better for a backing of good hedge. One day I will take a few acres and plant nothing but hedges—a kind of mind-maze without the slightly banal jiggery-pokery that conventional mazes have.

My ducks are growing into charming big creatures rather than charming small ones, and they shame the chickens by comparison, but now they are settled in I want to put them to work. Every day I open their run and shoo them out into the orchard, urging them into the garden to hoover up slugs, but so far they sqawk a lot, waddle round and round the pen and pant a bit before plopping on to the pond with a 'can't-catch-me' wriggle of the tail.

19.08.01

I got home yesterday after crossing the finishing line of the jaunts round Britain and Ireland that I have been making this year for Channel 4. This last trip started in Dublin and ended on Aran, taking me pretty much in a straight line across the centre of Ireland, trying, with the predetermined clumsiness that only television can construct, to get a slice through the country.

The Aran Islands were really my goal. I had wanted to go there ever since reading J. M. Synge's *Riders to the Sea* 25 years ago. I love all islands in principle and most in practice, but the Aran Islands, perched at the very edge of the Atlantic, seemed to contain the necessary harshness to whet the edge of the true romantic. This, of course, is their undoing. Nowhere else in this eight-month trip around the British Isles was so dominated by tourism. Two thousand visitors a day pour off the ferries from Galway, more than doubling the population of the largest island, Inishmore. Every one of these comes with a huge weight of earnest expectation along with their cagoules and trainers, and the islanders charmingly and sensibly fleece them for every penny that they can. I am certain that this is the only sensible thing for them to do—the tourists, after all, are just another crop or catch, but a much more profitable and less arduous one than potatoes or mackerel.

The purpose of the series I have been making is to find out what gives places their identity and what binds people to them with loyalty or kinship. In Inishmore this level of belonging runs below the daily life like a seam of rock, completely covered by a layer of commercialism. The image is apt because the islands are a continuation of the limestone of the Burren, surfacing out of the sea in layer upon layer of crushed bones and shells before ducking back down into the Atlantic. To understand the place—and I do not presume to do so—you have to first understand this stony physical presence. The visitor arriving at Kilronan is momentarily seduced by the trees, fuchsia-filled hedges, hanging baskets and gardens with flares of crocosmia, magenta dahlias and gladioli, but as soon as you take the road leading out up the spine of the island the reality is literally exposed. It is a place scraped raw by wind and literally melted by rain. The limestone lies either in great smooth plates or else in cracked shards. The grass grows only in the fissures and hollows. The landscape is divided into countless tiny fields, many no bigger than a town back garden and all bounded by exquisite walls as open, intricate and fragile-looking as lace, but necessarily so, so that the wind can bluster through them and dissipate. There are apparently over seven hundred miles of walls on the three islands with the biggest, Inishmore, amounting to only fifteen-odd square miles and the smallest, Inisheer, just 1400 acres. In families where a dozen children were common, the fields divided the land up, giving a stake in the island to hundreds of people at a time.

When they have cleared the fields of the loose stone, using them all up for the walls, they are left with a barren, rocky surface as inimical to growing things as a tarmacked road. The islanders then brought in huge quantities of seaweed, mixed this with sand and grew their potatoes, cabbages and onions on this 'soil'.

On the north-eastern side of the island, more sheltered from the westerlies, there is a natural layer of thin soil where hay and cereal crops are grown on areas hardly any bigger than a lawn. The meadows are as much flower as grass—oxeye daisies, dandelions and bugle, nothing fancy, but the assembly as rare and remote from modern British farming as the horse-drawn plough. These fields are still all tended by hand, the hay cut with strimmers, and tractors only used to carry loads along the few roads. I visited one household run as a self-supporting community by a former Catholic priest, Dara Molloy, who now describes himself as a 'Celtic priest', plus various transient volunteers. Their small garden was, according to Dara, particularly well endowed with soil as it had been cultivated for decades. Certainly what soil there was on the lazy beds was black and rich, but when I plunged my hands through the soil the smooth rock was only inches down. However, what will grow at all tends to grow well. Aran hardly ever gets frosts and, if you make shelter from the tearing winter winds, is positively mild. Despite this, to attempt any degree of self-sufficiency on the island involves a measure of self-denial.

Easier by far for the locals to harvest the tourists, driving them by pony and trap or hiring them bikes and serving burgers or fish and chips for the price of a three-course dinner. During a break in filming I asked Padraig, our own pony and trap driver, whether he was OK. Fine, he said. No problems at all. It is only whether my English is good enough. This was not modesty. English still made foreign shapes in his mouth. His English, of course, was both beautiful and articulate, spoken with the gentle, singing lilt of all western isles. Despite everything—the remoteness, the political sensitivity of any historically aware Brit visiting Ireland, the painted, thoroughly un-English houses and the road signs in Irish—this still is a shock. Everywhere you go in Ireland is abroad in a way that Wales or Scotland can never be. Padraig told me that when he left Inishmore for Boston in the early 1960s, he spoke no English at all. In Boston, on the building sites, more Irish was spoken than English. On all three of the Aran Islands, until perhaps 25 years ago, Irish was the only language spoken by the islanders.

My final image of Aran is not of wild flowers, sea, tourists or walls but of going round the back of the youth hostel at dusk in search of a meal after walking along the boiling coast in the rain and being astonished by a phalanx of madonna lilies, all in pots and in flower, tucked out the back with the gas bottles. But perhaps the surprise is part of the patronising attitude that the islanders so resent. They are part of modern Ireland, not an emblem of Irish purity, and modern Ireland is a sophisticated, well-heeled, not very pure place.

Much more totemic, to the outsider at least, is the Burren. This is a hundred square miles of carboniferous limestone in County Clare, south of Galway. It is staggeringly beautiful, combining a larger landscape as bleak and harsh as any under a northern sky with endless micro wonders, both of stone and flora. The limestone has been split by rain in parallel striations, called grykes, running like tramlines out to the horizon. In places these make crevices six foot deep. Walking is slow, ankle-twisting and invariably focused on the ground at your feet. This is not so much to maintain your balance as to absorb the incredible diversity and arrangement of flowers. From the road the hillsides seem lunar in their grey absence. Beautiful, but empty. Up close they are filled with plants. Most grow in the cracks and crevices, so a harebell will seem to sprout from a smooth flank of stone, its roots tucked into a few millimetres of soil. I am no botanist but could easily identify fragrant orchids, bugle, field and devil's bit scabious, wild thyme, marjoram, bloody cranesbill, wood sage, harebells, oxeye daisies, *Rosa pimpinellifolia*, and—having checked with my flower book—mountain avens. The extraordinary thing is that you can find all of these growing side by side within a few square yards. Add to this heather, thistles, vetch, the various ferns and 23 different orchids that you can find everywhere, then you have a miraculous collection of plants that collect together nowhere else on this planet. Mountain avens is a plant of the arctic tundra or alpine mountains, but thyme and marjoram belong to the Mediterranean, and heather abhors lime and yet grows with its roots in tiny pockets of peat sitting in a rain-worn hollow in the limestone. Where there is a thin layer of soil, as in Inishmore, the flowers outnumber the thin grass. And this was in August—in May it must be astonishing, with the added spectacle of the

252

gentians, wood sorrel and anemone, and the mountain avens not just occurring sporadically but in great carpets.

I can't work out whether the Burren makes me properly appreciate rock gardens for the first time or just confirm the artificial coldness that they normally seem to invoke. Certainly I saw for the first time what people are trying to achieve with a rock garden, that astonishing combination of stone and plant tissue that, in precisely the right proportion, looks so stunning. And equally certainly I saw that almost every attempt at this in the garden is bound for failure. Gardens are always artificial; they are meant to be so. At best they mirror the interior of our own minds. At worst they make a caricature out of a beautiful landscape. But to keep your garden firmly rooted in introspective fantasy, where it belongs, you do need to get out every once in a while and see the real thing.

27.08.00 **My Roots**

Whilst I was away I picked up a paper and was reading an article in the *Independent* [If you appear on television you are fair game for a range of criticisms, most of them inaccurate but inoffensive. But this piece—which delighted my children—barely contains my spluttering rage against the unnamed critic who dared question my capabilities with a spade. What's more, I was 45 at the time. Is there any other area of human activity where anyone under fifty is considered young?] about garden make-overs—agreeing with almost every word—when I saw words to the effect that putting young gardeners like Monty Don on the cover of more traditional gardening magazines will harm sales. It went on to imply that you could tell that I did not know how to garden by the way that I held my spade. I tried not to mind—after all you are not going to be loved by everybody, but to my annoyance it really niggled at me, as one of the things I think that I can do as well as anybody anywhere is to handle a spade—especially my favourite stainless steel Bulldog one, ten years old now and worn unevenly at the corners through hours—weeks, months—of hard use. You can do anything you want to do but uh-uh lay offa my best spade.

Weeks and weeks overdue we have cut the long grass in the orchard. The main problem of doing this every year is getting the machinery. I have done it before with a scythe, but it does take ages to do it not very well. Our rotary mower will not begin to do it. If I hire an Allen scythe it will cut it but leave the grass in long, hay-like lengths which are very slow to compost down. A rotary cutter is best, but they have to be exceptionally powerful to do the job. I finally got hold of a Honda machine which looked as though it would not mow a lawn, let alone cut the orchard, but I have to say it has been quite brilliant. It quietly trudges through the grass—all of which has been battered by rain and become matted, and turns it into rows of compost-to-be. I spent a happy Sunday in the drizzle, opening out the orchard and raking the grass into great heaps, fantasising about challenging effete, urban scribblers to a double-digging contest waged to the earthy death.

254

25.08.02

I am in front of the bay window at Lower House. The sun is shining its hardest on my bare legs. I think I might be happy. York stone. The hot smell of box and the trees shuffling with birdsong and breeze. It must be afternoon. It must be 1961. Women and children wear their legs bare. Men only wear shorts for sports. Here, said Jennifer, try this. She took one of the pink and purple flowers tumbling off the bush and broke it, snapping it expertly at the base. Go on, suck it. It won't hurt you. A little perfumed tube, curiously firm between my lips. Drawing till the roof of my mouth hurt, half expecting disgust and screams of laughter. And then the merest hint of sweetness, a fleeting glimpse of taste. A moment inside the life of a bee. Nectar, said Jennifer. You could live off that for ever.

I tried scores more fuchsias that day, showed the trick to anyone who would bear with me, and I cannot resist taking a draw on the occasional fuchsia even now. But I have never recaptured that exact, elusive sweetness.

Not that fuchsias have crossed my path very much. At my friend Henry's house in Usk they have boxes of fuchsias standing on a row of saddle stones and have had for the past thirty years at least. The boxes have a home-made four-squareness, and the combination of plants pouring out pink, magenta and purple, plus earthy loam, wood and stone is deeply satisfying, but belongs to that place. Copying it would cross the divide from

255

inspiration to theft.

About fifteen years ago Sarah came back from Chelsea with an enormous standard fuchsia, flogged off on the last day. Because it had been forced under cover for the show, most of the flowers dropped off after a few days of being outside in Hackney. But it came back more modestly and entertained us for the rest of the summer before being frosted. It was more like an exotic bird than a plant. It was never more than passing through. We did not really grow it.

In fact, I have never grown a fuchsia. This is nothing to do with the plant. They are not difficult if you attend to their modest needs, and if you are into taking cuttings—which I am—then they are easy to propagate, so essentially cheap. But not in this garden—yet. I like it very much in other people's gardens and swaggering along the Cornish hedgerows. I like the way that the flowers parachute off the branches like floating ballerinas. It has just somehow never felt appropriate. Perhaps they are too present in memory to have room for them in the here and now. There was, of course, sometime embarrassingly late in life, the delight of discovering that fuchsias were named after someone called Fuchs. Did all plants get named like this? Were there Dickias, Bottomleyias, or Prattias? Could grown-up life hold that many delights? As it turned out, it could not. Dahlia, Forsythia and Stewartia do not promise the same delicious thrill.

Fuchsias were not actually discovered by Leonhard Fuchs. His contribution, beyond having a funny foreign name, was to be a German sixteenth-century professor of medicine who had written a herbal describing native German plants. In fact the first fuchsia was bought to the attention of the west by Plumier, a French Catholic priest, who came across the plant that is now classified as *Fuchsia triphylla* whilst on a plant-hunting expedition in the Dominican Republic in 1695. His samples were shipwrecked but he published drawings in 1703. The first fuchsia arrived in London in 1788 and was given to the Royal Botanic Gardens in Kew. With the enormous increase in plant collection, combined with cheap fuel and cast-iron technology that made large greenhouses and conservatories possible, fuchsias were grown with hothouse intensity. This was largely unnecessary. In the Gulf Stream-coddled west *Fuchsia magellanica* (which is one of the hardiest species—although they cannot have known that then) was planted as hedging, and by the 1830s it was widespread as a hedging plant in the Isle of Man. But the idea of them was exotic and the Victorian plant consumer was not to be denied. All over Europe people bred fuchsias ferociously, all in glasshouses. By 1848 the first book devoted to fuchsias, by the French botanist Felix Porcher, listed 520 cultivars. Now there are more than eight thousand hybrids and cultivars.

Right up until the First World War the majority of fuchsias had lots of small flowers. In the 1920s and 1930s they began to be bred in America, and—hey whadya know!—the flower size increased dramatically. In many cases more did mean better, and varieties like 'Texas Longhorn' had flowers eight inches across. (Texas Longhorn? A breed of beef cattle to describe a fuchsia? When it comes to the naming of plants people often get silly or odd.) American and British growers began to

257

concentrate on hardy varieties that did not need greenhouses, fuel or labour. Like the dahlia, chrysanthemum, sweet pea or rose, it was something that could be grown in a small garden or allotment, lent itself to competition and became a way in which working men could show their expertise and add colour and exotica to hard lives. It is easy, in our soft, post-modern, untested age, to sneer at these shows, but I love them. I love the passion, skill and unsung graft that go into winning a local, nickel-plated trophy. These flowers are cosseted and wooed into symbols of freedom and dignity.

29.08.99 **My Roots**

Last Saturday we had a delivery of forty metres of local stone slabs. Why does one always feel guilty about things like stone slabs, even though they are a good deal, much cheaper than York stone and much nicer than man-made ones, whilst happily paying the same kind of money for bricks or sand for the building work? I can't help feeling that paving is a luxury, and walls or bath fittings a necessity. It looks a pathetically small stack, too. The slabs are all of different thicknesses, which will mean fun and games laying them, but the yard that they are for will look great. Luxurious even. We know that even forty metres will not be enough to do the job, so are already committed to using cobbles in squares, like a patchwork quilt. The cobbles are all from the ground here and have been gradually accumulating over the past couple of years. The yard had to be levelled, so we dug a few inches off it, which amounted to a colossal heap of soil put next to the heap of sharp sand that we will lay the slabs on. The yard is full of heaps.

We also found some broken medieval tiles and I spent half a blissful day on my knees with a pointing trowel, archaeologising like mad, and uncovered enough segments to make up four complete tiles. I shall take them to the county archaeologist for dating. I am constantly reminded that this is an ancient site [Our house is merely the latest surviving structure on the site. We know that there was a thirteenth-century hall/house and have pretty good evidence of an earlier building in what is now the front garden.] and we must be careful with its history, doing nothing that will damage it in any way for the sake of a quick horticultural effect, or anything at all that is irreversible. That is why the flagstones are a good thing, because they are like a protective shell over the past.

At the back of the house there has been a curious ennui, a kind of late-summer blues. Nothing new in this—as long as I have gardened people have talked about the August slump—but perhaps we have had so much telly, so many photographs that it is as though the place has withdrawn into itself a little. I quite like this. It has to be wooed back. So I spent a good day just weeding, not as a grand project, whizzing the hoe over the place, but gently grooming. It made me feel better.

September

03.09.95

'Autochromes' were the predecessors of the modern colour transparency. The process of making them was, by modern snap-happy standards, a complicated and inexact process, relying on as much luck as judgment. Red, blue and green transparent starch grains were baked in a thin screen on the emulsion of a glass negative. The grains acted as a colour filter when a photograph was taken, ensuring that eventually, after a lengthy developing process, the result could be viewed as a reasonably accurate colour slide.

'Accurate', of course, begs far more questions than it answers. In the end we want a colour picture to record the 'thingness' of an object more than we need a measurement. The smile caught in a holiday snap tells us more about the emotion of the moment than the muscular organisation of the face.

Flowers have attracted photographers from Roger Fenton to Robert Mapplethorpe and Don McCullin. Some of this is down to the obvious attraction of the flowers themselves—the same thing that has drawn painters and gardeners. Some of it is practical—flowers do not fidget and will do as they are told. But there is something else. They are ephemeral and constantly changing. Show me a rose and I will show you another quite different. And another. All three from the same bush. It is this unfixable yet familiar quality that makes plants endlessly fascinating. So no photograph can hope to be definitive (although the work of Roger

Phillips has, in a low-key, common-sense way, gone a long way towards that). To be good it has to strive after the essence of the thing.

I was visiting a prize sweet-pea grower the other day. He grew a thousand plants in his back garden, each tended with obsessive attention. From those thousand plants he would select ten thousand flowers and try and group them into identical specimens for each variety. 'Every night before a show,' he told me proudly, 'I'm all night—and I mean all night—going through them all under a magnifying glass, selecting perfect identical groups for each vase.' Whilst there is a lunatic human attraction to this behaviour, it has little to do with looking at or 'seeing' the flowers.

Leendert Blok was born in Lisse in 1895. He learned photojournalism in South Africa before setting up as a photographer back home in Holland. He had two specialisations, both unusual for the time. One was the production of huge panoramic prints—up to seven feet long—and the other was colour. Until his death in 1985 he was producing colour prints for virtually all the Dutch growers and exporters of flowers. His autochromes were discovered in a box by Frido Troost and published by Van Zoetendall Publishers in Amsterdam together with a series of modern prints by Jasper Wiedeman, photographed as a direct response to Blok's pictures. Together they make a stunningly beautiful book, without any of the glossy pretension of almost all garden books filled with colour prints.

Blok's pictures are not intended to be anything other than a record. As such they compare unfavourably with modern colour prints in terms of colour exactitude or detail. But as a distillation of tulips they are without peer. They have a drama and still intensity that transcends prize-winning exactitude. Fiercely descriptive, they are made into poetry, whereas so many 'poetic' portraits of flowers end up as just more inaccurate cataloguing.

Take the 'Blue Parrot'. It is an intimate, almost shocking portrayal of a flower. It looks as though it has just been hit by a bullet. 'Rococo' is like a gestalt print, almost wholly abstract. The two flowers in the picture titled 'Mr Dames' are only just there, growing up out of nowhere and leaning back into the dark, but he has the delicacy and potency of the tulips exactly.

'Remarandttulp' reminds me of trendy fashion plates from *Vogue*, the effect so carefully strained after by arty photographers. Would it make any difference if we found out that Blok spent hours manufacturing this staining and scratching of the negatives? Yes. Everything is vested in the truth and accuracy of the image. To be true to any flower the art must be artless.

Tulips have always had a particular attraction. They inspire obsession and devotion, not to say greed, because for a long time they were fabulously expensive. There is something in the form and detail of the flowers that manages to be decorously beautiful whilst being outrageously sexy. They, perhaps more than any other flower, have perfected the 'duchess in the drawing room, whore in the bedroom' qualities that conventionally men long for in women. We describe a woman with a narrow waist and full hips and bottom as 'tulip-hipped', meaning it only as a mark of admiration. The admiration is sexual more than aesthetic. The folded leaves around the swollen bud are vulval, delicate yet promising richness—the absolute opposite of *vagina dentata*. At the same time they are overtly and precisely phallic, knowing no comfortable sexual boundaries. A tulip is the visualisation of what good sex should be—open, dirty and delicately sensuous. If you think I am going over the top, have a look at Blok's various prints of 'Queen of the Night' or his print 'Darwintulp, Copland's Rival en Copland's Purple'.

This sexuality is beautifully caught by Maria Heiden in a prose poem in the book, telling the story of a Dutch crayon seller travelling Europe in the 1920s. Everywhere he goes he stops and draws tulips with his coloured pencils. People flock to watch and buy the crayons. In love with his work, he travels from town to village around the continent. Then he comes to the island of Elba:

> In the market square, surrounded by curious onlookers, he began to draw. For some reason he seemed to be having more trouble than usual that day. He didn't know why. The sky was cornflower blue, the crickets chirped lazily in the fields, the soothing gurgle of the fountain made everyone drowsy. There was a heady fragrance in the air that he couldn't place. When he looked up he saw only her mouth. The top lip gently scalloped, the bottom lip sensuous and as full as a ripe fig . . . 'Two lips,' she said, pointing to the drawing. 'Tulipa, tulips,' said the Tulip Man, gazing at her mouth. It was the perfect tulip, etched moist and tranquil in the shadows of the sunbaked market place in an unfamiliar

266

village, where lovers clung to each other behind closed shutters . . .

Tulips are best planted in the middle of November. When you dig your holes in the brown coldness of this autumn to drop the smooth bulbs into, remember the sexy drowsiness of that Elba marketplace and those perfect, moistly etched, Two Lips.

03.09.00 **My Roots**

I suddenly got very dejected about our garden this week. Some of this is because I have got to go away next week (on holiday, good for the exhausted TV presenter/writer but bad for the gardener and his garden in harvest time), and some of it is because there are times when you walk round the garden and suddenly see that it is not good. It does not come up to your own standards. Obviously those standards are influenced by your image of the garden. We all have an idealised picture of the garden that we have carried around in our heads from the moment it became ours and which, I guess, is never the same as the growing reality. Over the years that the garden is coming into being that image carries you forward and inspires you, but when things reach maturity, the cold light of reality can be harsh. As it was the other day. It seemed that this entire garden, in all its thirteen different components, was unrealised, dull and wanting.

So what to do? I started by doing what I always do in this position (it happens every year, usually about mid-July) and spent a long day in the vegetable garden. By the end I had removed every weed I could see, sown Hungarian rye-grass as green manure, planted out the last of the cabbages and broccoli, planted a bed of radicchio (dozens and dozens of plants, but what the hell, they'll last most of the winter), transplanted the strawberry runners pegged into pots a month ago (all with good root systems), dug up a bed of Charlotte potatoes for storage and rotavated the ground, spent ages squashing caterpillars (don't get sqeamish on me now) and watered the lot. It was a start and I felt better for it.

The jewel garden is still a disgrace, overlush with flopping flowers, undeadheaded and mildewy. I exaggerate, it is still lovely—but not lovely enough. We shall rationalise the planting this winter in the light of the weather that we are all having to cope with. I think everything needs more space for ventilation and less feeding of any kind to reduce lush growth. I think that the skill will be to create an effect of rich lushness without the debilitating results of crowded sappy growth.

Why have my tobacco plants (all *sylvestris*) grown so variably this year? Some are their usual fat-leafed selves, whereas others just feet away are puny, runtish things? It is an odd thing. I suspect that when I dig them up I will find that the stunted ones have not got beyond their slightly pot-bound rootball. Increasingly I am learning that the timing of potting on and planting out in relationship to an individual plant's root development is really important. In the end, what makes the garden shine is healthy plants, and the detail of that kind of timing can swing the balance between the happy and the dejected gardener.

07.09.97

In some larger gardens you may come across an area of hazel called a nuttery, planted in a similar way to a coppice but managed very differently. The garden version tends to have the new growth cut back each year after the general framework of the bush is established. This fixes the plants in a frozen maturity as well as guaranteeing a steady supply of hazelnuts. But a proper coppice is a crop of wood that is harvested as deliberately as a field of wheat. This process utterly transforms the landscape from dense woodland to almost open field, although a few standards are usually left to mature in every acre of coppice. Unlike a plantation, it is entirely self-renewing and can last for thousands of years. Consequently there are a set of plants, butterflies, birds and insects that have adapted to thrive within the terms of these cutting cycles and the changes that they impose on the coppice, from the newly cut, shadeless site to the dense undergrowth just before harvest. If you can extract those conditions and fit them into the intensive jigsaw of a back garden then you add more than just the sum of its plants. As much as anything else, it is a matter of being in tune with a particular association of a group of plants, light, soil and human need. All things that are manifest in a coppice, which, after all, is not a piece of natural woodland but a carefully controlled space for growing plants. Just like a garden. You do not need acres to do this. A corner that you are prepared to give over to this permanent cycle or even a couple of hazels that you cut to the ground every five years will have the required effect.

However, I am fortunate to have a strip running like a band across the width of the garden, about fifteen metres wide and thirty metres long, with a widening bulge at one end. For the past few years this has been kept cut as short long grass. I sprayed this off with Roundup (glysophate) [At the time glysophate was organically sanctioned, but that was probably the last time I ever used it.] in mid-August and it has started to look very wan and burnt out.

The next stage is to gather up all the self-seeded hazel seedlings that have been popping up all over the place—spread mainly by squirrels hoarding them from our one mature (huge) hazel. I have already potted up about a dozen, which are growing vigorously. I like the idea of spreading the seed of our own original hazel rather than buying in plants. These will be planted in a grid about three metres apart, rather closer than a commercial coppice but leaving both room for them to spread and space to walk between them. These hazels will be allowed to get established with a good root system and then, after perhaps three years, cut back down to the ground to form a 'stool' which will sprout vigorous straight-growing stems. Hazel is perhaps the obvious choice of coppice plant because its cycle is quickest, being cut usually every seven to ten years, but it is not the only one. Most deciduous trees respond to coppicing, but the one that probably takes to it better than any other is ash, and I shall be mixing ash in with the hazel in equal measure. [I didn't do this, but there are half a dozen standard ash trees, now (2005) each about twenty feet tall.] It is a much neglected plant, considered to be more a hedgerow weed than a wonderful field or garden plant, which it most certainly is. It is typical of our ridiculously perverted horticultural view of things that gardeners only get interested in the rarer mutants of a species and fail to relish the indigenous plant right in front of our noses.

Like hazel, the ash is a tree associated with magic. Much of this must stem from its amazing usefulness in an age that relied on wood for every aspect of sustainable life. Ash will coppice for a thousand years, during which it can be cut every ten years for the best tool handles and thirty years for the best firewood. It can be steamed and bent and has amazing flexible strength along the grain. Do you need to know this for your garden? Do you care? You should, in the same way that you should care about your lettuces tasting good as well as looking the part, or that basil makes the best accompaniment to tomato. For many of us the garden is the only link we have to a wisdom of things that is slipping between the technological cracks, and gardens become most interesting when they leap beyond the confines of the garden fence.

Ash grows best in a heavy soil over limestone but, given sufficient moisture, will grow anywhere that hazel will, although an ash coppice has a different character to a hazel one. Hazel forms a dense canopy near the end of its coppice cycle, whereas ash's leaves are slighter and more spaced

271

as well as being one of the last to unfurl. In consequence an ash coppice always has a luminous quality and, as a result, a slightly wider diversity of flowers growing on its floor.

After perhaps five years the growth should be thick enough to shade all the ground, which keeps the weeds down. But until then we shall have to mulch to smother weeds. I have a load of old straw bales I want to clear up, so I shall spread them out about six inches thick and they will rot down over winter. Any planting will be done through this layer of straw, which will have to be renewed, with any spare manure, annually. In time the fallen leaves of the bushes will enrich the soil and create that particularly spongy leaf-mould soil that you find in any type of deciduous woodland.

What to plant? The main thing is to keep it simple, otherwise you get back to a border-with-shrubs, which I want to avoid, and keep it to the plants that one might find in a working coppice. These tend to be ones that like some shade, but not too much, and which have adapted to the cycle of shade and light which comes from cutting the crop. They need some years of light to flower profusely and create seed but also some years of shade to suppress the grasses and other weeds that they cannot compete with. It is a very delicate and subtle balance, yet one that is much easier to maintain than a wild-flower meadow. All you have to do is cut the hazel and ash to the ground at regular intervals. As the coppice matures I shall divide it into three, cutting each piece every ten years, thereby providing the varied levels of shade and cover that the birds and insects would need in a larger wood. Just to think in terms of ten-year cycles is exciting and life-enhancing.

I shall have primroses, certainly, but strictly *Primula vulgaris* only; no primula cultivars (which I always find an aberration except the moisture-loving candelabra primulas). The oxlip, *Primula elatior*, is lovely, a kind of bashfully cocked primrose on a long stem and not a cross between primrose and cowslip (which, confusingly, does exist and is known as the false oxlip). I have seen the oxlip by the thousand in Madingley woods outside Cambridge, but it is confined to a small area of East Anglia. I see no reason why it should not be encouraged in my little wood here on the other side of England. It will not flower every year, because of the variation in shade, but should do really well in the second and third years after felling.

I must, of course, have the bluebell (*Hyacinthoides non-scripta*), which will eventually spread and become invasive, hurray. No messing about with the less intrusive Spanish bluebell, *Hyacinthoides hispanica*. Wild garlic, *Allium ursinum*, is as vigorous as bluebells but, according to Richard Mabey in *Flora Britannica*, rarely occupies the same space. I must check this next spring, but perhaps I shall put them either side of the main path that will divide the space. Wild garlic stinks but it is a good vigorous smell and its heavy strap-like leaves have a rich green that contrasts well against the yellow green of the emerging leaves of the trees. These leaves can be eaten too and are much milder than their scent indicates.

The wood spurge, *Euphorbia amygdaloides*, with its evergreen leaves and brilliant yellowish-green bracts, is as pretty as any of the cultivated euphorbias and responds vigorously to the influx of light after coppicing. According to Oliver Rackham, the seed can wait dormant at least a century before germinating in the light.

The wood anemone, *Anemone nemorosa*, is one of the first woodland flowers, perhaps because it will not flower in shade so needs to appear before the leaves grow on the trees. If you come across a large carpet of them you can be sure that the wood is very, very old, because they spread incredibly slowly—no more than six feet every hundred years.

Violets may seem more delicate than the wood anemone but establish and spread much faster. The common dog-violet, *Viola riviniana*, and *V. reichenbachiana*, which is more petite, are both woodland plants which increase enormously the year after coppicing. The dog-violet looks lovely but is so-called because it does not have a scent. So perhaps *Viola odorata* should be planted too, to add the distinct but fleeting violet fragrance.

In time I shall cut my first harvest of bean sticks, and ash poles for tool handles and firewood. In time perhaps a nightingale will nest there and sing to us in a clear moonlit night in May with the bluebells ghostly blue and the curlews calling across the water meadows. Gardening is so much more than just growing plants. [I did make the coppice and it has become everything and more that this piece dreamed of. Now, in late winter 2005, as the primroses and violets are in full flower and the bluebell leaves are pushing through, I am about to harvest my first bean sticks. One of my favourite dogs is buried there and it is the most secret, calm place in the whole garden. But, as yet, no nightingale.]

07.09.03 **My Roots**

I have been on holiday for the past fortnight. I told everyone that I was going to Norway, which was a surprisingly effective means of closing the conversation down. In fact I stayed at home and gardened, blissfully, all day and every day, not leaving the curtilage for days on end. [In fact I often do this when not filming. I took my children to school this morning and realised that it was the first time that I had been outside the house or garden for eight days. I simply had not noticed.] The weather, of course, was better than Norway, or Barbados for that matter. Perfect. For most of the year my gardening is terribly purposeful and project-driven and I am impelled by the need to make the best possible use of available time. For the past two weeks there has been none of that. I have pottered, sat and drunk cups of tea outside, looking at the shape of things, and lain on the grass and watched the sky for ten minutes at a time. Unthinkable.

Much slow, fiddly time was taken up with cutting hedges and giving the various bits of box and yew topiary their annual trim. I have been increasing the height of many of the hornbeam hedges from six to twelve feet, and this year they all got topped off for the first time. This makes a huge difference, even though in many instances it was merely a matter of secateur pruning. How I love the juxtaposition of straight lines and abundant planting in a garden!

The box balls nowadays only need one cut a year thanks to the box psyllids that have completely infested them all, sucking the sap and stopping most of their annual growth until July. This does not seem to be a problem and cuts the work by half, although it still takes a good two days to cut and clear up all 67 properly. And there were seeds to be sown for over-wintering vegetables, and grass cutting, and lots of harvesting of courgettes, tomatoes, plums, basil, onions, beans and of course lettuces of every description eaten at every meal. There would have been more, but the unspeakably horrible chickens got into the vegetable garden whilst we were taking the dogs for a walk and laid waste to scores of cos. Ripped them to shreds. I think I swore. I know I swore loudly and vilely. The neighbours were just the other side of the fence. But that's what holidays in the garden are for—to roundly curse the hens and know that the depredation of a few lettuce is the worst that the day has to offer.

22.09.02

I am writing this as the first light is creeping up the sky, pushing through the mist that caps the trees like a cloud layer. The garden is made into a gothic Chinese landscape, colour not yet awake, everything revealed in silhouettes and shining half-light. Extraordinary how this light can be so sharp and yet spread so thin, the edge of every leaf and blade of grass glowing and as fragile as strands of a spider's web.

Tomorrow is the autumn equinox. For only the second time this year, day and night will be perfectly balanced before the light tips gently down into the winter dark. There is no need to be depressed about this as we have had our share of sunshine. In fact it has been an exceptionally lovely month, bathed in that softness of light that only September gets absolutely right, but it does change things irreversibly as far as this year goes. It is more than weather, more than season even. It triggers a switch that gently turns most of the garden off, because light matters so much more to the gardener than weather. For instance it has been a good summer. It could have been made better with a bit more rain, but on the whole the combination of weather and light was kind. To the gardener it doesn't matter if it rains and there are clouds as long as there is plenty of sun between the showers. Gradually, as you get to know your own garden, you learn what the sun does to it. You see where it reaches and the surprising pockets of shade, the way it rounds buildings and how perverse and reliable it can be. And how it changes from week to week.

It has taken years, but I can now map the position of the sun over this garden at any given hour on any given day of the year. When I plant anything I know where the light will fall on it. Admittedly this is made complex by the steady growth of trees and hedges that are imperceptibly taking up more and more sky, but I know where I stand under the sun. I know the length of my shadow. The extent of variation is scarcely credible. In midwinter the sun hardly rounds the southern corner to shine down the length of the garden, setting exactly on the path running along the back of the jewel garden in a gap between two oak trees three fields away. [This is not actually true. On the most recent winter solstice (21st December 2004) we measured the exact spot where the sun disappeared over the horizon and it was even further 'back' than I had thought. But it did uncannily fall exactly into a gap and pathway in the jewel garden and we were able to draw a line from this to the edge of the garden. This felt a magical and deeply symbolic thing to do.] In summer it goes right along the end, bathing the orchard, and across the horizon to the north clinging to the sky past ten o'clock. This means that in winter evening is a concept of time rather than light, whereas in summer it is a place and a particular cast of low-slung light as well as the bit before bed.

The equinox is not just a marker on the calendar or a yardstick on which my own feelings about light can be calibrated. It is also triggering all kinds of things in the garden. Flowering and the timing of flowering are powerfully affected by the amount of light any plant gets. Every gardener has experienced this. Put three annuals grown from the same batch of seed in a shaded, slightly shaded and open position, and the sunniest will flower sooner and better than the partly shaded one and the one in full shade might fail to flower completely.

It would take a lot of the sting out of winter if we could grow things, sow seeds, plant them out on a blustery November afternoon and watch them grow to some kind of visual or culinary harvest. We can mollycoddle winter seedlings, use mulches, cloches and fleece and windbreaks to keep them cosy. But none of this is any good without enough light. It is not the chill in the evening air or the lashing autumn rain that carries the message, or even the weak sunshine, but the subtlest change in day length. I, in my profoundly unscientific way, find this astonishing. Falling light overrides fine weather, and increasing light (albeit of the same length at the spring equinox) makes it worth the risk of ignoring the cold and putting on growth. That a flower can tell the difference between a day of hot Indian-summer sun and a modestly mild one that has half an hour more daylight is dead spooky.

The falling light prepares the plant to cope better with extreme cold, and increasing spring days provoke a similar preparation for potential drought. Plants such as roses, ash and apples have their winter hardiness increased by exposure to shorter hours of daylight, so any of them grown under artificial light, even with temperatures that exactly mirrored those in natural daylight, would be less hardy than identical plants grown only under the sun.

Any garden is stuffed with plants from all over the world, and those that originate from near the equator are known as 'short-day' plants. They are programmed to respond to a steady rate of about twelve hours of daylight, every day. In British gardens these flower once the days start to shorten from July onwards. Most—like dahlias, chrysanthemums, salvias or leonotis—will go on flowering until cold gets them. Any plant that originates from a certain distance north or south of the equator (How far? Where? They never tell you this. Is there a line? A frontier where plants suddenly become radically more photoperiodic? A

279

no-grow zone?) will be a 'long-day' plant and react to increasing light by flowering, bringing this to a halt around midsummer and using the remaining summer heat to ripen seeds.

Commercial growers have been using this trick for decades. Drive through Holland at night and you will pass endless greenhouses glowing with blue light, all cajoling that extra urge to grow and flower. An early spring is as much a symptom of clear skies—and therefore more sunlight—as warm weather. If you combine extra light with extra heat, a whole group of plants respond by flowering, and therefore cropping, much sooner.

Then there are the clever ones, such as primroses, pulmonarias and violets and their ilk, which are all from the north so should by rights be long-day jobbies but buck the trend by responding to short days by coming into flower. This enables them to reproduce before the leaves of the woodland canopy, responding to their own long-day trigger, block out so much light that the plants of the understorey cannot photosynthesise.

So much we know and so little we understand. You cannot treat the garden like a laboratory without losing most of the things that make gardening worthwhile. The days are tipping into dark, so the garden and I start to retreat, catching light as we can, serving our dark time, waiting to be triggered into flower by light.

16.09.01 **My Roots**

Birds belong to this garden as surely as plants or people. The radio says that swallows are diminishing in London but the sky above this garden is filled with them. Actually the garden itself is filled by them, swooping in amongst the cabbages and sunflowers, wheeling through the cardoons and sweetcorn, using the paths as air corridors. The weather forecast is for rain, and they are stocking up on the insects forced down into garden range by the low pressure. Stocking up for the journey home. I often wonder what they consider to be home: these dozen or so nests around our house and barns that they unerringly return to, precise to a matter of inches over five thousand miles, or the streets of Nairobi or wherever it is that they go to over-winter. It certainly feels more like home for us when they are here, more like the complete thing. A peregrine crossed the vegetable garden yesterday, sending everything else racing, the immensely powerful sculling wing-beat just glimpsed from the corner of my eye as I weeded the celeriac. It is like a visitation, as extraordinary as an angel passing by. And there was a buzzard perched on the seat in the wild garden, clumsily finding air to fly in as I came round the corner, as awkward and panting as a dog with a ball.

The autumn raspberries are at their best and I have tied them back with yards of string. It feels very Heath Robinson and I don't know how to train them really. [It's easy. Treat them like broad beans—i.e. stop them flopping with string and temporary posts.] I tend to restrict training to removing all suckers growing more than a foot or so from the base of the plants, but I think that next year I will thin them more and tie them in as they grow, because otherwise they flop everywhere, whilst the pruned summer raspberries are as straight and tied as the strings of a guitar with supporting wires like frets.

The plans for the pond are formulating fast. I have found a local farmer prepared to do the job and take away the spoil to shore up the banks of the river where his cattle feed—he lost five metres of bank through last year's flooding. I reckon that we have dumped over thirty tons of subsoil on the spot, which has to be removed before we start digging. Then there will probably be as much again to go. I have also found a source of blue clay from South Wales for the puddling. The main problem is one of aesthetics rather than of principle. What we have at the moment is a useful area for the bonfire and for dumping subsoil and hardcore. What we risk replacing it with is a wet scar that leaks. But I envisage it as being a brilliant combination of crystal reflection and lush intensity. A New Dimension to the garden. We will call it newpond.com. Shares will be issued. [And like most dotcom ventures the plans for the pond came to absolutely nothing. A mound was made instead, looking on a good day like a Tudor mount or little castle keep and on a bad day like a golf tee.]

25.09.94

'If you're going to San Francisco/be sure to wear/flowers in your hair,' sang Scott McKenzie in 1967 (and whatever happened to *him*?), and the absurd instruction has lodged in my brain ever since. I am ashamed to say that I have just been to San Francisco and omitted to wear a single flower about any part of my person, but there you go, life is stitched together by a thousand such failures. It was a tantalising trip. I was making a film for BBC's *Holiday* programme, and the nature of such an exercise means being filmed or hanging around waiting to be filmed from morning to night. So any gardens have only been glimpsed. Whilst my mouth has been talking to the camera about holidays, my eyes have been scanning each street for their horticultural differentness and innovation that I have long since read about.

It was a Californian, Thomas Church, who in the 1930s wrote a book called *Gardens Are for People*. This was enormously influential because it advocated working garden design around the way that people live their lives rather than as a set piece that human beings would stand back from and admire. Thus he said that swimming pools—integral to West Coast life—should be boldly incorporated into the garden rather than hidden behind a screen. English pools tend to be standardly rectangular and treated in the same spirit as a tennis court or billiard table. Thomas Church made pools with sweeping curves and lines that related directly to the house and garden. It is

283

only one aspect of gardening but it is easy to overlook how extremely controlled a garden is. However naturalistic and 'wild' it appears, a garden is always an artificial environment made by people for people, so it makes sense to put the considerations of people—rather than plants—first. I have always thought that this is at the heart of all good garden design.

The lift in my hotel shoots out from darkness into daylight as it races up 36 floors. About a quarter of the way up it passes a series of flat roofs, all of which have gardens on them. These gardens have been brilliantly designed to be seen from the lift. They are defined in different-coloured stones and the planting all gazes up. These are gardens for People in Elevators. I visited Kensington Roof Gardens last year and was puzzled by them. It took me a while to work out why I felt awkward, and then I realised that they were pretending not to be on a roof. They had no relation to their extraordinary situation. [I went back the other day—ten years later—and had exactly the same reaction. Very odd.] It was deadening. You end up admiring them for the fact that they exist rather than for their beauty. California is—predictably—free from such humbug. A roof garden should treat the sky as its main element. Even when hemmed in by other buildings, they must have a sense of flight.

I have also failed to see the extraordinary redwood forests of this part of the Pacific coast, even though they are only half an hour's drive from the Golden Gate Bridge. Well, I did see them after a fashion, from a tiny seaplane that we took up for a spin along the coast. They looked greenish and unremarkable and made me long all the more to get down in amongst them.

In our last garden we inherited a line of nineteen *Sequoiadendron giganteum*, which we know as wellingtonias but the Californians much more romantically call the Big Tree—and I wanted to cut them down. This desire leaked out locally and ruffled a few feathers. 'You can't cut down the fern trees,' I was told several times. 'See 'em for miles.' This was the essence of my complaint. They stood out like American tourists in pink check golfing trousers. They had been planted too close together, so they were enormously lanky specimens, nearly a hundred foot tall and growing fast, without the spreading skirts that more space would have allowed them to develop. A wellingtonia needs at least 22 yards between itself and any substantial neighbour if it is to get enough light and space.

My argument was that they were imposed on to the gentle Herefordshire landscape with brutal lack of forethought and that they would be fine in their own environment. I was too obsessed with my own little world to consider what that might be like beyond an intellectual knowledge of where it was on a map. Gardening in Britain is an introverted business—all of us with our little patches of escape from the overcrowded clutter.

Well, now I am here in their environment, [I wrote this in Vancouver, during the second leg of that particular trip. Between 1994 and 1998 I made over fifty such trips, which meant that I often filed my *Observer* copy from far-flung corners of the world, in a climate, season and circumstances starkly different from those I was writing about. It probably accounts for the rather nostalgic, even homesick, tone of some pieces.] with unimaginable space and light, and again I have missed these regal cousins of my row of scrawny but distinctive trees. In a curious way it makes me the more homesick for them, those awkward intrusions that you could see for miles. It was a time of my life when most things ended up falling apart, and they were a truer symbol of my garden than the earnest attempts at harmony and integration around them. Better to be an awkward bugger and survive than blend seamlessly into the surroundings and go under.

21.09.03 **My Roots**

There is that chill in the air that you only get in September or May. It is lovely. August stands like a train at the station, sometimes exactly where you want to be but never really going anywhere. By now, regardless of the weather or where you live, we are definitely on the move. The air sparkles. Light bounces from yellow leaves like an echo. You step outside and know you can't go wrong. September gets in your sails and breezes you where you need to be. The plants know it: fennel, lettuce, chard, tomatoes, late carrots and all the squashes are finishing their growing with a final burst for the line before autumn closes in. Does autumn close in any more? It seems to linger around much longer, and then suddenly it is November and all that is left of the party is debris and a headache.

What doesn't linger after the summer we have had is the fruit. I have been working almost all of every day for the past three or four weeks and yet am trying to collect the apples before the wasps, ducks and general bruising make the windfalls unstorable. In theory one should only attempt to keep fruit that is perfect, unblemished by the tumble from a tree, but in practice I have not had time for this. So I have gathered the fruit from the grass in baskets and hope that they last long enough for us to get sick of eating them. It is still an uphill struggle to persuade my children that a lovely home-grown 'King of the Pippins' or 'Jupiter' is infinitely preferable to the bland conformity of a supermarket apple. But I suspect they do it to tease. There could be many worse things to rebel against. At this time of year our available storage space is crowded out with apples, pears, onions, garlic and all the tulip and allium bulbs that were lifted in summer and have not yet been replanted. They will not get done for a while either, till I have a little more time and I get my help back again in three or four weeks' time.

Enough of that—it is important to relish this lovely time, with its evenings cool enough for a jersey and a fire and the crystal mornings that slip so delicately over the hill into this garden.

29.09.02

The sky is busy with swallows frantically stocking up for their long flight. Down below, insignificant in their swooping world, all the work of the last six months in this garden is rolled up into a few weeks of abundance. Instead of spacing things so that we

287

get a steady stream of goodies across the months it tends to all come at once, producing far more than we could possibly eat. So it has to be stored and saved, and for the past few weeks the garden has been inundating us with mountains of fruit and vegetables. The kitchen (for that read Sarah) is a processing factory with sauces, jams, soups and bags of stewed fruit filling three freezers. It is a bit of a tyranny (not *another* wheelbarrow full of tomatoes!) but there is a long winter ahead and we have never yet had enough of anything to be wholly self-sufficient. Too much of the garden is given over to flowers and general dalliance for the eye for that.

However, as autumn becomes undeniable, the flowers get just a passing nod as we scurry around the garden trying to bring all the many harvests home. But the pears get treated with solemn respect. I check them every day, taking the weight of each one and gently flexing it on the stalk to see if it wants to come away. Too soon and it will not ripen properly. Too late and it gets woolly and rotten in the centre. You can bully an apple into edibility, but with a pear, timing is essential.

However, for all my precious pear care, yesterday morning I went and found a dozen lying like golden odalisques on the ground. There were only fifteen fruits on that tree and none had seemed ready to pick a day or so earlier. Then all at once they leapt like lemmings on a pear tree. There is a mangle of emotions in this. The last thing I want is for the fruits to fall and get bruised. But the fact that they fell means that they are ripening and—hurray—the first (uncooked) pear since last October.

Long-term readers will have read me complaining about my pears over the years. The chuntering has become as much part of the garden as the pears now. The heart of the matter is that I love pears. I love them to eat, to look at on the tree and their blossom in April. I love mature pear trees, although you hardly ever see such a thing nowadays, standing fifty feet high high and sailing across an orchard when in blossom, like a clipper in full rig. I love the deeply riven bark of a large pear tree, cracked into square chain mail.

So when we came to this garden a decade ago I wanted to grow some, as much for the performance of the growing tree as for a supply of fruit. I bought a job lot of eighteen 'Comice' in a tree sale. I think I got them for a tenner. 55p each. A steal. They had trunks the thickness of my finger and I could carry the bare-root bundle in one hand, but they seemed fine, although when I untied the bailer twine there were only seventeen. 'Comice' is 'Doyenné du Comice', prince of pears, each one worth a dozen good apples. I did not know it then but it is lateish too, usually ready about the time you read this. I planted them flanking what was to be path in what was becoming a vegetable garden. The idea had been to grow them as standards, but after a few years I decided to espalier them and pruned them accordingly. This is not hard to do as long as you are brutal with the secateurs and remember to do your pruning in winter to instigate the vigorous growth where you want it. But vigour will not, initially at least, produce much in the way of fruit, so you must prune in summer to create fruiting spurs and to restrict growth.

This pruning regime converted the shambolic

would-be standards into half-decent three-tiered espaliers perfectly well, until I noticed that the ends of the new growth kept dying back and fissures were appearing in the bark. The few fruits that did grow had the same kind of fissures and shrivelled before ripening. I looked it up. Canker. *Nectria galligena*. Caused by poor drainage. Cut out all afflicted parts and burn. So I cut and burned—couldn't do much about the drainage, let alone the incessant rainfall—but you are supposed to go back to clean wood and this would have meant practically coppicing them. The rumble of pear discontent began.

The truth is that pears don't like a wet, windy site. Books will tell you that they suffer cold and damp more readily than apples, but that is not my experience in this garden.

Every year I would decide to grub them out and burn them, and every year I arrive at September falling in love with the golden fruits that seem to get better and better. Yes, some of them are cracked and scabbed, but most are luscious and irresistible, provoking a food-lust only matched by figs, and when lit by soft-focused early-morning or evening sun, they become a kind of garden centrefold, decidedly softcore but shamelessly ripe.

One of the supposedly 'Doyenné du Comice' trees turned out to be 'Williams' Bon Chrétien' which is notorious for getting canker and scab but adds to the diversity. It is earlier—hence the single tree dropping all its fruit before the espaliers that it was joined to—and ensures fertilisation by cross-pollinating with the others. Like apples, you must have more than one pear to cross-pollinate, although 'Conference' is self-fertile.

I did have another dozen pears growing as an avenue of standards up in the orchard, perhaps trying to create that vision of billowing, bountiful trees that the espaliers were intended to be, but they were a total flop. The wind raked through their branches, contorting them into hunched old men, and the leaves blackened and fell. The odd fruit that did appear fell off before ripening. I pulled up the 'Comice' and 'Williams', figuring that I already had enough of those, kept two 'Concorde' which, as I write, are clustered with hanging hard green fruits. 'Concorde' is perhaps the easiest pear to grow, a hybrid of 'Conference' and 'Doyenné du Comice', with the easy temperament of the former and the taste of the latter. I potted up the pair of 'Conferences' and stuck them behind the compost heaps along with three crabs and three quinces that I had not found a home for. The other day we cleared and tidied this area and I put the crabs—all 'Golden Hornet' with Christmas-tree golden bobbles of fruit clustered along the length of the minaret trunk— in the jewel garden and planted the better of the two 'Conferences' against the south wall of the barns. The wall will warm it and soak up excess rain. After three days it already looks more handsome and established than my poor espaliers. But I will not threaten to dig them up any more. They belong.

26.09.99 **My Roots**

I spent the better part of last weekend sussing out the orchard. Forty-two trees, all carefully chosen for their regional relevance and idiosyncratic qualities of taste, all planted with labels and—this is the bit that really galls me—all mapped out on a beautiful and neat plan. Then I lost the lot: plan, labels and all. I ransacked the same drawers and files countless times but couldn't find anything. The labels had rotted and faded. So I went back through planting diaries (this I can be smug about, for over the past two years I have recorded everything planted, all weather, flowering and harvest details in a desk diary, and it is proving invaluable) and reference books and identified all but four of the trees, from rarities like 'Tillington Court' and 'Stoke Edith Pippin' to hoi-polloi like 'Blenheim Orange' and 'Newton Wonder'. I loved it. The orchard, on a sunny early autumn weekend, was as good a place to be as any, and painstakingly identifying fruit, bark, leaf and shape of tree to match an identity parade was fun. [This became a regular game every autumn for the subsequent five years or so. I think that it was as much therapy as a desire to sort it out.]

I planted out all the box cuttings taken in June, all much bushier and bigger than any box cuttings I had dared plant before. Most had rooted enthusiastically and are now over-wintering in the veg garden. Last year's September box cuttings are now half this lot's size and also still in rows outside. I think the solution is to go big in June. In front of the house we are planting eight new large box cones to replace yew ones that have floundered over the past few years. We made the change because the yews drowned in our wet winters on very compacted, stony ground. They were fine at first in their planting pits, but as the roots grew out they met the pounded clay and stone, didn't like it and, as the water collected and drained too slowly, suffocated and died. The box will be tougher and shallower rooting, so be less susceptible to this fate.

We have been processing pounds and pounds of tomatoes into sauce and the surprise stars have been 'Gardener's Delight', which I had thought of as just an easy-to-grow salad tomato. Not so. Crammed into a pan and roasted or boiled whole with olive oil they make the thickest and richest sauce of all the varieties we have tried.

A friend gave me a new type of hoe the other day, called a 'circle hoe', which works remarkably well, and I found myself hoeing enthusiastically beyond the call of any product placement. I think that it is American. It is a hoop on the end of a handle, sharpened on one side. You pull it through the soil, cutting weeds but not slicing adjacent plants. Simple but very effective.

October

10.10.04

I recognise that there are certain things about myself that only surface at certain times of the year. As September rolls into October (and could you wake in the dark and know the difference? Whereas the first and last days of October are in different seasons) I become obsessed with apples. Now obviously this is provoked by the ripening fruit on the trees in our orchard, but it is as though all things pomological ripen in me too. I eat apples all day: I have stewed 'Reverend Wilkes' and 'Arthur Turner' for breakfast, munch 'Tydeman's Early Worcester', 'Worcester Pearmain' and 'James Grieve' at my desk and as I garden, and make crumbles, tarts, pies and bakes of the cookers as and when they ripen. I want to devour them in every way and become painfully aware of how little I really know.

I should like to dignify this as scholarship and dress my little learning as burgeoning expertise, but in truth there is a trainspotting, shelf-arranging aspect to it that is probably no more than mere blokishness. Apples began to appeal to the scholarly mind in the 1790s, with Thomas Payne Knight breeding apples at Downton Castle just up the road from where I live. By the beginning of the nineteenth century the prospect of classifying and collecting hundreds of different varieties became intoxicating, and the Victorians took to pomology with zeal. It is all about subtle degrees of order and control, and even the physical placing of the different apples in their proper places in the apple store is an important part of that. Apple store? For sure. Sarah is always telling people that we built our apple store, which is in reality little more than a large cupboard with slatted shelves from floor to ceiling, years before we had shelves to put our linen on—as if everyone did not think that storing apples took precedence over storing sheets and pillowcases. An apple store sounds grandiose but makes sense. If you have more than a few early apples (as a rule, the later an apple ripens, the longer it will keep) then it seems a pity to waste them. A few shelves in a cool, dark place will give you a supply of apples well into the new year.

Why would you want to grow them rather than buy them from a supermarket? For a start apples make a marvellous garden tree, ranging from a small semi-standard that you can prune to fit your space to a magnificent mature Bramley that will house a tree house, a swing and dominate a garden. Their blossom is exquisite. They make an ideal setting for long grass and bulbs. Birds will sing in their branches. If space is really tight you can train them into espaliers, step-overs or cordons. Oh, and there is the fruit. An apple from your garden is gathered and eaten ripe, when the sugars are properly ready and not when the 'food producer' decides that they are fit to travel. You can choose from scores of readily available varieties and hundreds of rarer ones to have a real range of tastes and colours rather than the half-dozen bland, tasteless travesties offered up in the name of an apple. It is the difference between processed cheese slices and a perfectly ripe Cheddar or goat's cheese.

And you can have trees with *meaning*.

Everything in twenty-first-century life is so homogenised and uniform that anything that can inject identity and idiosyncrasy into your domestic world must be grasped at and relished. The other day Sarah came back from the Abergavenny food festival with a little booklet I had not seen before called *Apples of the Welsh Marches*. It was utterly fascinating because it both told me intimate, local details about apples I grow and whetted my appetite for others I do not. Take 'Crimson Quoining' as an example. I grow 'Crimson Queening', which is a bright red, rather oblong early cooker with curious, ribbed, almost square, corners. In Payne Knight's *Pomona Herefordshiensis* it is called 'Old Quoining', and he says that it was a cider apple in the seventeenth century. The name comes from the quoins of a building and now when I look at the apple I see the buttressed supports of Hereford cathedral—which certainly every seventeenth-century grower would have been familiar with. So the connection is made and life is richer for it. And every area would have similar detailed, personal apple history that can live in every garden.

04.10.98 **My Roots**

Some of the days this week have been the best of this year and the garden is looking wonderful. I feel no ownership of this, just glad to be part of it. The important thing is to note what looks best and make sure we have more of the same next year. The biggest gap is the dearth of the russety brown sunflowers—which were so spectacular last year. This year they germinated really badly in spring and we were late replacing them, so we have far too many developing sunflowers without flowers, or much sun really, poor things.

I took cuttings from penstemons and *Salvia elegans* and *guaranitica*, with a view to increasing our stock for next year. They normally strike very easily, but it has been so hot that it is tricky stopping them wilt. I long for a mist-propagating unit, but that means putting electricity into the greenhouse, which means digging up the yard, which means . . . and so these things get put off because of the hassle.

We gave the orchard its final cut of the year, raking up the long grass and then cutting it again with the collector. It is a big job—George, who has been helping us one or two days a week for the past ten years, did it for a day and a half, and I did a day. But now we have two large blocks of composting grass and hay and one immaculate orchard with 55 young apple trees looking rather startled in their trim grass. Sarah says that it is a bit park-like, but the park-keeper in me loves it.

This garden is now reaching the point where we are cutting back things we have planted. I (and my seven-year-old son Tom) cut down a row of poplars that were planted five years ago as an emergency windbreak. It has opened up an area that extends our coppice garden. This business of opening and creating boundaries is endlessly exhilarating. I love it. It is somewhere between moving the furniture around and rebuilding a house.

At this time of year we are practically self-sufficient in fruit, veg and herbs. There is an overwhelming sense of harvest and abundance. One of the biggest changes is that the children now enjoy this as much as we do and they are trying all sorts of things like artichokes, squashes, celery or yellow beans for the first time rather than turning up their noses and reaching for baked beans. However, our pear crop has always been sparse and this year is no exception. But the 'Williams' looks good and I am watching them like a hawk to see the wasps don't get them.

One of my mini-obsessions this year has been to grow decent celeriac. This is difficult as it needs industrial quantities of water to get the bulbs to swell beyond golf-ball size. [Not so. They need a long growing season, rich soil and regular but modest watering.] This year I dug in masses of manure before planting and have watered them diligently. They are now swelling nicely. But they can flatter to deceive by having a wide top with no substance beneath. Only after they are dug can one tell. It is tantalising. But I love celeriac and celery and it is worth the trouble.

13.10.02

My biggest regret in this garden is that I did not plant a walnut tree ten years ago. By now—judging by the trees that I did plant back then—it would be at least twenty feet tall. The other day I found myself picking apples from a ladder resting firmly in the upper branches of one of the orchard trees planted in '97, and I hauled my fourteen and a half stone up the mast of the 'Raywood' ash (*Fraxinus angustifolia* 'Raywood'—fantastic plum-coloured leaves in autumn) that was small enough for me to plant single-handed nine years ago. There is this tendency to fix trees in one's mind either as immutable mature objects or else as tokens of themselves that you plant for your grandchildren. Both ideas are wrong. Trees grow fast and change every year.

In my last garden there were two large walnut trees (they pollinate erratically, so it is best to plant more than one to ensure a crop of nuts) and once I found two owlets on the ground, fallen from the nest, and was torn between bringing them in to protect them from foxes and leaving them to sort themselves out. In the end I left them under the care of the walnut, and they spent the whole summer using it as a base and growing astonishingly tolerant of our visits.

I was reminded of these owls the other night when a tawny owl, shockingly big in the torchlight, drifted up in velvet-winged silence from the coppice. The hazels are now big enough to take owl weight if not quite my own avoirdupois. The coppice has now become what I imagined when I put the hazels in less than five years ago. (Garden diary, Wednesday 14th January 1998: 'got home from London 3.30 and went outside to plant hazels. Dug up 2 from spring garden and also 3 other smaller ones I had potted up. Put no manure under them as don't think hazels will properly appreciate it.') Why did I think that the hazels would be so unappreciative? It is a nut thing and makes some sort of sense, but nowadays I would give them a bit of encouragement via a bucketful of compost. However, with and without manure, 73 hazels got planted, every one a self-sown seedling from nuts secreted away by squirrels and voles. They had fallen from the huge hazel outside our back door that was the only tree on the site when we came. The voles cannot resist a hazel and the owls love a vole. Hence my visiting owl.

And now, such a little time later really, it has become a mini wood, where you can enter another world and hide. At this time of year, when the leaves are just beginning to turn yellow and the nuts are deep brown, it is one of my favourite places in the garden. The hazels meet to form a canopy, so that just dappled light falls through to the ground. The effect of this is to make any grass grow thin and straggly, so the primroses, violets, wood anemones, ragged robin and bluebells can flourish.

I discovered that hazels, like walnuts, do not like being moved, and for a year they did not grow at all. But gradually they got used to their new home and started to grow. They initially did this, unsurprisingly, by simply getting bigger. Then last year nearly all of them suddenly threw up very strong-growing stems from their base. Whereas most of the primary growth was kinked and haphazard in shape, this new stuff was dead straight. These hazel stems, or 'rods', are what the hurdler uses and what makes the best bean sticks for the gardener, although to restrict them to supporting beans is a criminal waste. I use them to make wigwams for clematis, hops and sweet peas, to make fixed fences, low and high, and as the framework for all our pleached limes. When they eventually become too brittle to be useful they then make marvellous firewood. Endlessly renewable on a five- to eight-year cycle.

But at this time of year the hazels exist for their nuts. Growing nuts for deliberate harvest is rare in modern gardens, but until the twentieth century they were a much valued crop, a nuttery being a refined coppice. The major difference is that the biggest nuts are produced on old wood, so the hazels are never cut flush to the ground, but pruned to get the right amount of light and air to them, fixing them in a perpetual maturity where coppiced wood is always reinventing itself. I will compromise by coppicing a few bushes each year.

The wild hazel of woodland is *Corylus avellana*, or the cob. It carries its nuts in clusters of two to four, the squat nut sleeved by a short husk. The plant has always been defined and known by its nuts. Cob comes from 'cop', the Old English for a head, and the word hazel derives from the Saxon 'haesil' meaning a head-dress—which must surely come from the appearance of the nut in its ragged bonnet. Christians named it after St Philibert, a seventh-century Benedictine whose saint's day is 22nd August—which is about the time when the nuts start to be edible. This has become 'filbert'. Confusingly we now classify *C. maxima* as a filbert and differentiate it from a cob by the way that the husk completely envelopes the nut, which, in turn is rather longer than the more rounded cob. Even more confusingly, one variety of filbert, the Lambert filbert, which was introduced in about 1830, is also called the Kentish cob. Other varieties include the frizzled filbert and the Cosford nut.

The truth is that the species interbreed very

easily and there are many hybrids. The big hazel from which all our smaller ones have been grown seems to be a hybrid itself, as it produces a mixture of long-sleeved husks and shorter, more cob-like ones. What I did not know, when I carefully dug up and grew on the seedlings, was that hazels grown from seed—the nuts—never come true. Certainly the coppice has both some bushes that are pure cob and a couple that are pure filbert. If you want the exact copy of the parent it is best to take a root sucker, detaching it from the parent at this time of year and replanting it in a nursery bed until big enough to fend for itself. Hazel does layer very easily and this is the traditional way that coppices were extended or gaps filled.

To get the best nuts, hazel needs to be grown on poor, stony soil, rather like fig. If the ground is too rich and damp the goodness will go into the wood instead of the fruit. That explains my somewhat pompous note in the garden diary about the hazels not appreciating manure. Personally I would rather have lots of wood and some nuts, so in future will add lots and lots of manure. [What is certainly true, from my own observations, is that hazels like moisture and light, so too much dry shade from standard trees is the worst thing for them. They hate being moved and hardly grow at all in the first year. They then get going with a vengeance.]

10.10.99 **My Roots**

There is a stage of every year when I lose contact with the garden. It goes its cantankerous way and I go mine and we are like niggling spouses, locked in a petty row that we know time will heal but unable to short-cut the process. I squidge round the garden looking at all the things I have left undone and all those things that I ought not to have done and curse myself and life for having saddled me with this grumpy lump of ground. I say 'squidge', because it is now thoroughly sodden, certainly too wet to get a lawn mower over it, and the grass holds moisture just long enough for the next shower to refresh it. The series of paths we made last winter are in fact acting as drains and channelling the water to the broad grass walks, so these are now wetter than ever. One of the big jobs this autumn will be to put land drains into these.

At the time of writing (a couple of weeks before you read this) I have belatedly given all the box hedges their late-summer trim, so that they go into winter crisp and neat and even. They look nice. There is no reason why you cannot collect the longer pieces of these hedge cuttings, stick them in a row in a corner of the garden and leave them to root, without any more ceremony. It is surprising how successful this can be. But we have masses of box cuttings at the moment, so I burnt mine. Their shiny evergreen leaves give a bonfire a particularly smoky, autumnal feel. I always think of my mother whenever I light a bonfire. She gardened furiously, but I don't think she ever enjoyed any of it really, except the bonfire. This she loved, and would keep it burning thinly for days and days on end.

We harvested all the squashes the other day and now they are sitting on the trestle table outside the back door like a cartoon crop, mounds of them, all huge and knobbly and wildly excessive. We will keep them there until the first frosts, so that they can ripen further and the skins can harden, which will mean they keep better.

Sarah pushed a wheelbarrow into the house the other day with thirty kilos of red tomatoes—there are as many green ones still to pick—and spent two days working on different tomato sauces with different varieties of tomato. All were frozen. I don't mind the odd glut when you eat far more of one fruit or vegetable than normal for a month, then do not taste it for a year, but there are very few things that cannot be stored or frozen to be eaten across the year. The one question always asked when we show someone round is what do we do with all the food we grow? We eat it.

24.10.04

One of the first signs that things are going awry [Although it is pretty well documented, I relapse each autumn into a state of chronic, but usually manageable, depression. It makes work very difficult to execute but does provide material and a kind of perversely gloomy direction that I try and

307

harvest with as much levity as possible. My actual mental state at these times is not really one of gloom, though—more an absence of . . . anything really. Exhaustion. Negativity. Nothing good.] is when you start to measure your life in song lines. No, not in a Chatwinesque, sub-aboriginal way but more a Leonard Cohen, Radiohead, Nick Drake kind of manner. I wouldn't dismiss this approach out of hand—like every other melancholic, middle-aged man I am an inveterate sucker for poetic gloom—but real darkness needs lifting not indulging. You have to find some light or go under. The garden is not offering much in that way. It is damp and unkempt and reminds me of a basement flat that has not been lived in for a while. If I were a visitor I wouldn't know who gardened here or what they were about. Yet, of course, I live here, it is my home and it is all my fault, one way or another. Look at it another way. It is like a marriage. We live together, the garden and me, share the same space for a minute or two (there I go again, another line; the temptation for second-hand emotion is overwhelming) but we are clearly not spending enough meaningful time together.

But I make myself go outside and look for the good. In the vegetable garden the artichokes have regrown with the same new vigour they show in spring. Although this is a triumph of hope over experience because the frost will surely cut them down, it is stirring to see. The 'Doyenné du Comice' pears are just at the point of picking. I am loath to gather them off the espaliers any sooner than I must—and yet once they drop it is too late. I counsel others to check them all every day but don't do it myself of course. If only. The late sowing of beetroots worked and there is now a whole bed of golf-ball-sized beets with very edible tops. Chicory all dandy, the radicchio and 'Red Treviso' turning their winter crimson. I am good at chicory. This is not hard but the knowledge and reminder of it cheers me up.

Then on into the damp garden, ravaged by neglect. No, on closer inspection that is my cast of mind. The eyes form a kinder judgment. A bit weather-blown perhaps, but mainly just unvisited by me. We are strangers to each other and I resent this very much. You have to do it together, you and the garden. We need each other to make any sense out of it. I see that the comfrey has grown back lustily from its cut-back just a few weeks ago, and the lovage and cardoons are brown echoes of their summer selves. But there, solitary and at first hidden, is the best thing I have seen in this garden for weeks and weeks. A solitary quince, pear-shaped, downy and lime green.

Just five yards away is another quince tree, literally bent double with the weight of its fruit which are much rounder, apples to the other's pear, and smaller. These are good too—no, fantastic, a gift—but familiarity has bred a little contempt. The other is the first fruit of that tree and I am jubilant, claiming credit where absolutely none is due. These are *Cydonia oblonga*, not *Chaenomeles*, although the latter will make edible fruit as a by-product of its flowers. But *Cydonia* makes trees, albeit scruffy ones, and although the blossom is as good as any *Chaenomeles* imaginable, that is the warm-up act, presaging the real thing that is the fruit.

The single quince is 'Vranja' which is the most

upright of the four varieties I have growing in this part of the garden. The fruit is very large, but then if a tree has only one fruit to put its energy into it *ought* to be a whopper. According to my garden diary, I bought the tree on 6th November 1997, but it only reached this final position in the garden two years ago, which was its third move in five years, so no wonder it had refrained from fruiting until now. But in theory 'Vranja' is an early cropper and one of the few quinces that can successfully be trained against a wall as a fan shape, as they tend to grow in a messy sprawl.

The tree laden with fruits is 'Lescovac'. Two years ago it had 47 fruits but last year not one, despite an incredible blossoming. Quince blossom is the best of all, a sugar pink that is never sickly. It comes very late and stays for too short a time but is always breathtakingly beautiful. This year there must be over sixty fruits. We still have plenty of the membrillo that I made with the bulk of the crop two years ago, which is a coarse but delicious sweetmeat that is ideal with a slightly smoky cheese, game or added to gravy like a jellied stock cube. But a little of it goes quite a long way, so maybe I should make marmalade and wine this time around, although I have just found another membrillo recipe that involves boiling the fruit in wine and honey rather than a sugar solution, which sounds worth trying. The edible point about quince is that it is aromatically, deliciously sweet but this only reveals itself, in the northern hemisphere at least, when cooked. It also has a great deal of pectin, so jellies easily and therefore can be stored conveniently. This is a kind of alchemy, and the tree has always been revered as being magically benign. In fact, eating quince in any form has been in decline ever since cane sugar became popularly available and the idea of preserving fruit became a chore rather than a stored-up treat.

My other two trees are 'Champion' and 'Portugal'. 'Champion' has roundish fruits, whereas those of 'Portugal' are more oblong, a sort of irregular pear shape, almost orange and very woolly with down and are noticeably early to ripen—if they appear. I see a quote that says it is 'slow to start bearing and a shy cropper'. Shyness is potentially attractive, but something in the fruit line would be nice soonish. The down that covers the fruit is part of their odd, rather confusing charm, even though to the uninitiated it can look like a particularly virulent mould. Just rub it off before cooking.

Growing quinces successfully depends upon rich, rather wet soil, although Jane Grigson refers to them doing well in 'the driest of upland fields and the hottest of small village gardens' in France. Certainly they need sunshine but don't gamble on the dry upland bit. If you have a wet patch of ground they will reward you for it. Order or buy a quince now (it is worth shopping around the internet and nurseries for the variety you want) and plant it any time between now and March. Plant it like any other fruit tree, which is to say with care but not reverence, digging a wide, but not too deep, hole, loosening the subsoil and adding no organic material below the roots but plenty as a mulch on the surface in a one-metre radius around the tree. It will need staking for its first three years but no special care or pruning again in its life other than keeping it weed-free.

They are self-fertile—so you can have just one and expect it to fruit—and grown on their own rootstock. Pears are almost inevitably grown on quince roots as well. This keeps pears small, whereas on its own roots a pear tree wants to become a large, even magnificent tree, more like a full-grown ash or beech than a back-garden bush. Quince tames and reduces it with three possible measures of quince vigour, 'A', 'B' or 'C'. A few pear varieties, of which the best known is 'Williams' Bon Chrétien', are incompatible with quince and have to have an intermediary graft or 'interstock', compatible with both quince and pear, to connect the rootstock with the scion. This is called 'double-worked' and will usually make the tree more expensive as it adds a year on to its nursery life.

On its own roots quince is sprawly and gangly, and it is a waste of time trying to clip or prune it to your preconceived ideas of beauty. Go with it. Be astonished at the blossom. Be unreasonably proud of the fruit. Drink in the incredible fragrance with which a single quince can seduce a room and feast on its pomaded sweetness. It will, I promise, brighten your northern sky.

14.10.01 My Roots

At time of writing we have had some of the softest, best autumnal weather possible. It has felt a crime to stay indoors. Last week I wrote bemoaning my lassitude, but a combination of the weather and a week at home has lifted that like a sea fog and I have got a lot done, although not necessarily in a proper, grown-up garden expert [I have always hated being labelled a gardening 'expert', even though I am probably legitimately that by now. It implies an aspiration that I never held.] kind of way.

I started by cleaning out the cold frames before winter. We always have a bunch of plants that should have been planted out weeks, if not months ago, as well as plants that were too sickly to plant out at the right time and are even more sickly now. They were all chucked on to the compost heap. But I did have hundreds of box cuttings that Gareth took last August. They were all in pots and had shown no signs of life at all. I suspected that this might be because he had used soft builders' sand in lieu of the sharp sand that makes up 50 per cent of our normal cutting compost. The pots were filled with weeds, capped with moss and generally looked miserable. But they did not look exactly dead, so I took them all out to see what was there. Once I cleared the rubbish, I discovered that every single one had vast tentacles of white roots. I can only guess that the sand had just enough nutrient in it to enable them to survive, but not to support any foliar growth. Anyway, I transplanted the lot into the vegetable garden and I will be very surprised if they do not treble in size next spring. This feels like finding a tenner in an old pocket or an uncashed cheque in a drawer—a complete bonus, and will provide stock for completing the hedges in the jewel garden.

We cleared the kitchen fireplace to mend it and I took a barrowload of wood ash to the gooseberries. It was one of those 'quick' jobs that lead inexorably on like a devious flow chart. First the ash had to be sieved, which meant finding the sieve. Then the gooseberries had to be weeded, and whilst I was about it, so did the strawberries, and whilst I was doing that I discovered that I had forgotten about all the runners that had been pegged down weeks and weeks ago, so they had to be transplanted to the bit where the surplus hawthorns were heeled in, so they had to be moved and watered in, and then, finally, I spread the ash around the gooseberries—but there was quite a lot left over so I thought I would put them round the redcurrants, which had to be weeded first . . . And so it went.

I liked this. I am very happy with a mazy, unfocused kind of process. In the milky sunshine glowing back from the yellow leaves, it is as good as a holiday. And probably the nearest I will get to one this year.

28.10.01

I suspect that the garden is a story that we make up to explain ourselves. It is often a pretty flimsy excuse, coming out as something between a police statement and a fable. The truth flits in the spaces between things. At least, this is the only way that I can make sense out of my apples. I chose them, planted them, have tended their every need far beyond the call of apple duty, but I keep losing the damn things. For the past few years I have been trying to nail them down, as long-term readers will be only too painfully (or patiently) aware. [I told

314

you . . . I am seriously convinced that the apple obsession and the Lost Trees are all part of the onset of winter depression.] Last year I spent days—literally—painstakingly working out what variety was planted where by a process of detection and discovery, and reckoned I had all but three in their right places. Somehow this year I was drawn into going through the process again—whether because the story needs to be told this way in an endless annual loop for psychological reasons of stupendous banality or because just a little more perseverance will actually give me the answer, I am not sure. Either way, I found myself on the apple treadmill again over the past few weeks. I should say that all the apples in this garden have cropped stupendously this year, every tree laden with fruit.

The site that the pumpkins temporally filled this summer is the subject of much debate. It is shaded and very weedy and does not feel like a growing plot. Too tucked away. I think we will move the compost heaps there, although this will shelter the cordon gooseberries a little and I wanted them to be as exposed as possible to blow away the sawfly. [In fact I cleaned it with a crop of potatoes and then it became the nursery bed.] This area of soft fruit is beginning to assume its own shape after a couple of awkward years. What on earth do I mean by this? Well, it goes back to the garden telling a story. You make up bits and play with them to see if they ring true. Sometimes this works out first time and all is well and good, but as often as not you have to fiddle and reshape until it is right. And sometimes, like with this soft fruit bit, you just have to wait and let the plants work it out for themselves. I will confess to a pang of pleasure

315

every time I see the summer raspberries pruned and tied ready for winter. Some of this—probably too much—is a desire to control and discipline unruly nature, but there is a simple aesthetic in the repetition of the canes, as regular as railings but as slender and elegant as bamboo, the light burnishing them a warm, tawny brown. They make a good shape and pattern. It is a simple pleasure.

And more than anything, I am aware that the year is gathering in. You will read this with time lurched out of kilter, the clocks thrust rudely back. My hatred of this is only mitigated by the delight of them going forward in March. But it is a long wait. Soon enough the apple trees will be stark branches, cropping only memories. Perhaps this is why I would normally grow as many apples and squashes as I can, not just for a sense of self-aggrandisement, but to fill the storage shelves with that amazing intensity of colour, the black reds of 'Spartan' or the streaked crimson of 'Tom Putt', as well as the pumpkins' orange and golden yellow, so I can open the door with scarcely space to stand and bask in their light while the wet leaves flap around in the dark outside.

29.10.00 My Roots

I have hurt my shoulder. I did it in August, drunkenly lifting weights at midnight. I know, I know. Pathetic. But there we are, the damage was done and the hurt remains. Only driving, writing with a pen or reaching for anything in bed hurt more than gardening. A couple of hours' digging or planting guarantees a couple of days'

316

real discomfort. I find this curiously depressing, because it cuts out a whole tranche of life that provides happiness. [This proved to be quite a long-term and serious injury that cramped my style for the next couple of years.] The garden does not always need me but it rams home how much I need the garden. I have always been an evangelist of muscular horticulture, digging, banging, pushing and sweating for a personal victory. Now I potter, trying not to reach for anything with my right hand, in a constant little swamp of private pain.

This is much on my mind because I have been digging up all the ligularias in the jewel garden and moving them to the new 'damp garden' to join the hostas that I have also moved over the past few weeks. The 'new' damp garden has always been damp and has occasionally been gardened but has never been organised and designated before. So now it is official. As with the hostas, the astonishing thing was how much space the ligularias took once they were painfully dug up and transplanted. I split the bigger clumps and left more space than they had been accustomed to, but the transformation is dramatic. I moved them because we had found that even in the heavy soil of the jewel garden, they only looked happy in wet weather. A day or two without rain (admittedly rare enough) and they would wilt and flop appallingly. In turn this has left spaces to be filled in the jewel garden, but, hey, a space is not a loss but an opportunity. Mainly to thin out and redistribute the various grasses that we planted far too close together to get an instant effect for an American magazine that came to do a feature on the garden last summer.

We have had a couple of very light frosts, but not enough to damage anything other than the outdoor basil and certainly not enough to kill off the caterpillars on the brassica. I find that they always start on the green plants, like broccoli and cavolo nero, and then move on to the purple plants like curly kale and red cabbage. I am still picking off dozens from these plants, which we grow as much for aesthetic as physical nourishment, and tattered, shredded leaves don't look good. But it has been a particularly good season for rocket, all of which I have grown in soil blocks for the first year and planted out, rather than sowing in rows and then thinning. But it seems to be hotter than normal. Is this the weather or the seed? By the way, I like getting email from you (montydon@observer.co.uk), although I reserve the right not to reply if I am not moved to do so.

November

05.11.00

On 2nd April this year, I finished the 'My Roots' bit of this column with the sentence, 'A solo garden must be tinged with loneliness.' The response to this was instant. A single man emailed me to say: 'I have lived alone for all of my adult life. I am not lonely, I enjoy my own company and the company of others. You are profoundly wrong in implying that single gardeners must be lonely. Worse, by putting that view in writing, you are promoting the myth that the single lifestyle is inherently worse. Frankly, the thought of having to share decisions about my garden with someone else horrifies me, but then we are all different. Please respect that diversity.'

And a single woman emailed me to tell me about the 'people' (plants) that filled her garden: 'I have to take issue with your last remark today in "My Roots". My garden is a solo effort, and even though I always work in it alone, it is thronged with people . . . it is only a scrap of land (though in the most beautiful dale of all), and I've had far bigger in the past, but it is so full of lovely people I sometimes pause in a smiling reverie, trowel in hand—and forget what I went out to do!

'My garden is . . . the making of a space in which I can be, and give expression to, what is truly me, without compromise, reservation or distortion . . . Perhaps now you have a glimpse of a cottage garden in North Yorkshire that proves that solo does not necessarily equal lonely.'

There were others, all in a similar vein. The

truth is that although I enjoy my own company I have a horror of being really alone. I need a mate to feel complete. This might be because I am a twin and thus have never known separateness without loneliness, and might be because I am sufficiently undeveloped as an individual to make it on my own. Either way I don't think that I can imagine the degree of self-sufficiency needed to make a garden entirely by and for myself. But I accept that this is a failure of imagination and is clearly not universally true. Many people are alone because they choose to live and garden alone.

Their garden then takes on a different role. It becomes garden as companion and gardening as an interactive thing. Of course it always is in that no one other than television make-over artistes just does gardening to a bit of outdoors in the serious expectation of making a garden. It doesn't work like that. You give, the garden takes, the garden gives back, you take. Pullme pushyou all the way. Now if there is more than one of you involved (and I believe that it is impossible to make a decent garden with more than two people involved at a creative level) a lot of that to and fro is done between the people. You discuss. Argue a little. There is an awful lot of 'Whadya think?' and 'What if . . . ?' It is a genuinely collaborative effort.

One of the most interesting aspects of filming *Real Gardens* over the past three years has been seeing how the dynamics of a household affected the garden. [This involved visiting two gardens, each on alternate weeks, for two days at a time, to garden with them. These visits took place across three to six months, so I got to know the gardens and the households pretty well.] I never visited a gardener who lived alone. I don't think I ever knowingly have. In almost every case there was a dominant personality who 'did' the garden. The spouse often initially played a very low-key role. But as time went by it became apparent that they invariably had a powerful influence over every aspect of the garden, even if it was a negative one. A garden made despite other occupants of the house is a storyboard of anger and frustration, another measure of an unfulfilled life. Think of all the primped and tightly dragooned gardens run by tight-lipped, angry old men whilst angrier women clean the house to death indoors.

So gardening alone can definitely be a liberation of sorts. There is something exhilaratingly creative about deliberately pleasing yourself. The first thing to do is to define the degree of privacy that you need and want. Different strokes for different folks, but I know that I want my garden to be entirely private if I am to enjoy it to the full. In my experience the only way to avoid the horror of loneliness is to enjoy being physically on your own, and the first stage along that route is to create a domestic aesthetic where the only value judgments are your own. For me this means not being overlooked, if at all possible, and no uninvited human presence. In an ideal world this means screening the edges of your garden with a combination of walls, fences, trellis and hedges, and even if that is not possible, creating an inner sanctum within the more public gaze of the garden at large with a genuinely private area where you can see the parts of the garden you want but cannot be overlooked.

Then clearly that privacy gets filled by an

extension of yourself. On one level it is impossible to advise or instruct on how that might manifest itself without contradicting the notion of glorious individual, solitary freedom of expression. But on another I think that it is even more important to read and look like mad if you are making a garden on your own. The reading is easy, if potentially expensive, although most local libraries have a fairly decent selection of gardening books. It always astonishes me that people would rather go to the trouble of writing to someone like me to seek advice or inspiration than pop into the library and get a book that will do the job better. I am writing this with shelves behind me holding over a thousand gardening books. Reading plays a very important part in my own gardening and it is a practice that is, by definition, solitary. I suppose that a good half are in some way or other practical, but half are inspirational. However creative you are, you need challenging and stimulating to respond well and, short of a gardening companion, books play that role supremely well.

Looking involves going and visiting other people's gardens as much as possible. Always take a notebook and pencil and if possible a camera too. In fact I cannot recommend too highly the practice of taking pictures of your own garden—however basic or humble—on a regular basis. It is astonishing how you forget what you have done and the combination of photographs and a daily garden diary adds greatly to the pleasure and success of a garden. By looking at other people's gardens—even the huge, thronged gardens of the great and the good—you can expand the solitary possibilities of your own private backyard.

However private, there is an element of all gardens that is pure theatre. I simply cannot imagine not wanting to share that with others. Tucked in behind that statement is the suggestion that solitary gardeners have no one to share with—which I realise is absurd. But I think that it means a different kind of sharing. If you garden with a companion you share small, intimate moments: the light catching the leaves just so, that hour when all the tulips/roses/primroses/purple-podded peas/apples are poised on the edge of glory. A solo gardener rolls out the garden like a performance. It is part of entertaining, a tool of friendship. This is fun and I wish that we did more of it—I suspect that this side of gardening gets sublimated in the casual sharing of coupledom. Balanced against presenting the garden as a performing, all-singing, all-dancing personal work of art is the simple pleasure of gardening. Quietly pottering with just a radio for company is one of the great secrets of happiness, not doing anything for show or public acclaim but simply for the love of it. Alone.

09.11.03 **My Roots**

The dominant horticultural fact of my week has been that the ducks have hit puberty. All summer they have waddled around the orchard in their three pairs, wing to wing and beak to tail, one happy and harmonious band. They spurned the pond we made, but we sunk an old tin tub in the ground and although only two could get in it at a time, they loved this and spent most of the day paddling in and around it.

Then a week or two ago I noticed that one pair was dominating the water and chasing off the charming white drake. This got increasingly fierce and whilst I was fifteen foot up a ladder picking the last of the 'Norfolk Beefing' apples I looked down to see the pair of them systematically drowning him, one standing on his back whilst the other pecked his head. So I caught the bullies and penned them in on their own. This took hours as they didn't want to be caught, and the pen then had to be made with posts and chicken wire. But it was a beautiful morning and the truth is I love this aspect of rural gardening. The remaining four immediately settled back into their prelapsarian harmony.

My two prisoners were demented, spending all day desperately trying to break out. The next day they did just that and the conflict continued, only this time the other white duck started bullying one of the erstwhile tormentors. The area around the sunken tub became a frenzied and scurrying cross between a corrupt school playground and a pub car park at half past eleven on a Saturday night. So Tom and I pumped the stagnant pond out, refilled it and spent another hour coaxing them in, which consisted mainly of catching them and throwing them in. It worked. They swam and washed in apparent harmony. Then I went off and spent another hour or so on the internet and discovered what any informed duck-keeper would have known straight away. This was not war but sex. The drakes were establishing a pecking order whilst seducing and shagging the ducks. Also I worked out that instead of the three pairs that we were sold, we actually have four males and two females. The white 'duck' is in fact a particularly lascivious drake. So two will either be given away, or prepared for the table, but I am ashamed to say I am rather sentimental about ducks and will find it hard to wring their necks.

11.11.01

There is a Shirley poppy hanging on in the jewel garden as delicate and bedraggled as the poppies in our buttonholes are stiff and opaque. It cannot last, of course, but I wanted to see if it would make it through to today. If I were of a mind to gather around a cenotaph then I would be tempted to pick and wear it. God knows that there are memories enough to mourn in every village and small town across the country. These are shameful days and they will be back to haunt us long after our absurd politicians have been deflated, put away and forgotten. So no cenotaph. No picked poppy. No faith in God and not a lot in man. I revert, as ever, to the garden, tiptoeing between despair and hope.

It is a good place for this, my garden in November. Last year I felt resolutely glum, rolling myself up into the month as if it were a duvet, but this year I feel fine—albeit in a constant state of appalled and angry dismay. Perhaps this is the best cure for the winter blues.

On the eleventh hour of this the eleventh day of the eleventh month I shall not find my poppy but pluck a sprig of rosemary for my remembering. Most of us well-read, soggy-liberal *Observer* readers think of Shakespeare and Ophelia when it comes to remembrance and rosemary, but the plant had the memory habit well before Tudor times, featuring in funerals and weddings since the Egyptians. At funerals a sprig was placed in the hands of the corpse, and at weddings the bride wore it dipped in scented water twined into her bridal wreath. Sprigs decked the bridal bed. Why? What was being remembered? Innocence? Chastity? Neither, I think. The wedding connection comes from the plant's original dedication to Aphrodite, the goddess of love. At times like these it is a good link, taking your hefty kick against the pricks, picking a sprig of rosemary and remembering love and the little deaths of the bridal bed. Although Sir Thomas More wrote, 'As for Rosemarine, I lett it runne all over my garden wals, not onlie because my bees love it, but because it is the herb sacred to remembrance and, therefore, to friendship.' Perhaps the bridal rosemary symbolises the wisdom of good marriages bound together by friendship. Certainly the medieval and Renaissance mind liked the constant duality of the flesh and death, and they would have played with the sweet-smelling emblematic *memento mori* that grew with icy blue flowers. I am sure that the scent had a lot to do with sweetening the process of death, especially in the summer heat.

Rosemary hates our wet winters but can put up with a surprising amount of cold. But combine wet and cold and it gives up the struggle. The secret of getting it to be lusty and really intensely oily is to grow it in very poor soil indeed—pure chalk or building rubble with plenty of limestone mortar is ideal, as long as the drainage is good. I suspect that

Thomas More's rosemary was rooted in his walls as well as running all over them. I used to lose plants all the time here until I started planting them in great pockets of grit, trying to keep the roots away from our fat Herefordshire clay loam that almost everything else thrives on. Another tip is to plant it hard against a south-facing wall so that all the moisture is sucked up by the bricks. I have about a dozen plants in a cold frame that I took as cuttings two years ago in readiness to replace last winter's losses which, thanks to the grit, never happened. I have completely neglected them this year, which they have loved. They are as healthy as anything in their root-bound, unwatered pots. We grow and use lots and lots of it, roasting potatoes and lamb on faggots of the stuff, throwing it on to the fire to fill a room for a moment or two with the resiny, dry fragrance of southern sun.

Nothing serves memory so well as scent, which, alone of all the senses, connects directly to the core of the brain on a very basic, functioning level. We remember fragrance exceptionally well, albeit often after we have long forgotten all the associations that went with it. Ask a person to recall an orange and they will describe a fruit or incident from the past week or month. But ask them to recall the scent of an orange and they will instinctively delve into childhood for the truest description.

There is not much that belongs to this season that is truly fragrant. The cidery tang that soaks the October air around here as surely as if it were an oak cask has completely gone. In its place there is the smell of gentle decay, quite unlike anything else that we normally associate with that word with its redolence of soggy compost heaps or bodies under rubble. It is entirely leafy. The smell of leaf fall blows back from childhood with a damp, fungal intensity, and the grass has a thin, wormy smell in the sun.

But even though it is dark and the days are drifting away from us, I want to be outside, whatever the weather. I will take the scent of rain and sticky soil and not wallow in my own or any one else's memory. This garden, here and now, is the touchstone of my reality, even if the scent of humbug does hang in the wind.

15.11.98 My Roots

Some of the best things about this garden never even enter it. At about seven thirty, on one of the indeterminate grey mornings that have clogged this autumn, I fed the chickens tucked away in the far corner of the orchard and did my usual tour round the place, taking stock, renewing intimacy with the series of small cameos that make up the larger place. Now that the herbaceous perennials are dying back and the annuals have been removed, the small paths that run through the borders make this easier and more complex. Summer is about the grand sweep, but winter gardens are all about detail—an affair conducted in glances and half moments rather than high passion. I remembered that we have a *Callicarpa bodinieri* tucked away at the back of one of the large borders (not hard to forget—it does nothing at all for nine months of the year) and went round that way to look at it. Sure enough, the purple metallic balls that make its berries were clustered round the leafless stems in its characteristically weird way. Tiny leaf shoots flared from the branches, already prepared for next year's round.

Moving away, I glanced up—and there in the low sky above me was a peregrine falcon, long sharp wings beating with a muscular confidence, his flight running straight down the path bisecting our garden, heading directly to his horizon. (His? Well, you can tell, and for those of you who know too, it was a tiercel.) I watched with heart-leaping wonder until I lost him in the greyness, although the caucus of crows meant that he was not far.

This, remember, is no mountain or cliff but Herefordshire: soft, old-fashioned countryside. We get curlews collecting in early spring in the water meadows next to us, and from February to May their lovely call is a feature of the dark. Ravens nest nearby and spend hours of every day in unhurried business around our airspace. Herons are common and last week there were six in the field together, picking up frogs drowned by the flooding. Swans swim to the garden fence and geese and ducks skim the sky. We have a great spotted woodpecker working away at the rotten branches of the hazel and a sparrowhawk that rounds the corner of our kitchen like a stunt flier. Last year I saw a goshawk flying over, and its presence was confirmed by local bird watchers. The full list is much longer, but the point is made. Birds love gardens. Birdsong improves a garden as much as any flower.

I have had the opportunity to look around more than usual this past week because I have been out of action with a slipped disc. Walking around is about the only thing I can do without too much discomfort. It is ironical that this should happen at one of the windiest, wettest, darkest, coldest spells during an exceptionally wet, cold and grey year, but never before have the hornbeam hedges seemed so lustrously gold and orange. Never before have the grasses—especially the ochre ones like *Carex flagellifera* and *C. buchananii*—seemed so rich and subtle; never before have the cabbages seemed to have such a powdery coat of blue over their green leaves. Either the world is extraordinarily beautiful or the painkillers are having more entertaining side-effects than I had realised.

12.11.00

This piece was supposed to have been written to coincide with the clocks going back. But I forgot. Just as I forgot to order the garlic, broad beans and 'Feltham First' peas for sowing. It all slips through my unworked fingers like water. This is not a memory thing—my memory, I'll have you know, is a slickly running whatdoyoucallit—but a quiet, futile rebellion at the drawing in of the year. I want to forget. At this time of year I am ready to give in. I want out.

It is not as though there are not things to do. November is the ideal month for all deciduous tree and shrub planting, whether it is a beech hedge, a climbing rose or an orchard. The ground still has enough warmth to tease some growth from the roots without any demands being made by the leaves. There is all that vegetable garden stuff: the ground should all be dug and the globally warmed weeds removed. Runner beans finally tidied away. The herbaceous borders can be all cut back and split where appropriate. Tulips and daffodils planted. Paths made or repaired. The work so long, the time so short. Stop whingeing. Get out there and do it.

But I forget. I forget these things in the same way that I forget to shave or put on clean trousers. I can feel the bristliness and am aware that that is dried mud on my leg, not decoration, and yet . . . You know the scene. This is well-rehearsed territory. It bores the shit out of me. It is low-quality stuff.

All this on Remembrance Sunday, and I am mainly reminded how I always forget how much I hate this time of year. Put that statement into context. Go back to mid-May. I love my garden then, love the season, regardless of weather, regardless of what is specifically happening outside. It is always as good as can be borne. Fast forward to here. Same garden, same place, same view from my window, same plants on the whole at a different phase of their being. Now I don't hate my children or wife or friends for being under the weather or tired or older or a pain in the arse. It is them. I accept them for all that they are, rough and smooth alike. But when the clocks go back a light switches off. Now some of this is familiar Prozac territory and nothing to do with the garden, but what with sun lamps, positive thinking and a wife who knows just when to kick me up the arse and when to bind me into her arms, we have that under control. I know I will come through. This is something else.

333

This actually happens. It is not a slightly miserable palling over of my state of mind but an actual process that is happening right now as I write and you, some future away, read. Out there in the cold, harsh and remorselessly unappetising garden. And because of that it is a very real and significant part of my gardening year. It happens every October, rising to a whimpering peak around Christmas and then on Boxing Day I shake myself, sniff the air and get creakingly back into the groove.

Of course this is to do with the sodding light slipping away. It is a rum thing. Most people accept it as part of the season—you have autumn, all ochres and russets and misty mauvey light, and that works into winter which is cold and dark. But when it comes to the garden the two seem to have independent trajectories. You can test it against the weather. On a lovely bright autumnal day the quality of the light seems to make up for the quantity of it. Sunlight slips inside the leaves. Soft sun dancing. Sunlight leaning so low across the garden that the shadows are pulled impossibly to the horizon, shimmering at their edges, frayed with light. There are still penstemons, dahlias, chocolate cosmos, white annual cosmos, *Nicotiana sylvestris*, marigolds, leonotis, knautia and, improbably, the occasional hysterical poppy. Sure it gets dark by five, but enough good light has been stored in the mind's batteries to make that potentially a cosy, natural summation. The day folds itself like a freshly laundered white towel into sweet-smelling log fires, lamps, books and a good meal. But if the sky has remained leaden all day long, smearing an oafish light across the face of so-called daylight, and the browns and greens of the fields and hedges disappear into a non-colour, a kind of tonal and pigmentary vacuum, then five o'clock arrives with all the charm of used dishwater meeting a plughole. Same season, different land.

I blame drivers, fuel-guzzling householders, big industry and, of course, the bleedin' government. If they didn't all use so much energy we wouldn't have global warming and if we didn't have global warming we wouldn't have so much rain and if we didn't have so much rain we wouldn't have so much cloud and—stick with it—if we didn't have so much cloud we would have more LIGHT. It is, of course, too late. The globe is warmed and cooking up nicely. Which means that it can only get worse in our lifetime and unless we do something really, really serious about it, which no government seems morally or politically capable of, in the lifetime of our children and grandchildren too. To call it a bad year or a damp autumn or a gloomy day implies that there is some kind of communal objective correlative. But there is no better time. Only in memory. The clouds are here to stay. [It was a genuinely appalling autumn. We did not see the sun—literally—for over forty consecutive days in November and December. There was flooding all over the country, and Sarah and the children moved out to a hotel in December because we had no drains (so therefore no loo, bath, washing machine, sink etc. etc.) between the end of October and January. No wonder I was feeling more glum than usual.] So what to do? Lawrence Johnson, he of Hidcote fame, had an answer when he decamped to Menton in the south of France each winter and carried on his gardening there. It is a good wheeze but assumes (a) greater funds than I have at my disposal, (b) someone to look after home for the winter months, (c) no children, and (d) . . . well, (d) is the perverse one, because it also assumes that you don't really need the gloom. And I think that I do. After all, how you going to go up if you never been down? Even in the heavy-clouded nuclear winter the sun chinks through the odd gap and dazzles the rain for a few moments. You need to see bare branches to know the full astonishing shock of the new leaves come next April. You need the flat, brown emptiness of the mixed borders to measure their summer fullness. In short, you need to know hunger in order to properly appreciate the feast when it arrives.

And I should miss the planting. It matters a lot that I have planted just about everything in this garden and have coaxed winter soil around the roots of plants that were naked and not up to much when they went in. It gives me my most meaningful stake in the place. There is an important bit of me buried out there in the mud with each plant and I have learned to trust that it will grow with renewed enthusiasm around the middle of next February, beginning of March. With any luck I might be up to a bit of flowering too.

But for a while I, like the flowers, lie underground, under memory, nibbled by worms. I like worms, encourage and nurture them and hope for a few in every handful of soil I pick up from the garden. (Do you not handle your soil? You should. Keep in touch.) But around the beginning of October they start casting on to the lawn and grass paths, turning the surface of the ground into a knobbly slime. Let's not put too fine a point on it, worm casts are a kind of clean excreta. Walk across the lawn in the dark and your shoes skid on a neat pile that feels exactly like Pekinese poo on a pavement. I really object to this. It spoils my day. Reduce the quality of my grass and you lower the quality of my life. I don't mean a buttock-clenched attention to the horticultural standard of the lawn—couldn't give a fig for all that rubbish—but the sensuous texture of grass and the surface of the ground under my feet. How the ground feels is pretty much how I feel. And come November we are both starting to feel pretty shitty.

19.11.00 My Roots

Did I say that we had got through the floods unscathed? I spoke too soon. Between writing last week's words and these, the water has lapped at our door and laps yet. To try and provide drainage we have dug a trench right down the length of the garden and laid a perforated land drain. It was dug fast, by eye, and curves and twists subtly. The floods rose again as this was being done and the trench promptly filled to the brim with flood water without making any noticeable difference to the water levels in the garden. The trench was cut down a grass path, but the rain made the sides collapse overnight and parts of jewel garden borders had to be evacuated so that this could be repaired.

Whilst this emergency digging went on, Poppy, our Jack Russell terrier, inspired by the action, went on a manic vole-hunt, digging dozens of holes in the borders, spraying tulip bulbs at every pass and destroying the roots of scores of plants. Sort of funny, but also sort of the last straw.

Although the canal/trench is a thing of sinuous beauty, in any other circumstances a dramatic piece of radical garden theatre, there is a huge amount of soil thrown up from it. This is now completely saturated. An utterly sodden seventy-metre mound of mud. The demarcation lines between grass, flood and mud are indecipherable runes ploughed into the ground. It will have to be made good—and I know that in three months' time no trace will remain—but that is a joke for the moment. The truth is that if we knew then what we know now, we would have laid this garden out in a completely different way to accommodate the inevitable flooding. Over the past week I have toyed with taking a JCB to the place and doing just this, but baulk a little at that. If I inspect my motives honestly I have to confess that I do not feel I have displayed what we have done enough. I want more public sharing in this place before I rip it apart. Vanity or altruism? Neither really. Just a natural born show-off.

Despite the waters rising, we have continued the process of cutting four new two-metre brick squares into the jewel garden. This means digging up hard paths, potting up plants, removing topsoil and putting in scalpings and sand before laying the bricks. It is worth the trouble tenfold and has dramatically improved the garden, even though we have only done two in the week. This garden has always been very long on places to delve and hoe and short on sites to sit and consider, and it means that now that the large beds revolve around these small seating areas—just big enough for a couple of chairs and a table—and we can go out and drink our champagne in one of five spots according to the light and state of performance of the various plants. Dressed, of course, in waterproofs and waders.

18.11.01

If I am feeling slightly bereft of inspiration before writing one of these weekly pieces, my mind as blank as the screen, I go and mooch around the garden, letting it come to me in a way that the busy gardener does not often allow. For sure we look and stare and think, but for proper inspiration you have to allow yourself to become passive and let the garden come to you.

So this morning I strolled round, open, receptive and inviting inspiration, but there was nothing there. By now the flowers have been all but used up. That could, of course, be a function of this garden and a measure of my own land-locked insularity, but all that are left are survivors and stragglers, hanging on into the wrong season like the last to leave a party. At no other time of year is there such a tangible, measured absence. This is both disconcerting and curiously surprising. Curious not in that it happens but in that I am still surprised that it happens. I suppose that this is the pendulum that balances the astonishment of every spring. However you justify the need for this dormancy in the greater scheme of things, the truth is that the garden lies exposed.

And here lies the inspiration. We have a corner of the jewel garden where self-sown nasturtiums have taken over for the fourth consecutive year, swamping the grasses and box hedging around them, but in October they look fabulous, scrambling half-way over the hedges and up the roses like a beautiful and benign bindweed. Nevertheless I have to hack them back at least three or four times during August and September to stop them suffocating the young box hedging that has been grown from cuttings. Now the frost has done the job for good this year, reducing their orange and yellow flowering sprawl to a shrivelled heap of black rags, like a burst balloon. The box hedging, that is to all intents and purposes invisible for half the year, suddenly leaps out. Instead of being not-flowers it becomes the garden. Or, at least, the strongest and arguably best thing in the garden.

This is true of all plant structure at this time of year and the best argument for having topiary and trained plants embedded into the design and structure of any garden. We have another bit of the garden that is made up entirely of 64 box balls or cobbles (each one is irregularly roundish) with brick paths running through them. In spring they glow with new growth but by summer, although neat enough and stylish in that kind of Conrany, metropolitan way, they occupy the space but not the eye. They are the minimalist's idea of horticultural heaven because clipped box has no mess, whereas flowers are—at their ecstatic best—little more than a gorgeous exclamation of mess. But for the coming three months they are the best thing in the garden, and every winter I wish that we had more such topiarised shapes all over the garden.

We have got some. There are more box balls dotted about the various borders, which are almost totally hidden for the summer, and 26 yew cones in front of the house. Some of them are a great deal more convincing than others because I have sporadically added to them, using excess hedging plants, and they are struggling to achieve cone-maturity. But that is part of the point of topiary. The idea has to make as sharp and fulsome an outline in the mind's eye from conception as the final thing will do on the sky. Everything that you do to it will be geared towards reaching this point from which you mentally began. If you are working in yew and box—and they are generally reckoned to be the best things to make topiary from—this will take some years. We are not in make-over territory here. Topiary is slow sculpture. Having said that, it is always surprising how fast it actually grows. You can make almost any shape of almost any size out of yew within ten years, and after thirty years things look ancient and are hard to date.

I don't quite know where the fashion for peacocks, squirrels and teapots came from. I once saw a field of box teddy bears in Holland. The image still punishes me. It has been suggested that peacocks were introduced by the Crusaders in an attempt to mimic the Byzantine aviaries, but this doesn't ring true to me, and I cannot think of a single medieval representation of a peacock. The history of evergreen topiary has been driven by the Dutch, who took to it in the seventeenth century and are still snipping away today by the thousands of hectares, hence the teddy bears. Initially the

341

cones, pyramids, spirals and balls in the formal gardens of the late seventeenth century were deliberately modest in scale. As and when they got too big they were removed and replaced by a smaller model, grown and clipped in readiness so that the picture was fully formed from planting. You can see a good example of this in the Privy Garden at Hampton Court. But beyond the palaces and really grand houses this was too extravagant. You can see a county squire just about agreeing to one of these dam' newfangled gardens, but drawing the line at digging the things up just to replace them as soon as they got growing.

The landscape movement that became a craze from about 1740 onwards meant that many of the topiary gardens were dug up and replaced with lawns and artfully positioned clumps of trees, but some did remain or were planted, soon outgrowing the tight demands of seventeenth-century formality. So the yew and the box bulged and grew and were fiddled with to preserve symmetry and control. An overgrown bulge became a bird. That curiously British trait of regulated bolshiness suits topiary very well. We keep clipping and training but let it go too, liking the overgrown and the wonky, carefully preserving the plants' eccentricities as they form, whereas on the continent they are altogether more logical and directive about things. Hence the difference between their immaculate parterres and topiary gardens and ours, which tend to look as though they have recently been rescued from years of abandonment.

The Arts and Crafts movement liked topiary a lot because it fitted exactly into their idea of decorative order and structure that could be made and go on being made every year. And so our Victorian gardens, from the grandest to the smallest cottage patch, started sprouting birds, hilariously phallic shapes and growths—anything to break the tyranny of a clean line and to allow the subconscious to romp a little.

We all know about evergreen topiary. You plant a healthy specimen and train the leaders in the direction you want growth whilst cutting back hard to stimulate bushy thickness. You can tie the leaders to canes or, much more expensively, make formers to sit over the bush so that it grows through and then is clipped back to that outline. But there is no need for that degree of expense and elaboration. Anything can be trained and clipped to almost any shape with some patience and a little skill. It is an entirely free form of expression and as such is, I think, entirely wonderful. But the things to remember about this kind of topiary are that nothing in a garden stands in isolation. The relationship between each shape and outline is as important as the piece itself. In other words, topiary usually looks best *en masse* and as part of a considered piece of design. This can grow and change organically—indeed it should and almost certainly will—but the overall concept should be there from very early on. This inevitably leads on to the other question of manipulating and understanding the bits that are not there. I would take this further and say that the best bits of almost every garden are the empty spaces between things. These spaces have to be shaped and maintained just as carefully as the objects that define them.

In winter, when there is more space than at any other time of year, the gardening of emptiness is at

343

its hardest. Anyone can make a green path flanked by immaculate tall hedges look good if they are in the full flush of midsummer health, but a grey November day is less forgiving. The eye does not wash over rough grass, straggly branches and floppy evergreens, but sticks at each irritant. Hence the importance of topiary. But topiary does not have to be restricted to cones and spirals. Any kind of training and pruning that is done for effect rather than the health of the plant amounts to topiary. Deciduous plants are perfectly fair game for this. All you have to bear in mind is the basic principle of pruning, which is that if you cut a shoot back, the new growth will be more vigorous. This is because the terminal bud of a stem produces a chemical that inhibits the growth of any buds below it. Remove that terminal bud and the others will leap enthusiastically into action. The harder you cut back, the more uninhibited is the subsequent response. So if you have a plant that is intended to be symmetrical and one side is growing weaker than the other, the correct thing to do is to cut the weak side back hard whilst gently pruning the vigorous side. It goes against instinct but not nature.

Hornbeam is particularly good for training, as is, in a bushy kind of way, hawthorn. Limes are also very trainable and we have quite a few limes (*Tilia cordata*) here that are all pleached hard each winter to three tiers of interlocking branches spaced two feet apart with the lowest six feet off the ground. That detail is lost by the end of May in a flurry of leaves and hectic shoots growing as much as six feet from hundreds of buds. But when the last leaf drops I will cut all this year's growth off and return to the stark outline that dominates this garden for four months of the year. It is an important part of accepting winter for what it is rather than seeing it only as the absence of summer. And the bits I like best are the rectangles of sky between the branches.

25.11.01 **My Roots**

Last Tuesday we had a delivery of three cubic metres of readymix. Readymix concrete comes into my life every few years and always causes the same brand of planned panic. You know what it is for and where it is to go but nevertheless it always seems so much and so wet and the pile never seems to bear any resemblance to the space allotted to contain it. In this case it was a path, 52 metres long and nine inches wide. Gareth had dug the trench in preparation and put in a foot of hardcore along the length of it with the intention of finishing it with brick pavers. But that would have cost a fortune, especially considering that this was strictly not for show but a working access. We rather timidly plumped for concrete, with self-conscious genuflections towards modernity and post-modernism rather than the raw 1950s brutality that was also the possible outcome.

Four of us barrowed it in and it took an hour or so to tamp it level, making sure that it was just below the flanking grass but making no attempt to get it flat. So, as it began to get dark and the rain thickened from a drizzle to fat drops, this dead straight, undulating line of grey concrete formed down the grass path that leads to the tunnel and the soft fruit and chickens and will, in time, also lead to the new compost area. The rain did it no harm and at ten o'clock that night I went out and brushed it with a stiff yard broom to get a suitably coarse surface. In the morning we all gathered to admire its straightness and dry hardness. There is something rather abstract about even the concrete solidity of a long, very narrow path set into grass. It is wide enough to push a single-wheeled barrow without treading on the potentially muddy bits on either side, and it is broken with three two-metre concrete squares where paths turn off at right angles into different sections of the garden so you can get round the corner. It has cast a long line of pleasure down the garden—not least to the boys, who are already using it as a motorway for their bikes.

Just as I wrote the above I got a phone call to tell me that George, a friend who helped me a great deal in both this and my last garden, had died. The garden is filled with his memory, especially in paths he helped make. He would have liked our concrete slither, liked the way that we made a tidy job of it. I cannot tell you how much I mind not showing it to him.

22.11.98

At this time of year the garden is like a dog that has been rolling in something unspeakable, smeared in dirt and utterly at odds with the sheltered comfort of the house. But as going outside is less and less of an attractive option it is worth considering the garden from indoors. By a quirk of Tudor architecture my house has only one upstairs window that looks out on to our back garden—which is by far the bigger part of it—and this window belongs to the loo in the attic. Occasionally I go up there, climb on the seat and squint through the skylight to get a fresh take on affairs on the ground, but as a rule it means that I look at the front garden every time I get up in the morning but the back garden hardly ever. But last week the builders who came to re-roof our hop kiln put a lovely scaffolding armature round it. So I was able to look down on the whole garden from a vantage point roughly level with the top of our chimney. Even in this sodden, muddy, God-awful season it looked beautiful. The structure, which we have worked hard at for the past six years, was laid out just like my plans and drawings that I originally did five years ago, powerfully influenced by the wonderful drawings of the late Sir Geoffrey Jellicoe. It was an astonishingly fresh realisation of all those plans and schemes—even though I have been furrowed down in its soil making it to those plans all this time. This structure—the clichéd 'bones' of the garden—would not have been nearly so evident in summer, smudged over by flowers, foliage and the general floppy spillage that stops the garden looking regimented. The scaffolding will be down in a few weeks and then we shall only have the photographs I took, but it has made me think about how important gardens are from indoors, especially from upper-floor windows.

There is, of course, nothing original in this line of thought. Since the late fifteenth century gardens have been designed to be viewed from a first-floor window, with Tudor knot gardens the first manifestation in this country showing interlaced lines of low hedges creating a geometric 'endless' pattern.

These came originally from designs on carpets imported from the Middle East in the fifteenth century, and full appreciation of the transference from warp and weft to foliage obviously needed an elevated viewing position. We have become accustomed to the convention that hedges are a framework or container for flowers of one kind or another, but the essence of a knot is that the intertwined lines of clipped evergreen hedging plants, usually box, but also santolina, hyssop or even thyme, are the sum and substance of the design. They did not rely upon any floral infill to complete them, running to no more than different-coloured sands or stones to occupy the spaces between the lines of hedge. Although Francis Bacon famously derided knot designs as being no more than the ornamentation of the kind found on a pie or tart, this kind of translation of two-dimensional patterns into three growing dimensions is always extremely satisfying, be it manifested as a knot, maze, parterre or any other organised layout. Or pie crust for that matter.

Flowers can hide space, and the space between objects is usually as interesting and aesthetically satisfying as the objects themselves. I guess that this is very elementary architectural theory, but certainly not enough attention is paid to it in garden design.

In seventeenth-century France the essentially modest knot was developed into the parterre, which was at times a very grand sequence of geometric patterns, containing flowers, statues, gravel and water. This was soon copied in Britain, Holland and Italy, and the paintings and engravings of Leonard Knyff and Johannes Kip show many parterres attached to the great houses of England at the end of the seventeenth century, almost all to be brutally swept away in the subsequent fifty years.

Maybe the parterre never really suited the British attitude towards gardens. It is too grand and public, going off into knobs and twiddles and ending up in the worst excesses of neo-rococo Victorian park bedding. A parterre never had the contemplative intimacy of a knot, which is more humble and domestic and which never really grew beyond the scope of a carpet. We like our gardens to be private and intimate, even claustrophobic. When we idly gaze down from the stair window at our brown piece of garden under a grey November sky, what we most want is to draw it back into our territory, to unite house and garden in the same easy, seamless way that the opened windows and doors of high summer make possible, not to stand amazed at the scope of our mastery of the countryside around us. There may be nothing much going on outside, but the opportunity to look

349

down and enjoy the nothingness between the patterned skeleton of a garden is one of the perks of the season.

It is easy to lose possession of the garden at this time of year, but perfectly reasonable to be fully connected to it from inside the protection of a closed window. After all, the garden is mostly what you perceive it be—regardless of where and how that perception is formed. The view from inside the house is as much part of your garden as the view of the kitchen from the end of the garden belongs to your house. It makes sense to compose it so that it fills the window frame as pleasingly as possible.

On one level that means lining up the lines and paths on windows in the house. Not only will this look more harmonious, but also it immediately includes the view as part of the garden. Open the curtains and look down a garden path and immediately you want to go on down it. On another, only slightly more sophisticated level, you can learn from knots and construct the hedges, borders, paths and permanent features of your garden so that they create a grid or pattern that pleases you without any assistance from flowers. Edge borders with hedges, line paths, plant trees and shrubs so that the space revolves rather than just occurs around them.

However, this does not mean pushing everything to the edges of the garden. It is amazing how many gardens have a few shrubs and climbers planted against the fences with a thin ribbon of border framing an expanse of lawn, muddy from worm casts, football and poor drainage. As soon as the flowers fade in autumn this becomes utterly empty. It is like a room with all the furniture pushed back against the walls, waiting for the party that will never happen. Far better to have space around the edges and to fill the centre of the garden with hedges, trees, ponds or whatever excites you. The difference between interesting, uncluttered space and dreary emptiness is absolutely critical. Work it out in plan, and if the resulting drawing satisfies you on paper, the chances are that its appearance in the garden, viewed on a blustery wet day at the fag-end of the year, will bring you a surprising amount of pleasure.

30.11.03 **My Roots**

The fox got my ducks the other day. I went up to feed them in the morning and knew instantly what the silence meant. I found one half under the fence minus its head and another buried neatly in a shallow grave, covered with leaves. Of the others only bundles of iridescent green and black feathers remained. I am a countryman and am not on the whole sentimental about nature, but this scene, which I have had to encounter over half a dozen times in the last ten years, always distresses and depresses me. I think that I shall not keep ducks in this garden any more, as a life safe from foxes is incompatible with any degree of freedom for them, but maybe one day I will move somewhere that is large enough to take a big pond with an island where they can safely roost.

The ducks are gone but the tulips are all in, nearly six thousand bulbs planted in a flurry over three days. Some of these, like 'Ballerina', 'Abu Hassan', 'Negrita' and 'Queen of Sheba' are more of what we already have in the ground. Some, like 'Black Parrot' and 'Queen of Night', are bulbs that we lifted in spring and are replanting. Subtle differences count for a lot with tulips, and the only way to really see if one is as you want it is to try it and see, and then, if it works, bulk out with plenty more of the same in subsequent years. But we have some new (to us) varieties as well. 'Texas Flame' is a buttercup yellow with a red flame, 'Flaming Parrot' is described by the catalogue as 'barium yellow flamed chrysanthemum crimson', and although I don't know what barium yellow is, I will surely find out when they appear next spring. We are also trying one called 'Va Bien', which is 'primrose yellow flamed blood red'. We wanted 'Recreado', which is a deep plum stained with a violet flame, but it had sold out (as ever, we were late with our order) and we have the very different and very pink 'Menton' as a substitute.

I also planted a hundred yellow 'Pagoda' erythroniums in the spring garden. I have long admired them but never grown a single one before. This is one of the advantages of being a self-taught amateur—there are so many new experiences to be had.

December

01.12.02

There is an H. G. Wells short story [This is from thirty-year memory. I hunted for the story but could not find it.] in which a typically ordinary Wellsian figure suddenly finds himself capable of extraordinary feats of magic. Astonished at his own facility, he confides in a friend and, to reveal the extent of his gift, he points at an object on the table with the command 'Be a bowl of vi'lets.' Over the years I have often thought that being a bowl of violets is the sublimest of all aspirations, but actually if I were to be a plant it would be a yew.

Our modern gardens are stuffed with common yews (*Taxus baccata*), mostly as soberly clipped hedges or slightly kitsch, camp topiary. As garden gear these are fine. No other evergreen has the dignity or substance of yew. As yew trees, however, these suffer frivolity by biding their unimaginably long time. The tightly clipped cones either side of the garden path will outlast you, every trace of ancestry issuing from you, the garden, the house, the roads and every object in vision. When everything else is old they are hardly troubling their adolescence. Just occasionally you find yews that have broken free from their clipped shackles and become trees. There are marvellous ones at Killeruddery just outside Bray in County Wicklow, Ireland, that were planted in 1711 as topiary but after a hundred years were ignored, left untrimmed and grew away into trees like sculptures escaping the stone block. But these are babies, a mere three hundred years old. They have a life expectancy of at least ten times that.

No, I would not be a topiarised yew, garden-worthy and crisp of edge, but a scraggy ancient tree that had avoided removal by way of an iron-hard trunk of vast girth that deterred the handsaw for centuries. [My parents-in-law cut down a large yew (not good—but it did, of course, regrow vigorously) and I salvaged some large sections of trunk which stood outside in our yard for ten years. In the autumn of 2004 I carved eight of them into large wooden pebbles (thinking of our clipped box pebbles)—which took hundreds of hours of hard graft—so I know exactly how hard the wood can be.] Yews make new horizons out of time. Geology and astronomy dizzy the mind with abstract numbers, but yew trees in the here and now unravel years in the same way. The yew at Fortingall in Scotland may be nine thousand years old. It will get older. There are some, in Wales, more than five thousand years old, and it is reckoned that as many as a hundred are in excess of one thousand. But dating yews is an imprecise business. According to the most famous dendrologist of them all, the late Alan Mitchell, there are only fifty large yews of known date. Can this be true? It seems a fantastically small figure. These fifty vary from thirty to 1100 years old and tell us almost nothing because yew is on the one hand so good at regenerating itself from the bare stem—a gift that age does nothing to diminish—and on the other hand is almost invariably attacked by fungus that rots the interior of the trunk and large branches, making accurate dendrochronology impossible. The incredible tensile strength of yew wood—which is what makes it suitable for

356

longbows [My son Tom and I are very keen on archery and are making some yew bows. Apparently the best yew for bows in Britain (Spain historically produced the best) is from the Welsh Marches—i.e. exactly where we live.]—means that a thin shell with a completely hollow centre can still support huge branches for hundreds if not thousands of years. No other tree can do this.

They are magic trees, much older than western civilisation, often older than the churches that shelter by them, capable of almost limitless life as their branches slowly bow down to the ground and take root. To cut an old yew down is vandalism of a shocking order, although it will almost certainly regrow. To grub one up is inviting catastrophe, the worst of all bad luck.

I would give a very great deal to see time unfurl in this garden alone, watching the changes that I can only intelligently guess at, skipping down the centuries from Norman through Tudor, Carolean, Georgian and dingy twentieth century like clouds in a speeded-up film, setting the fragile present into context. Because that is what age does—creates a context that is bigger and broader than the white room of the moment. The experiences of the present are shuffled to fit the expanding pack of years, changing everything a little and making all change seem, well, little. Imagine the viewpoint of a 3000-year-old yew! Lesser trees would grow and fall like mushrooms, woods would be cleared, cultivated and grow rank before turning into housing estates. The garden would make its thousand thousand micro-changes, each one a week or season of wonder, shifting like sand-ripples between the tides, accumulating its story like geological layers. All my planting is merely the embroidery on its surface and only old age—not human old age but yew age—would give me any kind of insight into it.

As it is I must bide my time. Gardens as ordered and measured spaces are always young. A man may make two or even three gardens in his time and see them mature in a way that necessitates cutting back, re-ordering and making radical alterations to avoid unwanted change. But after ten years much of the work is geared to making them stay within their bounds, instead of getting old in the way that they naturally incline to.

I have known only two men who were born, lived and died in the same house and garden. Both were old men when I was very young. Both are dead. One was a cowman in the little village I grew up in. He loved his garden but there was practically nothing in it that made it a garden as a place. There was a block of ground in which he grew vegetables and another block kept for dahlias and chrysanths. They all won prizes. There was a patch of grass, nowhere to sit and a hedge he cut in May and September. He was out there in all weathers until dark despite having been up at four to milk the cows. Every year he did the same things, grew the same things in the same seasons. Every day was new. When he died, forty years ago, the cottage was taken over and the garden all grassed over. Within six months it was as though it had never been there.

The other old man was at the opposite end of the social scale but in many ways not so different. Rudge Humphreys, the father of my friend Henry who appears on these pages from time to time, [He

358

does seem to have cropped up quite a few times. Go and see their garden when they have an open day. It is fantastic.] lived at Usk Castle all his life. Henry has done so too, for nearly fifty years. Rudge excavated the castle and made a garden within it, spending all his life working in it. It is open to the public via the *Yellow Book*. The castle goes back to the twelfth century and for all its astonishing grandeur and history, it has more charm than any other garden I know of, not least because it is filled with Rudge and Henry's quirky, batty sculptures, topiary and conceits. My favourite bit is tucked around the front of the gatehouse where Rudge made 21 topiary balls to celebrate his twenty-first birthday seventy-odd years ago. They are now perhaps one, even two metres across and, although tightly clipped, all different from each other. They are, of course, of yew.

02.12.01 **My Roots** [I have always wanted to take a sabbatical from the *Observer* from the beginning of November to the middle of December. These pieces are a real struggle to complete. If they become drearily repetitive, I can assure you that a huge amount of effort is devoted to making them more positive than they might otherwise be.]

I have been fighting off an attack of the winter blues. This is no big deal, not even unusual really at this time of year, but it does clog the system. It gets in the way. The symptoms are always the same and always confuse me. First there is the inability to raise enthusiasm for anything beyond domestic chores, computer games and rearranging the apples in the apple store. No pleasure. Then there is the constant foggy tiredness coupled with an inability to sleep for more than about four hours. And lastly a batch of physical ailments that feel as though the body is winding down, like an old car. The confusion comes from the way that this creeps in, infiltrating the system with its swill of intolerance and bad temper, and it comes as a relief to finally realise what is going wrong. I heard on the radio the other day that Macy Gray, who is also a manic depressive, although by the sound of it far worse so than my own rather inadequate version, was told that a balanced diet of exercise, sex and sleep was the best cure. Whilst I am unreservedly enthusiastic about the first two and would willingly do more of the sleep bit if I could, I would add another essential component: gardening.

Because I have written about this before I am aware that I risk becoming a bit of a bore on this subject, but, for what it is worth, I am deadly serious. You see, behind the easy flippancy and ability to manoeuvre through the day, I don't feel very well at all. The options reduce themselves to the best of a bad bunch. So yesterday I took myself into the garden as therapy, even though I regarded it with about the same enthusiasm as a barium enema. Now, in this state, there is no point in attempting anything that involves decisions or energy. That will only lead to failure, which just makes things worse. You have to potter with intent. Pruning is always a good idea. So I pruned back in the spring garden, removing hellebore leaves that were splaying on to the path (and fully aware of the great debate about when to cut back hellebore leaves. My policy over the past few years has been to do it by degrees between November and February) and cutting back the hedge where it was narrowing an entrance. Strange how you accept the gradual blocking of things. When I had finished, it seemed liberated and radical, as though not to have done it was an extraordinary oversight. There is a metaphor lurking in there somewhere. I cleared the jewel garden of all frosted and slimy leaves, producing barrowloads of ex-nasturtiums, dahlias, sweet peas, salvias and pulling up bundles of *Verbena bonariensis* that had self-seeded in wrong but beautiful places. I dug the dahlias up, filling a large barrow with just the 'Bishop of Llandaff', as the tubers were swollen with diocesan plumpness despite the abject surrender of the top growth. When I had done this, Sarah, Tom and I made a bonfire, with orange pellets of light scattering into the tea-time darkness and the hellebore leaves crackling in the flames. And at the end of a remorselessly grey, chill November day in which the only life that had any meaning was entirely domestic, entirely unambitious in scope, I still felt pretty bad, but I liked myself and this garden a bit better. Perhaps it is one and the same thing.

07.12.03

Tomorrow is my youngest son's birthday. He will be thirteen, which is a landmark just as big for us parents as for the teenage Tom. And although he will not be the least bit different in any perceptible way, everything will be different. We will slide seamlessly from midnight into tomorrow and somehow he is not really a child any longer. [Well . . . not always.]

He was born in a blizzard. I had just enough time to race Sarah into Hereford for an emergency Caesarian before the snow trapped us all. It took me four hours to half drive, half shovel my way the ten miles home and another four days for the roads to clear before I could get back and see both of them. Our business had just been broken up and sold for a fraction of what we owed, and the house and nearly all our possessions were in the middle of being sold to make up the difference. Yet the arrival of the baby spread a huge ripple of calm over the household that autumn and winter. We moved out on Sarah's birthday in February. And apart from a year or so whilst we sorted the house out, he has grown up here and the garden has grown around him. I have pictures of him in an anorak and nappy and wellies, clutching a bloody great hammer. Always a hammer or saw in his hand, and before long a power tool or two. For his seventh birthday we bought him a shed which he immediately kitted out as a workshop and filled with my tools. He is now on shed number four and the garden has three of them dotted around. Their insides are bright, brilliant and surprisingly domestic, like surreal frontier cabins. Although temporary and subject to the fancies of their creator—he has built them all himself—these are as much part of the garden as the hedges, trees and plants that they are set in. I like this idea of having buildings cropping up on a whim, something between toys left lying around and monstrous woody plants that have muscled their way up from the soil.

This, of course, is completely disingenuous. The control freak in me—I am a gardener after all—is horrified by the idea of buildings of any kind that are not precisely factored into the horticultural scheme of things. But that horror is part of having children in the garden. They loose the bonds that tie the garden together. Now that they are all (almost) teenagers, the garden has become less a play area for them than a kind of neutral space like the landing or hallway. Not particularly interesting in its own right but nevertheless part of home. I made a garden that seemed to me to be as full of delight as it could possibly be for child or adult alike, but I was wrong. Children live in a quicksilver world that flows from moment to moment, whereas we adults are lumpen and plodding. My garden was a grand plan that was laboriously executed and as such completely unappreciated by the children. Their garden was always being broken up into new worlds, whereas mine was always being carefully assembled.

So how would I do it again if I were to cater for the children in the garden rather than merely tolerate them? I would make *places*. Places can have magic regardless of the details that they contain. We grown-ups go on endlessly about the minutiae of differences, whereas children simply don't care about that any more than they care about the furniture at home. A flower is almost just a flower. The places I have made in the garden have mostly existed to frame their details although, occasionally, by accident, they were child-friendly They loved the willow circle that was made from cuttings of a particularly vigorous salix hybrid that grew six feet a year and formed a willow henge almost over one summer. Nevertheless I grubbed it out after three years because it did not fit into my grand plan. They have never forgiven me.

A couple of years back we got a digger in and sorted out ten years of subsoil and bonfires into a low mound with a flat, square top. This was an instant hit with children of all ages. Why? Because it is a place to go. When you are on it you are king of the castle. This summer there was a pool on it and now in the winter a trampoline. Both could have gone elsewhere, but somehow that felt the rightful place for play. I remember when I was lodging in a house in Cambridge, over twenty years ago, I made a mount in the back garden, burying all the hardcore that I dug up from a driveway. This was then covered with soil and turfed. It was not much of a hill, but the children of the household immediately loved it. I wish I had done this at home ten years ago.

My children used to play all their grass-orientated games in the front, amongst the growing topiary yews where there wasn't much space. I had made a lawn at the top of the garden, ideal for football, bike riding or teasing the dog, but they never played there, preferring the front because it was near the house. The umbilical cord only stretches so far. I would now make an area designed for carefree play right by the house, because that is where the cares are freer when you are small.

And as they got older they wanted their own piece of the garden. Like a fool I interpreted this as a desire to grow and cultivate their own patch. Nothing could have been wider of the mark. They wanted an uncultivated, ungardened piece of outdoor home that they could make into a mountain bike track or a jungle or an assault course. Whilst I was busy trying to contain and control my world within a backyard, they were looking to create whole worlds from a patch of grass—and any old patch would have done. My eldest son Adam wanted to make a bike track in the orchard, but I forbade it because it would have messed up the pristine static image. I am very ashamed of that.

The truth is that a precious garden is not compatible with children, and the nature of most serious gardening is pretty precious. Both sides must compromise in order to accommodate each other. But I suspect that the adult gardener takes much more from the relationship than the child, because that spirit of play, of making things up and believing in them with all your heart but changing them completely after lunch, can make a garden dance. Grown-ups can make it into an exquisite tableau, but in a purely adult garden there would be no surreal sheds where sheds are not planned and, to paraphrase T. S. Eliot, the leaves would not be full of children, hidden excitedly, containing laughter.

06.12.98 My Roots

My father-in-law gave us two presents last week as part of their move from the farm (with certainly the most beautiful range of farm buildings in England) to a smaller house. One was a huge pile of logs and the other an old tractor. The only proviso was that I get both tractor and wood from his house to ours by the time that they moved—which was the other day. So I rang my friend Brian.

Brian lives just over the border in Presteigne. He is small but very fast and has a bobcat—a kind of Reliant Robin with a front bucket with a Welsh Ronnie Corbett at the wheel—and a lorry. He said that he could do both jobs. This is because he always drives a ten-ton lorry with a trailer and the bobcat on the trailer. As he lives just down the road from a quarry, it means that he invariably delivers a load of something to someone where he is bobcatting or somewhere along the route. He then loads the lorry with the bobcat before returning and dumping the load. Bingo—three jobs in one.

So one of the provisos of hiring Brian is that he brings a delivery from the quarry with him. I chose scalpings—the grey mixture of stone and dust that forms the sub-layer of roads—to use as a drainage layer for the paths that we are laboriously digging out in the kitchen garden. The paths entail digging out a foot of topsoil and putting in a six-inch layer of these scalpings before the layer of sand and finally bricks. We have only done about a fifth of the paths and already there are mounds of topsoil to be spread—by Brian with his bobcat when the ground is dry enough for him to ride over and get to it.

The only day Brian could do I had to be in London, so I left him and Gareth—who is helping with the paths—to do it. The major problem was where to put twenty tons of my father-in-law's logs. The first trip involved dumping the scalpings in the middle of our yard, filling and blocking it to all but a wheelbarrow's width. The second was the load of wood, plus the tractor on the trailer. The firewood was dumped in the lane, blocking it completely, and the tractor put in our driveway, filling it. Then Brian used the bobcat to push the log pile—by now of beaver-dam proportions—along the road until they were piled neatly along the verge by the house. Try doing that in Islington or Ruislip.

The tractor has a 'box' on the back—a kind of shelf that can be hydraulically raised and lowered, and Adam, my eldest son, has mastered this and started ferrying the wood in the box on the back via the muddy field to the gate into our orchard, where it will be out of the way. There are ruts and tyre marks where six months ago the grass was waist high, swishy with pollen, but it is reparable.

Is this gardening? Well, country gardening certainly, and the reality of making this place work. My family often accuses me of running the garden as a complete control freak, but my line is that I see it as an athlete that has to be monitored and fine-tuned to rise to peaks of performance.

Weeks like this last one amount to reconstructive surgery.

10.12.00

James Turrell's Skyspace stands on Cat Cairn, a promontory looking right down the seven-mile length of Kielder Water like a watchtower or blind lighthouse. The first analogy might appeal to the romanticism of the situation as it is just eight miles from the Scottish border, but the second carries a more accurate indication of what it actually is. To get there at all you must come through miles of the largest planted forest in Britain, covering nearly 250 square miles, and skirt along the shores of Kielder Water, which is the largest man-made lake in Europe. Given that the purpose of my trip was to look at a piece of art set in landscape, this long, increasingly impressive approach sets you into the right scale by expanding your cloistered city or village horizons and then drawing them back to the turret on the crag.

I am shamefully ignorant of this part of England, having once paid a childhood visit to Hadrian's Wall and otherwise seen the North East as one of those mysteries like the Black Country or the Fens—knowing that they have something that people love and feel passionate loyalty to, but not having an inkling of what that is. There is no fool like an ignorant fool. Thankfully it is never too late to learn. [I have just spent a very good weekend in Newcastle—so I am slightly redressing the balance.] For a start, it is a staggeringly beautiful part of the country. And there is a breathing space from the writhing south, which is always a good thing. With the trains all over the shop and only a day to get there and back, I took a 45-minute BA flight from Birmingham of such cramped discomfort that it felt like a joke (except the price of £280 is distinctly unfunny). [Since I wrote this piece, cheap inland air travel has transformed the way people get about in this country. The flights we took to Newcastle the other day cost less than half the price of my trip four years ago. It is now often cheaper to fly around Britain than to go by train.] But Newcastle airport is downright sexy, and in minutes you are driving north-east towards the vast stretches of Kielder Forest and the Scottish border.

This is Viking country, raided from north and east for a thousand years, not for possession of the soil but to spoil and dispossess. To flex the border. Even on a grey November day in the wettest autumn for ever and ever, the light is pearly rather than lowering, and when you go in search of Turrell's work light is everything. It is his medium. Earth and stone are used only to contain and corral light, and to this end he has built 'Skyspaces' in his Arizona desert home, in Ireland, Japan, Israel, Holland and France as well as now up here in Northumberland.

I came across his work, quite literally, in June 1991. I was a freelancer then and got a commission to write about the gardens of the south-west corner of Ireland. We went to Skibbereen to see Creagh Gardens, which I had read were 'charming'. (Just a hint of condescension in that expression, don't you think? Grand cannot be charming, big cannot be charming, stylish can never be charming, but small,

369

muddly and eccentric can.) We popped into the local Irish Tourist Board office, where they suggested we go and see the Sky Gardens, which were just being made. So, before visiting Creagh (charming), we went and had a fascinating few hours there. The estate had been bought by a wealthy Swiss art dealer who commissioned James Turrell to make an installation there. When we visited it was still at the bulldozer stage, but Turrell also happened to be visiting and he was, er, charming. But not in a garden way. Rather grand and impressive. Memorable.

I was very taken with that Skibbereen garden because it was the first time I had seen a large outdoor space used by an artist in such a coherent, visionary way. Visionary is exactly the right word because all Turrell's work depends upon the way that you, the viewer, see things. As he has said about his work, '[it] is not so much about my seeing as about your seeing. There is no one between you and your experience.' That kind of remark can easily lead to the situation where it has to be pointed out to the emperor that he is wearing no clothes—unless there is an experience worth seeing. But with Turrell, there always is. He walks the walk.

The Kielder Skyspace is essentially an underground chamber, approached from a round tunnel cut through the side of the hill. If you visit the excellent website (www.kielder.org/index) you can see from a series of photographs that the chamber and tunnel have been constructed from reinforced concrete and then piled over with rock and earth, but the effect is subterranean, a modern tumulus. But what is buried inside is not a bundle of bones and artefacts to guide you into the dark, but light.

The ceiling of the Skyspace is a framed circle open to the sky. The light from this empty space seems to fill the oculus like a pulsating, glowing object and at the same time softly illuminate the chamber. It makes the space seem contained and rich and yet is exactly the same subdued, low grey cloud cover that you flew through and drove beneath. The details are monumental and very precise. White walls running seamlessly into white ceiling, making a circular frame round the open ring of sky. Massive concrete seats painted grey linking to the grey interior of the circular entrance tunnel. Faultlessly crisp edges to circles of door and sky, a circle of black gravel directly beneath the open roof. Sound bouncing round the walls. The effect is quietly transfixing. At dawn or dusk your entrance into the Skyspace triggers lights around the circular space hidden behind the seats, creating a ring of ambient light, and the white walls glow ochre and enrich the sky colour.

The experience of sitting quietly (albeit freezing) is enormously satisfying, even though sensation is stripped down and pared back as far as it will go. All superfluities are abandoned. I would love this in my garden. A building like this, subterranean or overtly external, is within the tradition of temples in the landscape such as you find at Stowe or Stourhead. To find that type of building—in itself lifted from temples and bowers of medieval, Roman, Greek and Byzantine civilisations—interpreted in this modern idiom is tremendously exciting, especially in the rather philistine world of garden buildings.

Don't get me wrong: I am sure that Turrell would be amused to think of this piece of art being compared to a summerhouse or a merely decorative stop in a highly manufactured landscape, but the analogy is nevertheless there. Gardens are our private, domestic landscape. Although seemingly a vast expanse of wilderness, Kielder Forest is in many ways as artificial and contrived as any garden. It is not an unpopulated space that is needed for this work so much as unpolluted light, free of the insidious ambient glow of streetlamps and car headlights.

Any carefully thought-out garden building, whether it uses light as skilfully as Turrell does, or is simply contrived to provide calm seclusion, adds a vital element to the garden as a whole. This obviously happens on an external level, although I would prefer it if the Skyspace had been completely submerged beneath its hillock of earth and rock, rather than clad in drystone and only the bottom half buried. But perhaps in a massive public space like Kielder the sight of the tower is needed as a signpost to announce itself. The thing exists entirely as a subjective experience from the inside out and does not, I believe, need any exterior at all. What really matters is what happens on an internal level. The building's manipulation of light and space strongly influences how you see the world and, in particular, how you use light and space at home, indoors and out.

Buildings in the garden world, both domestic and public, are on the whole retrospective and unambitious. The Skyspace and the other buildings at Kielder are ambitious, modern, grown-up works of art that can compete with anything else in the world. No doubt planning permission and the matter of expense (the Skyspace cost £300,000) would constrain all but the grandest gardeners, but I will be thinking very carefully how to include the lessons of Kielder into my own backyard [Tom's sheds.] and I urge you to make the journey there to do the same.

14.12.03 **My Roots**

Over the past few years I have been attempting to make a holly hedge-on-stilts. It is slow and is only just beginning to look as it might eventually end up—whereas if it had been hornbeam it would be a tightly clipped fixture by now. It is now at the stage where I can clearly see what is in the process of happening, but everyone else has to take it on trust as the visible evidence is a bit sketchy. The technique is easy—I have planted hollies at five-foot intervals, trimmed off all growth below three feet and trained lateral growth to three tiers of parallel canes that I have fixed between them. But it is coming into being and smothered with berries this year. Behind it is a brick wall, and the combination of glossy green and soft orangey pink is a good counterblast against the grey skies. I remember when I lived in London in the 1980s admiring a long, low box hedge opposite Chelsea Arts Club that was planted tight up against a white wall. The juxtaposition of wall and tightly clipped hedge usually looks good.

The truth is that I have done remarkably little

outside all week as I am immersed in finishing a book [*The Jewel Garden*. In fact we completely rewrote everything I did before Christmas that year and it was not completed until March.] and, apart from odd forays outside, have been trying to keep myself chained to the desk. This is where the chickens keep me sane, which, for most of the time, is not only an astonishing but also a remarkably unattractive thought. But the fact that they have to be let out and fed every morning, fed again in the mid-afternoon and shut up after dark means at least three trips up to the end of the garden. At this time of year that in turn means taking my shoes off, putting on wellies and some kind of coat—dogs all excited because they think that they are going for a walk—and going right down through the whole of the garden to the end of the orchard regardless of the weather. I hate them, of course—they are ugly birds and we haven't seen an egg from them for six weeks—but they are part of the set-up and must be cared for as well as possible. And, at a time when I can go for days and days without leaving the place or seeing anyone outside my family, they get me out. I taste the weather, see things. It is a reduced canvas, for sure, but all I can cope with at the moment.

23.12.01

We make Christmas up from the shards of experience and intentions that attach themselves to the festival and invariably this means returning inward. This applies down to every specific detail and explains why, on the whole, we don't like change at Christmas. It is a ritual to be followed to the letter, and the vestments and stations must be exactly observed. This is why it feels so disastrously wrong if it does not work out and why we long so much for it to be right. If the pieces all fit together then the still point of the world has been located, measured, and found to be just fine. Oh, and there is a religious thing too.

Most of this is to do with indoors. One of the supposed bits of the jigsaw is a white Christmas, but it works without that. Christmas, for most of us, is played under a closed roof. But not, you might have guessed, for me. If Christmas is an island of reassurance in my internal landscape, then the garden is the water that sits around it. It has to be placed within this context. Just as we all make up our own Christmas from memory, so I am going to make up my own Christmas garden from pieces of all the gardens that I have loved and known. They are all mine. Intimacy and meaning are everything. This is a solipsistic exercise and the gaze is turned fixedly inwards.

I was raised in a large Hampshire garden that had no horticultural ambitions or expectations beyond an ordered pleasure ground with a vegetable garden attached. There was a large copper beech tree near the house that towered over my childhood. You could curve your back into the fluted buttresses of its trunk. The leaves appeared each May, making the air shimmer with almost unbearable pleasure. The last time that I saw this was forty years ago, in 1962, as I was sent away to school after that. I have no recollection of spring happening at school, but I can remember the intensity of the knowledge given by that one beech that the world was slowly opening out and expanding into leaf. It was a terrifying, unbearable joy.

By summer—the summer of school holidays— the leaves were burnt purple on the outside and bright green as you peered up under them. The rooks bickered and roistered right up at the top, with occasional eggs and, worse, naked huge-beaked chicks, spattered on the ground. In winter the leaves fanned round the garden and all had to be swept with a besom, added to the leaf mould and eventually, a year or more later, sieved to make potting compost for the winter chrysanths. My Christmas garden has that beech in June, leaves still glowing with the sheen of arrival, at the edge of the lawn.

Ah yes, the lawn. You cannot have Christmas without a lawn to play on, especially when the sun is hot enough to make the grass scratchy dry on the skin of your bare arms. Lawns have only two purposes: to create a green interval between things, and as a play area. Both are completely valid in a garden. But many people get grass all wrong. A lawn is a passive thing. In itself it has no value at all. As a green space—effectively a glade—it can be wonderful, and there is much to be said for a circular lawn to play that role. I find it helpful to think of the average garden as essentially a piece of cultivated woodland (*pace* all permaculturalists) and any clearing that lets light and air in is always a good thing. But the glade should always be defined by where it ends and the edges need to be visually strong. It is a mistake to let grass taper away. As a play area we tend towards the definitions of pitches, be it tennis, cricket or football. I have nothing against this at all and would always want a cricket pitch in my garden to accommodate the passing cricketing fancy. But I do not pretend that it is a lawn. In fact, when we discussed making it into a lawn we ended up reckoning that the same effect would be better served by a long, shallow canal—which was prohibitively expensive. So the grass will continue to be created and maintained to the demands of the game that is to be played, rather than the other way round.

Talking of glades, in our last garden we had a two-acre wood and I want it back for Christmas. Any regular reader of this column will have come across the phrase 'our last garden' dozens of times. Let me explain. This was a forty-acre bit of land around a house on a Herefordshire hillside. We were only there for less than three years, but in that time it absorbed a lifetime's load of dreams and soaring, insane ambition. I loved it with every obsessed fibre of my being. There were lots of good materialistic reasons for loving it—the acres, the view, the mature trees, pond, privacy, sense of aggrandisement—but that is like contriving a physical tick-list of why you love your wife, when it is not the things about her that you love—it is *the* thing, it is *her*.

The wood, for example, was not an interesting wood. It was not semi-ancient, nor coppiced, nor containing rare and interesting specimens. It was on a steep slope and hard to get at, and in living memory it had been a larch plantation, was cut for timber in the last war and left to regenerate. Consequently it was full of the quick colonisers like sallow, birch, elder and crack willow, with some oaks, field maple and ash growing in the middle and a fringe of geans, or wild cherry, along the two flanks. There were snowdrops, violets, primroses, red campion and bluebells in spring, a large badger set and a fox earth. A pair of buzzards nested in the tallest ash and the young sat like young turkeys in our meadow, refusing to fly.

In many ways I think that a small wood is the ideal starting point for a garden. I often write about how fast garden-making is in the scheme of things, how twelve years will set up a garden of maturity immeasurable to most eyes, but a wood takes generations to become mature. To buy or inherit one fast-forwards you a whole lifetime. And once you have it, you can fine-tune endlessly. You can clear as much or as little as you want to create light, and you can work round the existing mature trees. You can plant climbers and bulbs entirely within the spirit of the wood. You can make walks, seats and cut views out to shape and guide your perception. I did all these things and was only beginning. I would like to continue the work in this made-up Christmas garden.

I shall also be taking the orchard as part of the seasonal package. This was large—nearly five acres—also on a slope and filled with over sixty fully mature apple trees. The apples, of course, were beside the point. Five acres is enough to keep a dozen families in apples, apple juice and probably cider as well. But all those apple trees created a magical space, the grid of their original planting imposing rhythm rather than restriction, and the sprawling, unpruned, lichen-smothered branches protective rather than lowering. It was a wonderful place to go and hide, as almost all of it was entirely hidden from anywhere other than the wood, and yet if you climbed into any of the trees you could see forty miles across to the Brecon Beacons. This is the perfect kind of privacy. Oudoors, unseen and yet able to see everything you wish to see.

I would also like the fishpond from that garden. It was unexceptional as fishponds go, although the bona fide medieval article, roughly rectangular in shape and perhaps a hundred feet long and thirty feet wide. When we got there it was almost completely smothered in brambles, dogwood and overgrown hedges, but when I cleared all these I uncovered not only the pond but also a rockery with watercourses, paths and steps that turned out to be Edwardian and had been covered over for decades. I cleared and tidied all autumn, revealing a wonderful space but not much in the way of plants. The next spring, however, there appeared gunnera, lysichiton, aruncus, astilbe, *Iris sibirica*, lobelias, rodgersia, rheum, and *Darmera peltata* (although it was known as *Peltiphyllum peltatum* back then).

You will notice that nothing of my current garden is included in this Christmas recreation. That is because it lives rudely in the here and now. It does not acknowledge Christmas any more than it notices birthdays or death. On Christmas Day I shall not return anywhere beyond pandering to the children's inevitable conservatism. But I shall be out in the garden, planting for the future.

379

23.12.01 **My Roots**

It is odd how passing fancies choose their moments to take you. The other day I suddenly got an urge for roses when I was cleaning the burnt pheasant stock from the saucepan. The pot turned out to be a write-off, but I think that the rose idea is a goer. I want to add roses to the orchard and little wood-in-a-box I am making. The orchard is infantile, but the latter is pretty much embryonic and has to be taken more on trust than any evidence that the eyes can offer. It is a good idea, the wood-in-a-box. It consists of a little wood with a clipped hedge, six foot high, all around it so that—and this is the cunning bit—from the outside you cannot tell that it is there and from the inside you are hidden as though you were in the middle of a vast wood. But first the hedge has to grow, and it was only planted this last March.

However, I want roses inside it. This is partly to deliberately upset the naturalism and keep the garden tightly manufactured. I know that not many roses like the dry shade that any wood inevitably creates, but I think that *Rosa roxburghii*, & *'Dupontii'* and any of the *pimpinellifolia* would do well enough. I like the sound of *p. 'double white'* and think that 'Stanwell Perpetual' would cope. The roses planted in the orchard would get more sunshine, but I want great mounds of rose, so whatever I plant must be vigorous, even boisterous, and have the delicacy of the species roses. Sarah thinks it is a barmy idea and will ruin the loose, carefree wildness of the grass between the trees, but that is where the problem lies. I would love that grass to be thick with bulbs and wild flowers, but it is too vigorous for that. The soil is too rich, the grass grows too energetically and nothing else gets a look in. By letting really strong roses spread I think it will add the right amount of restraint without losing the spirit of soft abandon that any self-respecting orchard should have. And I am going to plant climbers up all the standards. So my bedtime reading for the past few days has been roses all the way. [The roses stayed in my mind and the orchard remains a rose-free zone. Sarah was right—it was a barmy idea. I have lots of them every winter and very few ever come to anything.]

I did the final cut-back of the jewel garden, unable to convince myself any longer that the last soggy brown tatters of foliage were really interestingly tawny and structural. What did interest me was the extent to which one of the four standard 'Golden Milkboy' hollies had reverted to all green by being shaded by just this year's surrounding herbaceous growth. The other three are clearly and strongly variegated, green and gold, whereas this one is green and lime green. It will yellow up with a bit of wintry sun. And now we have skipped through the solstice, on the homeward run, there is sun increasing by the day. It sounds platitudinous but I really sense it. There will be roses blooming before we know where we are. Have a happy Christmas.

26.12.04

Was it happy? All those wishes for merriment and happiness must surely have hit some targets. Personally I have no expectations. I do Christmas as a ritual and enjoy the procedure for its own sake. When you have children the vicarious happiness is enough. You are happy because those that you love are happy. Perhaps that is the only measure of happiness. Anyway, here we are on the other side of that happiness curfew and this is where my own private pleasure starts to ripple out. It doesn't go far, nor needs to, to have full effect.

For the past few months I have battened down the hatches and sought no outside stimuli or contact at all really. I do what I must and very little else. This is the way that I have learned to get through these dour months. But Boxing Day is the pivot upon which my world turns. Today I open the door and take the first tentative steps outside. This has become something of a Christmas tradition. A lot of people around here will be going, as a result of one of the more pointless and illogical bits of legislation ever passed, to the last Boxing Day meet. Others will be visiting in-laws, going to football matches or going down the pub. But my Boxing Day is for gardening. Now if I was to read that elsewhere I would snort derisively. My children would die a thousand deaths if they were to read this (chances v. low indeed). Get a life! Well, I wouldn't be doing the job I do if I cared an iota about that, but it is a big day. Remember the importance of ritual.

There are no gung-ho projects, no long-laid plans. Everything is tentative. It might be pouring with rain, but rarely is. Often damp, dark and mild and sometimes cold, but I can only remember one stormy Boxing Day in the last ten years or so. However, it is invariably uninviting and vaguely resentful. The garden has slipped away from me over the past few months and I have to woo it back to me. To start with I give it time and admire all the things it has to offer. I will try and pick a few flowers for the little green vase on the kitchen table. In truth it is not much. A few primroses, hellebores and snowdrops in bud, the winter honeysuckle. This latter manages to be both modest and glorious at the same time. We actually have three different types of winter honeysuckle, *Lonicera fragrantissima*, *L. standishii* and *L.* x *purpusii*, which is barmy and, unless you collect such things—which I do not—completely pointless.

L. fragrantissima is the best-known and most common of the winter honeysuckles and has tiny ivory flowers on its bare, woody stems (although in mild areas it will be almost evergreen) that would scarcely be noticed in the hurly-burly of a May garden but which earn pride of place at the back end of December. The real point of these flowers, however, is that they have as delicious a fragrance as anything that will grow in the garden at any time of year. Sweet, haunting and supremely sensuous, they are produced best in mild spells and our bush grows on the north side of a wall, but where it pops over the top into the south-facing sunshine the flowers are produced in a modest mass.

There are still seed heads, although if December is wet they start to get a bit soggy by Boxing Day.

My current favourite is cardoons, closely followed by the almost machined precision of *Echinops ritro* and the delicate flat plates of honesty. This year we do not have the latter because all the stems carrying the seed heads got bashed and flattened, so were cleared away. I might well do some cutting back of things like the leaves of the hellebores. Cutting and clearing is one of the best active/passive jobs to get one going. There is hardly any thought or skill needed, but a lot of visual reward for the effort. I tend to cut the hellebores back in two or three passes between the beginning of December and the end of January, cutting off only those that have fallen past the horizontal, although I am not convinced that it would do any harm simply to remove the whole lot once you reach Christmas. The main reason for doing it is to allow as much light and air as possible to the new flower and foliage shoots that are starting to appear and will really get growing in a few weeks' time. Our oriental hellebores are rife with chronic blackspot, and although it doesn't seem to do the flowering any harm, I burn all the leaves. They have also interbred hopelessly, so although there are patches of wonderfully distinctive colours ranging from almost white to deep, deep purple, the majority are a bit muddy. I should mind, but I don't. Perhaps I would care more later in the year.

If this goes well and the flesh remains willing, I will move on to something a little more finite and significant but still in the realm of cutting. I like cutting. It feels like action and yet is somehow peaceful. I rarely feel robust on Boxing Day. It is all about gentle re-emergence, not galvanising into action. There will be time for that later in the year.

This has nothing to do with hangovers. I wish. I drink very little because my liver was damaged many years ago, so is not able to cope with it. I don't have to look far for things to do, as there are a whole raft of things left undone. One of the reasons why I don't like putting in a weekly list of timely jobs on these pages is that it would be so damned hypocritical and would only show up my own lack of purpose. But equally I know from long experience that it is rarely too late for anything. So there are summer raspberries to prune that should have been done three months ago, autumn raspberries that are ready to cut back to the ground and, most embarrassingly of all, blackcurrants unpruned. This will mean a reduced crop next summer, but we always have too many anyway. I had planned to give all my hedges a trim in October but scarcely started. Now would be a good time to do the inside of the ones surrounding the borders, as it would cause least damage to growing plants. But maybe hedge-cutting is too noisy and too macho. Anything bigger or more mechanical than secateurs can wait for the New Year. But I might begin the pruning of the pleached limes, which is a long job, taking a minimum of two weeks, so can be nibbled at in one-hour bites. It might make me feel that I have done something worthwhile.

That is what it is all about, of course. Feeling like I have re-entered and engaged with the place. Feeling like I am part of it again. And it will get dark by four o'clock and I will have had enough. But in a funny, rather weary way, it will be the happiest part of Christmas for me. It will feel as though I have come home.

27.12.98 **My Roots**

The garden came indoors at Christmas. For the first year since we have been here all our holly, ivy and mistletoe came from the garden. The birds have eaten all the berries on the holly, but no matter—it was shiny green and all from trees planted by us.

The birds resorted to the berries to fight the cold. It got down to minus 8 here last week, so that the gravel was iced together and lost its scrunch. People think of extreme cold as a big problem, but in the country frozen weather is so easy. It is the only time in the winter months that there is no mud, and for a few deluded days we walk outside in our shoes and push loaded wheelbarrows across the grass. Yup, give us half a chance and we know how to enjoy ourselves. It passes, of course, and it is back to the slither and slide of winter gardening. If I am honest I could have done with more winter gardening during the past few months of any kind at all. I have been trapped trying to write a book that should have been finished ages ago, hating myself for not working and not doing anything else because I had to work. [It is a familiar refrain. This time the book was *Fork to Fork*.] But whatever the consequences, I have given myself a break over Christmas.

I love the gap between Christmas and New Year and use it as a kind of horticultural retreat that I look forward to for months. If the weather is bad then there are gardening books to catch up on and plans to be made for the coming year. I mean plans literally—drawing up 1:100 and 1:50 plans for new developments and alterations to be done in the coming year. When everything about the last month or two has been a downward slide, there is something incredibly positive about working outside until dark, even if it is just pacing things out and really, really looking and then working on in the evening at the drawing board on the same project. I use these plans as a kind of list for the coming year. It never all happens of course, but is a fine way of linking mind gardening and the dirty-handed stuff.

The best bit of dirty-handing last week was the planting of six ash trees that I have had heeled in for eleven months now. The truth was that I ordered them and changed my mind between the order and delivery, so had nowhere to put them. They are a variety called 'Westof's Glorie', which is no more than a selected version of the common ash, although *The Hillier Gardener's Guide to Trees and Shrubs* says with a xenophobic glint in its eye, 'It is a commonly found street tree in continental Europe.' Anyway, I have planted them in a clump that makes sense of a larger area, [I have no memory of this at all. Anyway they must have been moved very soon after this, because for the past six years they have been in the coppice—and are growing very well thank you.] so now they shall be commonly found in a garden in Herefordshire for the next couple of hundred years. Planting trees is deeply satisfying and good for the soul, especially on a winter's day. It is the act of marking a long time. What else can a human do that leans so far into the future?

CHIVERS
LARGE PRINT
–direct–

If you have enjoyed this Large Print book
and would like to build up your own
collection of Large Print books, please
contact

Chivers Large Print Direct

Chivers Large Print Direct offers you
a full service:

- Prompt mail order service

- Easy-to-read type

- The very best authors

- Special low prices

For further details either call
Customer Services on (01225) 336552
or write to us at Chivers Large Print Direct,
FREEPOST, Bath BA1 3ZZ

Telephone Orders:
FREEPHONE 08081 72 74 75

166

891 27

857
338

1060

87

552

725